PAGAN
CHRISTMAS

Also by Christian Rätsch and Claudia Müller-Ebeling

The Encyclopedia of Psychoactive Plants
Ethnopharmacology and Its Applications
by Christian Rätsch

Marijuana Medicine
A World Tour of the Healing and Visionary Powers of Cannabis
by Christian Rätsch

Plants of the Gods
Their Sacred, Healing, and Hallucinogenic Powers
by Richard Evans Schultes, Albert Hofmann, and Christian Rätsch

Shamanism and Tantra in the Himalayas
by Claudia Müller-Ebeling, Christian Rätsch, and Surendra Bahadur Shahi

Witchcraft Medicine
Healing Arts, Shamanic Practices, and Forbidden Plants
by Claudia Müller-Ebeling, Christian Rätsch, and Wolf-Dieter Storl

PAGAN CHRISTMAS

The Plants, Spirits, and Rituals
at the Origins of Yuletide

Christian Rätsch and
Claudia Müller-Ebeling

Translated from the German by Katja Lueders
and Rafael Lorenzo

Inner Traditions
Rochester, Vermont

Inner Traditions
One Park Street
Rochester, Vermont 05767
www.InnerTraditions.com

Originally published in German by AT Verlag under the title *Weihnachtsbaum und Blütenwunder* by Christian Rätsch and Claudia Müller-Ebeling, ISBN 3-85502-8028
First U.S. edition published in 2006 by Inner Traditions

Library of Congress Cataloging-in-Publication Data
Rätsch, Christian, 1957–
  [Weihnachtsbaum und Blütenwunder]
  Pagan Christmas : the plants, spirits, and rituals at the origins of yuletide / Christian Rätsch and Claudia Müller-Ebeling ; translated from the German by Katja Lueders and Rafael Lorenzo.—1st U.S. ed.
      p. cm.
  "Originally published in German by AT Verlag under the title Weihnachtsbaum und Blütenwunder."
  Includes bibliographical references and index.
  ISBN-13: 978-1-59477-092-0 (pbk.)
  ISBN-10: 1-59477-092-1 (pbk.)
  1. Christmas. 2. Plants—Folklore. I. Müller-Ebeling, Claudia. II. Title.
  GT4985.R38 2006
  394.2663—dc22
                                                        2006019226

Printed and bound in India by Replika Press Pvt. Ltd.

10 9 8 7 6 5 4 3 2 1

Text design and layout by Priscilla Baker
This book was typeset in Sabon, with Charlemagne, Runa Serif, and Agenda used as display typefaces

To send correspondence to the authors of this book, mail a first-class letter to the authors c/o Inner Traditions • Bear & Company, One Park Street, Rochester, VT 05767, and we will forward the communication.

CONTENTS

FOR OUR FAMILY

PREFACE

We celebrate Christmas in the middle of winter, when the trees are bare and nothing in our gloomy, gray and white surroundings reminds us of the vivid green landscape of summer. Each year at Christmastime, we participate in a kind of ritual "summerfest" involving evergreen branches and winter-blooming plants, during the heart of the cold, dark winter season. Why? The simple answer is because it is exactly at this time of year that we yearn most strongly for green plants, blossoms, and the light of the sun. During the harsh winters of the past, our ancestors felt the same longing.

This book is about the ethnobotany of Christmas—a study of Christmas plants and their symbolic uses and meanings throughout the centuries. Looking at it in the glowing light of the candles in the Advent wreath and the festively lit Christmas tree, it is easy to see that plants contribute much to this feast season. During the dark time of Advent, we especially appreciate having a green fir tree and blooming plants in the house, such as poinsettia and Christmas cactus. We hang mistletoe and decorate our doors with wreaths made from fir, ivy, and holly. For roasts and baking, we use exotic spices from trees, shrubs, and plants of tropical regions. The children wait excitedly for St. Nicholas, Father Christmas, or Santa Claus, for whom they put out shoes, stockings, and gift plates, expecting marzipan, chocolate, apples, tangerines, and nuts in return. Many of these delights come from trees in warm, faraway regions from which we import their fruits.

Christmas is the most culturally pervasive and successful feast of all time. But what is behind our treasured Christmas traditions and customs? Why do green fir branches, flowers that bloom in the middle of the winter, Christmas spices, and incense still play such a central role in Christmas celebrations around the world? What are the symbolic meanings behind the use of these plants, and how have the old customs survived into the present computer age?

We discover amazing answers hidden in the darkness of history. A multi-layered background of symbolic meaning has made these plants a central part of Christmas rituals all over the world. The use of the plants that play such an important role at Christmastime originates not only where we most expect it—in the customs surrounding the Christian feast of the birth of Jesus—but also in ancient, pre-Christian, pagan traditions.

The symbolic meanings of these plants have roots in the distant past, when our ancestors were more intimately connected with the passage of the seasons. They were much more dependent than contemporary city people on the return of the sun and the plants after the long, dark winter nights. Depending on their values and beliefs, some modern people may choose to ignore or reject the history within which our well-known Christmas customs are rooted. Some react with interest to events and beliefs of days past; others feel that the historical sources contradict their religious beliefs or are otherwise irrelevant to our current Christmas customs. We can either profit from the traditions, beliefs, philosophies, and realities of life of other cultures, societies, and times—or we can ignore, refute, or fight them. We have the freedom to choose.

As individuals, contemporaries of a particular generation, or part of a given cultural, religious, or national tradition, we all have a past. How prepared we are to take a long, hard look at our own life, at our personal childhood and past, and beyond that, at our cultural, religious, and historical heritage, is entirely a matter of individual choice. But none can deny the essential role plants have played and continue to play in the midwinter celebration that we call Christmas.

C. MÜLLER-EBELING, HAMBURG,
IN THE ADVENT TIME OF 2002

Why a Book About Christmas Plants?

Fir trees, mistletoe, holly, golden oranges, red apples, ripe nuts, exotic spices, straw stars, cinnamon stars, mugwort roast, witches' houses made from gingerbread, and currant loaf *(Christstollen):* It's Christmas all around!

Christmas is part of the cultural heritage of the world, a global syncretism, a potpourri and conglomeration of elements that manifests itself finally, and most significantly, in the uses of flora from all over the world. From the familiar to the exotic, Christmas involves teas and shrubs from East and West, spices from the Orient and the New World, incenses from Eastern as well as Nordic sources. There are northern and southern fruits, herbs, and other plants to use and enjoy, including tobacco, magic mushrooms, and ingredients for special brews. There are flowers and other decorative plants from the rain forest, the desert, and the mountains—from all ecological zones and from all cultures.

Our Christmas ethnobotany explores the use of plants from all over the world that have become and remain a central part of the global Christmas ritual. Every plant comes with its own story with which to enrich the feast. Every plant's history hangs like a treasured ornament from the world tree that gives us a home in the universe. At Christmastime, the middle-class living room becomes the setting for shamanic rituals with deep roots in ancient traditions. Thus this book is not only about Christmas plants and customs, but also about the origins and historical background of the traditions that continue to inspire us and delight our senses.

For who doesn't like Christmas? Even Friedrich Nietzsche liked the feast: "You can't believe how much I am looking forward to Christmas, wonderful Christmas!" the philosopher wrote to his mother, Franziska, and his sister, Elisabeth, on December 5, 1861. "Christmas makes everything good!"*

C. RÄTSCH, HAMBURG,
AT THE TIME OF THE SUMMER SOLSTICE, JUNE 2003

*Nietzsche, Friedrich, *Autobiography from the years 1856 to 1869,* Schlechta-Index III, 935.

Preface

x

THE ETHNOBOTANY
OF CHRISTMAS

*Our ancestors are the worldly essences: water, salt, and acid.
They live within us, and yet, at the same time, they are always
leaving us. And then, time after time, they come seeking us
out again. Through the plants they remind us of a state of
timelessness, where human heritage is just a breath of wind on
a lake's surface. Human history is also plant history.*

SCHENK 1960, 7

Christmas is a Christian feast infiltrated by ancient pagan customs. On the other hand, it is also a pagan feast over layered with Catholic liturgical and folk rituals. It is the feast of the birth of the savior Jesus Christ and of the sun's rebirth; it is the time of midwinter "smudging nights" during which people smudged with herbs to cleanse their homes and stables and protect themselves against evil influences. This time, when the old year gives way to the new, is a time of gods and spirits, veritable orgies of gift giving, and rituals intended to ward off danger and ensure the fertility of the fields in the coming year.

Throughout the season runs evidence of a very rich Christmas ethnobotany, with ancient traces we will follow to their roots in this book. During this excursion into the past, we will learn much about Christmas trees and Christmas greens; about Christmas spices, scents, and incense; about protective rituals that have survived until modern times. The mythology of plants leads us to the origins of the culture of shamanism and the sacred botany (hierobotany) of ancient times—into medieval customs involving witches' magic, the warding off of demons, fertility rites, and rites of sacrifice.

The symbolic meaning of Christmas plants opens up to us a new perspective on cultures and customs of times long past: the mythical wild hunt of Germanic and Nordic origin, the Julbock and the feast of lights from the north of Scandinavia, the celebration of Saturnalia from the Mediterranean, ancient rituals commemorating the rebirth of the sun, and a tradition of protection against witchcraft from early Christian times (fifteenth and sixteenth centuries). It teaches us about folk *perchtenwalks*, nighttime processions of people dressed to represent the devil in archaic wooden goat masks and fur coats, and about biblical feasts to honor the birth of the Christ child, the holy three kings, the holy Barbara, and the holy Nicholas.

As with many other rituals, Christmas has a magic that is difficult to grasp and even more difficult to explain. The Christmas feast might be the most successful example of a mass ritual that has overstepped every international, ethnic,

Christmas plants on Christmas and New Year's cards: rowan berries, incense ball, fir cones, holly branches, mistletoe, box tree and spruce branches, sloe, ivy, and lantern flowers. (Coos Storm, ©Paperclip International, 1999)

religious, cultural, and political border. It is popular with people all over the world. Each culture has interpreted, incorporated, and applied the elements of Christmas in its own way into its own rituals and celebrations.

In short, Christmas is the most pervasively syncretic ritual of modern Europe and North America. It brings together traditions, ideas, and customs from all over the world and from all times. Christmas is no mere traditional folk ritual. It expresses itself as a constantly developing collage of diverse elements, all of which have their own history and legends. Whether you are interested in the true background of Christmas or not, the way in which it is celebrated today clearly takes meaning from the larger concept of a "feast of love" celebrated not only by the early Christians, but also by the pagan ancients.

Plants play an important but so far neglected role in our understanding of the roots of Christmas. The triumph of the Christmas tree started in Germany and the Swiss Alps. Mistletoe and holly came from the British Isles into the neighboring European countries and over the "great lake" to the New World. The poinsettia comes from Central America. The rose of Jericho hails from the deserts of the Near East. The Christmas cactus lives on trees in Rio de Janeiro in faraway Brazil.

In this book we will explore the symbolic meanings behind Christmas and the triumphant spread of Christmas ethnobotany—including Christmas greens and blossoms, the Christmas tree, and plants used for Christmas incense, ornaments, foods, and beverages—throughout the world. We will also explore the shamanic and pagan roots of Christmas customs many of us take for granted, including the origins of Santa Claus's traditional red and white garb and his yearly flight through the winter night sky in a sleigh pulled by reindeer.

Traditions, Rituals, and Customs

Rituals are the key to understanding the inner constitution of human society.

VON WELTZIEN 1994, 9

Nothing is more frustrating to the ethnologist than the fact that informants cannot always provide answers for certain questions. When I asked the Lacondon Maya of Chiapas, Mexico, why they strung up the skulls of the animals they shot, I received the curt answer, "Because that's the way it's done." Clearly, the sense and meaning of many ritual activities are forgotten with the passing of the centuries. This is exactly what would happen if an ethnologist were to take a survey among modern people to ask them why they celebrate Christmas, why they put up a Christmas tree, why they use a certain evergreen to decorate their rooms, and why certain scents are associated with Christmas.

Rituals are like theatrical plays or operas. With the passage of time, their content is continuously reinterpreted and imbued with contemporary meaning. Rituals are ideal surfaces for projection. They consist of symbols that are interpreted unconsciously or personally. Christmas is such a ritual. The way we celebrate it remains constant; individual approaches and interpretations, on the other hand, are always variable. Christmas is a complex ritual with elements of tree and forest cults, agricultural rituals, magic customs, applied folk botany, rites of sacrifice, mystery plays, feasts, and all kinds of social exchange. Christmas is also a "feast of love" involving symbolic plants; nearly all the plants of Christmas have a historical association with fertility, love magic, or aphrodisiac effects. Thus, for ages, Christmas plants have provided a safe haven and domain of contemplation on dark and cold midwinter nights, with their blessings and their dangers.

The forest is a theater of strange beings, friendly and unfriendly. What are those creatures crawling around underneath the elder tree? It is the old one and her troop of mandrakes, woodruffs, goblins, and wights? Are these ministering angels or threatening demons? The friendly and unfriendly dance merrily beneath the witches' weed; they smoke devil's tobacco and light up the underworld with the magic sparks of their druid's dust. Plant spirits appear in visionary consciousness as anthropomorphic beings that can speak with anyone, in any language. You need only ask—talk to them—and they will reveal the secrets of the normally invisible natural world to those eager for the knowledge. The shamanic world laughs and sings.

Ethnobotanical Plant Categories in the Christmas Feast

Symbolic and decorative plants
Wintergreen
Christmas tree
Floral arrangements
Blossom wonders

Oracular Plants
Incense
Aromatic essences
Spices
Food plants
Intoxicating plants

"On the Way to Reality" is the name of this episode of the cartoon series *Alef-Thau* by Alesandro Jodorowasky and Arno. (©1993, Carlsen Comics, Hamburg)

The Ethnobotany of Christmas

Christmas in the fairy forest: Father Christmas drives his sleigh through the world of fly agaric mushrooms, in the snow. (From a German children's book, circa 1920)

THE CHRISTMAS CALENDAR

The usual dates supplied for the traditional Christmas season start with November 11 and end on February 2. Here is a small survey of the most important dates in the Christmas calendar.

November

11. Martini or St. Martin's Day
Old start of winter; first slaughter feast after harvest time
25. St. Catherine's Day
Time to start Christmas baking
30. St. Andrew's Day and Night
Start of the new church year. Day of fortune-telling for love matches and weather for the coming year. Astrological lucky day.

December

1. Beginning of the Advent season and the Advent calendar. Start of the *klaubaufgehens* (wood gathering).
4. St. Barbara's Day
Time to sow the "Barbara wheat." In Provence, wheat is germinated in a saucer on Saint Barbara's Day. The higher the wheat grows, the greater the prosperity it foretells. On this day, one creates Barbara's boughs by bringing in branches of fruit trees and putting them in vases to force them to bloom. When they blossom, one can foretell an individual's luck in love as well as the quality of the fruit harvest for the next year.
6. St. Nicholas Day
End of *klaubaufgehens*. St. Nicholas brings presents to the children. Mexico: Houses are decorated with *Flor de San Nicolás*.
7. "Bad luck day"
8. Mary's conception
10. Astrological good luck day
11. "Bad luck day"

13. St. Lucy's Day

Old winter solstice (before the advent of the Gregorian calendar, this was considered the shortest day of the year). Night for driving away ghosts and witches.* *Perchtennacht* (blackest night); time to cut the hazel wood rod.

17. Christ Child gun salute[†]

Start of the Saturnalia in Rome.

19. End of the Roman Saturnalia (pre-Caesarian times)

20. Astrological good luck day

21. St. Thomas Day[‡]

Astronomical winter solstice. Most common beginning of the raw nights and start of the smudging nights during which house, court, and stables are smudged in purification rituals.

22. The sun enters the zodiacal sign of Capricorn

23. End of the Roman Saturnalia. (Saturday takes its name from "Saturn day.")

24. Holy Night. Night of Christ's birth; Christ's night. More modern beginning of the raw nights.

25. First day of Christmas.

Sun day. Winter solstice and rebirth of the sun *(sol invictus)* in Roman times. Birthday of Mithras, ancient Persian god of light.

26. Second day of Christmas.

Boxing Day. St. Stephen's Day. *Ilex* (holly) bushes are carried from village to village. "The time between the years." Oracle nights, lot nights.

27. Third day of Christmas.

Fudel (women beat men with life rod branches). St. John's Day (farmer holiday).

28. Fourth day of Christmas.

The day of the innocent children.

29. Astrological good luck day

31. Sylvester

Turning of the year, named after the holy Pope Sylvester I (ca. 314–335 CE). Night of St. Matthew.

January

1. New Year's Day

Start of January. January is named after the Roman god Janus.

2. End of the raw nights (in more modern traditions the raw nights end on January 5).

5. The last day of Christmas. The children plunder the Christmas tree.

In the night before January 6, Befana, the Italian Christmas witch or three king fairy, comes down the chimney and fills children's boots with sweets. To children who were not well behaved during the preceding year, she brings ashes, coal, and garlic.

6. Three Kings Day

Epiphany. Baptism of Christ. Birthday of Dionysus, Greek god of wine, vegetation, and ecstasy. Old change of times.

7. Old St. Valentine's Day[§]

February

2. Candlemas

Official end of the Christmas season. Time of light processions (grounded in Celtic Candlemas). Rituals performed for the security and protection of the fertility of the fields.

*In Bavaria, sloe (*Prunus spinosa* L., Rosaceae) was burned in the *glütl* (smoking pan) to smoke out witches and demons (Weustenfeld 1996, 107).

[†]In Bavaria, gun salutes are fired off every afternoon until December 24th.

[‡] In order to make fruit trees fertile, they are beaten with bags of peas on St. Thomas Day (Seligmann 1996, 100).

[§]Farmer's saying: "St. Valentine with a little hatchet puts Christmas Day in the bag!" (Fink 1983, 331).

The Ethnobotany
of Christmas

Christmas Songs of the Hard Winter

Listen closely to Christmas songs and you might be able to feel a really cold breeze coming into your centrally heated home. These songs speak out not about joy and celebration but instead about deprivation, the pitiless harshness and cold of winter that freezes stone and bone. A Christmas song composed by Karl G. Hering (1766–1853)* tells us, "It is a very hard winter when a wolf eats another wolf."

Today, it seems we seldom see a white Christmas. We yearn for a white Christmas as if for a winter fairy dream, and are happy when we hear the weather forecast predicting good skiing and sledding. While we glide down the hills in the cold and snowy weather in modern skiing gear that keeps our fingers and toes from freezing, it's hard to imagine that somewhere else (in Russia, perhaps), heating and water pipes are bursting in the cold. In lovely Switzerland, long before ski tourism began, the people were well acquainted with "Jack Frost"—the righteous man of winter described in these verses written in 1782 by Matthias Claudius:†

The Winter Is a Righteous Man
The winter is a righteous man
Strong like stone and enduring
His flesh feels like iron
And he does not shy from sweet or sour

Flowers and bird's songs
He does not like at all
He hates warm drink and warm songs
All the warm things

When stone and bone break from the frost
And ponds and lakes crash
He likes that sound, he does not hate it
He is dying from laughter

His castle of ice is far away
On the North Pole on the beach;
But he also has a summerhouse
In lovely Switzerland

Soon he is there or here
To govern, to lead us,
And when he walks around we stand around
And look at him and freeze

*Most Christmas songs were composed in the eighteenth and nineteenth centuries; others are from the thirteenth and fourteenth centuries.

†Melody composed by Jh. Fr. Reichardt in 1797.

The Ethnobotany of Christmas

Jingle Bells, Good King Wenceslas, and other famous Christmas carols played during the Christmas season in department stores and markets sound sentimental or kitschy to our ears. Who actually listens when caught up in the stress of shopping? The usually schmaltzy violin arrangements and the sweet bells fool us into believing that the content of these songs actually derive from "the good old days"—when, in fact, the real context of the times was anything but romantic and sentimental. These songs actually evoke experiences of deprivation, as in the following folk melody.

In the Middle of the Night
Oh, let God reign!
It is so cold!
Someone is likely to freeze
And lose his life
So cold goes the wind!
I am sorry for the children.

Oh, God have pity!
The mother is so poor
She has no pan
To cook for the little child,
No flour and no grease,
No milk and no salt.

It was much easier for our grandparents and great-grandparents to identify with the infant Jesus, nestled on hay and straw in the poor stable in Bethlehem, than it is for those of us living in an affluent society. In their time, they were content when their basic daily nutrition—sometimes just a mash of flour, grease, and salt—was secure. Only three or four generations ago, winter was the time when the infamous "Thin Jack" was the chef in poor households. Work in the fields was over for the year. Many farms were snowed in. Farmers and their farmhands gathered closer around the hearth fire and settled for provisions stored since the fall, foods that could endure the frost and the winter. Porridges, preserves, salted foods, *gepökeltes* (salted meats), and smoked and dried foods were on the table.

For people living in town, the days became shorter and the nights longer. Whoever lacked warm clothing and had no wood for a fire could—until the middle of the twentieth century—truly feel the harshness of the winter. One yearned for warm socks and a warm jacket, a merrily crackling hearth fire, hot soup, and something good tasting—like the apples, nuts, and almonds mentioned in numerous Christmas songs. In these times of darkness and scarcity, on what is practically the shortest day of the year, comes Christmas Day. Our modern celebration of the birth of Christ, with all its glowing lights, continues the pagan traditions of the winter solstice, during which the people celebrated the

A fir tree as in a fairy tale.
(Postcard)

*Translator's note: In the German original, there is wordplay here with *der Heiland* (Christ, the Savior) and the meanings of *heil* (wholeness, salvation, healing) that does not come through in English.

†Music composed by Friedrich von Spee, after a melody from the Rheinfelsische Songbook of the year 1666.

The Ethnobotany
of Christmas

return of the sun. Christ, the Savior, is also the one who makes the land whole again, who saves the land* and bears the hope of a new greening of nature, as expressed in this verse from the song "Oh Savior, Tear Open the Skies:"†

> *Oh earth, break into leaf,*
> *Break into leaf, oh earth*
> *So that hill and valley may become green*
> *Oh earth so this little flower brings*
> *Oh Savior out of earth springs*

The Christian feast of love and joy was intertwined with the birth of the Savior. It inspired in believers a feeling of charity for the poor and the beasts. For the poor, it nourished hope and a belief in the gracious generosity of those more fortunate. For children, Christmas promised the hope of Santa Claus, or Father Christmas, who brought ginger nuts, currants, and maybe even exotic colonial goods—like oranges from the Orient—in his sack.

Soon Christmas Comes
Melody: Hans Helmut; Lyrics: Karola Wilke

> *Soon Christmas comes*
> *Now Father Christmas is not far away*
>
> *Listen, the old man is knocking on the gate.*
> *With his white horse, he is waiting . . .*
>
> *I am putting hay in front of the house*
> *And Ruprecht, Santa's helper, is taking the sack out*
>
> *Ginger nut, little apples, almonds, and currants*
> *All that he gives to the good child . . .*

The verses of enduringly popular Christmas songs carry these experiences—the hard winters and the longing for warmth, food, and charity that our grandparents and great-grandparents knew so well—into our modern living rooms.

A PAGAN FEAST

*In the feast one finds the holy dimension of life in all
its richness; in the feast we experience the holiness of
human existence as a godly creation.*

ELIADE 1957, 52

The feast that takes place between December 24 and December 26 is what we normally call Christmas. In the countries of the high north, in Scandinavia, this time is called *Julfest*. To our ancestors, this time period was known as "raw nights" or "smudging nights." What does this mean? Where do these words come from? Entries in etymological dictionaries—those that clarify the origin and meaning of words—are no help. For example, in its 1963 edition, the *Grosse Duden* by Paul Grebe and Günther Drosdowski tells us that *jul* comes from the Nordic and described the winter solstice in pagan times, and that the word "went on, after Christianization, to indicate the Christmas feast." But there are no entries that explain what *jul* actually means.

Very few authors took the trouble to search for answers in sources from earlier centuries. One who did was the famous folklorist, Adolf Spamer. His detailed and informative book *Christmas in Old and New Times** provides us with many interesting clues. According to Spamer, in the early eighteenth century the word *jul* carried the connotation of "shout for joy" or "hurrah!" Later on, it was associated with the Old Nordic *êl* (snow flurry) or *jek* (to speak), as well as with a Middle High German word for "invocation of the sun." And this is a very logical explanation, considering the fact that in the north the sun never even reaches the horizon in midwinter. Spamer concludes: "It is clear that *jul* is the characterization of a long wintertime period."

Spamer is also on the right track when he takes old calendrical divisions into consideration. The Anglo-Saxons called the months we know as December and January *giuli*—similar to the Icelandic *ylir*. However, Spamer limits himself to vague declarations concerning the transformation of the once-pagan winter solstice celebration into the Christian Christmas feast. He delivers hard facts. He talks specifically about Hakon the Good (934–960), the third king of Norway, who situated Christmas during the time of the normal *Jul* festivities and is ultimately historically responsible for the merging of the two names, *jul* (=yule) and *fest* (=feast). In other sources, the Roman Emperor Justinian, who had converted to Christianity, is credited with changing the date of the feast from January 6 to December 25 in 542 CE, to honor the birth of Christ.

The German word for Christmas—*Weihnachten*, meaning "holy night"—first emerged in 1170. Spamer sees it as a translation of the Catholic liturgical

*Published by Eugen
Diederichs in 1937 in Jena.

9

The Easter rabbit with a cap reminiscent of the Christmas fly agaric mushroom. (Sticker book, Münster: Coppenrath Verlag, 1998)

word *nox sancta* (holy night), and believes it referred to the sacred nights of pre-Christian rituals. The ancient Germans started the new year with *Moraneht*, "mothers' night." So it was easy for early Christian missionaries to associate that day with the day mother Mary gave birth to the Christ child. In addition, until Spamer's lifetime, the term *mothers' night* was interchangeable with *twelve nights* in some areas of Germany. The folklorist also discovered the last remaining practice of a pre-Christian custom in Carinthia, which involved laying a table for the deceased on the holy night. This custom is the origin of the big Christmas meals of our time.

Everyone celebrates Christmas in his or her own way. For Christian believers, the night between December 24 and December 25 is holy, a symbolic return of the birth of Christ. Pagan and Earth-centered people continue to celebrate the winter solstice. To many, Christmas represents a traditional family feast day, a time of contemplation, a welcome respite from the yoke of work. For some, the meaning of Christmas is obscure, seemingly celebrated simply because it is customary. Others dislike the Christmas season because it can be a terrifying example of excessive consumerism. Others ignore it out of disinterest or spiritual conviction. For example, a Jehovah's Witness does not celebrate Christmas because it is considered a "heathen feast" in that faith. And some people have no associations with the Christmas season. Orthodox Jews still hope for the return of the Messiah; for them, the birth of the founder of a new Jewish sect has no meaning. The same is true for Muslims, who do not regard Jesus as a prophet of God.

In old Rome, December 25 was the day of *dies natalis invicti solis*—the

Spirits in the forest: fly agaric mushroom wights, fairies, Easter rabbits, a toad, and a full moon. (Children's book illustration from Elsa Beskow, *De Sma Skovnisser*, 1919, Carlsen reissue, 1996)

A Pagan Feast

birthday of the invincible sun. This day served as a time not only for worshipping the sun, but also for worshipping Saturn, the god of seed sowing and wealth. Far from the borders of the Roman Empire, another age-old pagan feast was celebrated—winter solstice, marking the rebirth of the sun, the return of light and life. This ritual—celebrated with intoxicating drinks and roasted meat from animal sacrifices—held a central meaning to many Germanic peoples.

Strangely enough, it never occurs to most people to ask why the birth of Christ is always celebrated on the same date each year, while the dates for his death and resurrection—Easter—change from year to year. The answer to this riddle is that there are two different calendar systems. The recurring date for Christmas is related to the course of the sun; the dates for Easter change each year because of the cycles of the moon. Easter is always the first Sunday after the first spring full moon.

Red and White: Colors of Christmas

The mystery of the recurrent and omnipresent red and white color symbolism at Christmastime—in the Christmas tree, with its red balls and candles, or in the dress of Father Christmas—has many possible interpretations.

One explanation has roots in very ancient symbolism representing the cosmic connection between man and woman. White, like the snow, represents light, pure spirit, the realm of the sky. White is also the color of a man's semen. Thus, in an intercultural sense, the color white symbolizes the male principle. Only later was white associated with innocence, celibacy, and pureness. The

White and red are the colors of shamanic clothing in Nepal.

A Pagan Feast

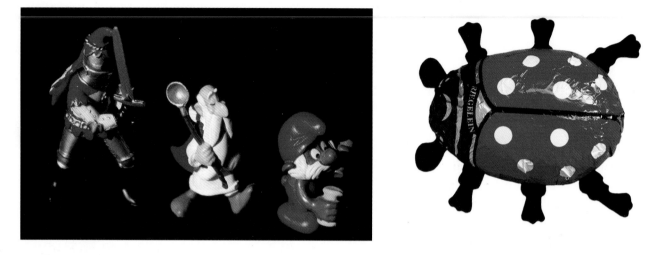

Left: The red and white guard from cartoon land.

Right: In pagan times, ladybugs were holy to the love goddess Freia (Freia=Mary). But why does this one—like the fly agaric mushroom—have white dots instead of the usual black ones? (Chocolate ladybug)

---

*Red is also the color of thunder (Braem 1995, 72), and the color of the thunder god, Donar (Germanic) or Thor (Norse). It reminds us of the color of the fly agaric mushroom, which was believed in northern European mythology to be created from lightning and thunder.

†*Zauberei* (magic, sorcery, witchcraft, conjuring) comes from the Old High German word *zoubar* (Nemec 1976, 100).

‡Circa 55–116/120 CE.

A Pagan Feast

color red* symbolizes, like menstrual blood, the universal female life force and principles of love, passion, and magic.

More clues to the symbolic meaning of red as a Christmas color can be found in a study of ancient runes. In old Germanic times, one entered the runes in stone with one's very blood. Runes were not ordinary, everyday letters for inscribing banal or mundane written content. They were magic signs that "came to life" through ritualistic cutting and blood-letting. They were *zauber,*† meaning that they were magic and had the power of enchantment (Krause 1970). Whoever had power over the runes could do magic spells.

The word *zauber* itself has to do with the act of consecrating the rune wand with one's own blood. The word *rune* means "secret" or "secret knowledge," but it also means "magic." Female Germanic prophets were called *alruna,* "the all knowing," because they could see truthfully. They were believed to have the gift of prophesy by nature and were highly esteemed because of that. In his work *Germania,* the great Roman historian Cornelius Tacitus‡ wrote: "The runes were originally conjuring formulas that were put together in a certain way and became a poetic song. The magician is a medicine man who has a way of seeing the medicine that makes it work or conjures it with a mighty spell" (Jordans 1933, 16f).

There is yet more to the meaningful connection between red and white. In the pervasive linkage of the two colors can be seen a kind of alchemy, a melding of two very different substances that are united in an alchemical wedding to become the Philosopher's Stone. The *Rosarium Philosophorum,* an alchemists' text, says about Mercury: "He is the whole elixir, whiteness and redness, the permanent water, and the water of life and death, and the virgin's milk, the cleansing herb of the purification" (Heinrich 1998, 234).

The Darkness of Midwinter

In the drunkenness of ecstasy we have climbed the winds.

RIG VEDA X, 126

Autumn brings darkness. The season ends with the shortest day of the year, the day of the winter solstice. Winter begins with the longest night of the year and leads us from the darkness back to the light. Winter ends when day and night are of equal length, on the day of the spring equinox. "Every year, on winter solstice, a temporal nativity is accompanied by the rejuvenation and renewal of the whole cosmos: The world tumbles back to the time of origin; chaos returns" (Giani 1994, 40). This is why the Christmas "feast of light" takes place in darkness. The dark carries the seed of light and vice versa, almost a European equivalent of the symbolic unity of yin and yang.

In midwinter, the snow arrives. The days become longer, and the snow reflects and enhances the light. Midwinter means renewal of life and holds the promise of new life force, the return of *viriditas*, the greening power. The Romans associated this cosmological state of affairs with the flower blossom miracle, in which plants bloom in the dead of winter: "On the day of the winter solstice, pennyroyal *[herba pulei]* blossoms are hanging underneath the roof to dry, and the bubbles they produce—that are filled with air—burst" (Pliny the Elder II, 108). All of this hints at the important role of evergreen and blooming plants in the time of the winter solstice, the ritual use of fire and candle, and a deeper meaning to the name "mothers' night."

The darkest night of the year was called mothers' night, because now the sun god, lover of the goddess, is reborn in the lap of the Earth. With him,

Shamanic Elements in Christmas

Astronomical date
Solstice, midwinter

Mythology
Wotan and the Wild Hunt
Christmas wights (creatures of the woods)
Sol invictus; the rebirth of the sun
Saturnalia

Symbols
Fir tree, world tree, tree of knowledge
Evergreens: mistletoe, holly, wintergreen, and others
Straw stars
Opium poppy seedpods
Fly agaric mushroom
Angels
Red and white
Green and white

Ritual Activities
Incense burning or smudging with herbs
Animal sacrifice, symbolic human sacrifice
Drinking rituals, *Jul* libations
Christmas presents
Potlatch exchange, gift-giving ritual in Siberian shamanism
Julklapp (Swedish gift-giving ritual)

Plant Rituals
Tree cults and the cutting of winter greens
Blossom miracles (plants that bloom in midwinter)
Oracle plants
Sowing the Barbara wheat

the light of life is renewed. It is the moment of quietness, of contemplation. The cosmic tree (shamanic tree, ladder to heaven) sparkles in the starry brightness under which the child of light is born, reveals itself in an inner vision. Fir greens decorate the rooms. They are smudged with mugwort, juniper, and other aromatic, cleansing herbs (Storl 1996a, 73f).

In this night the goddess gives birth in the darkest place on Earth, during the quietest hour, to the reborn sun-child. Human beings acknowledge the wonder of this sacred night in their meditations: They light candles, they burn oak or birch and let it smoke, they let the burning *Julblock* bonfire smolder; and they hang up the *wintermaien*—the original Christmas tree. The British Celts decorated their house with holly, mistletoe, and ivy; and on the continent, fir or spruce was used. The ashes of the *Julfire* were believed to be healing and were put on the fields to bring fertility (Storl 2000b, 150).

Sacred Nights, Smudging Nights, and Incense

*The dream whirls around the times, the rooms, the periods
of time, it chases them like a storm chases the fog. Through
glimpses of dream and fog, reality is shining.*

SCHENK 1960, 25

Our ancestors called the twelve days between December 25 and January 6—the time between the first day of Christmas and epiphany (the day of the holy kings)—the "raw nights."* They are now more generally known as the twelve nights of Christmas. They also recognized four "smudging nights" during which the people smudged their homes and stables with herbs to protect against evil influences.

Old tradition has it that during these nights—especially the nights before St. Thomas Day, Christmas, New Year's Day, and epiphany—the spirits are out, haunting. In these dark times, ruled by elemental powers, the spectral army of Wotan's wild hunt hurried through the clouds, uncanny spirit beings fighting the battle between light and darkness. In his unfinished epic, *Pharsalia* (also known as *The Civil War*), Lucan (39–65 CE) describes the emotions of people of a remote past:

Nature's rhythm stops. The night becomes longer and the day keeps waiting. The ether does not obey its law; and the whirling firmament becomes motionless, as soon as it hears the magic spell. Jupiter—who drives the celestial vault that turns on its fast axis—is surprised by the fact that it does not want to turn. All at once, witches drench everything with rain, hide the warm sun behind clouds, and there's thunder in the sky without Jupiter realizing it (Lucan, VI).

*Also known as twelve nights, lot nights (=nights favorable for augury and divination), and in-between-nights or undernights (=shady dark nights that attract spirits of the invisible world).

A Pagan Feast

Rituals were in order to ward off the demonic influences and to conjure a rebirth of the sun after the dark days. At nightfall, "house and stable were smudged with healing herbs: mugwort, juniper, milk thistle, fir resin" (Storl 2000b, 150). Because of these smudging rituals (originally pagan and later performed by Catholic priests), these nights were known as "smudging nights." People burned juniper and many other aromatic substances to drive out demons. The smoke transformed the aromatic woods and herbs into scent that was supposed to implore the gods to take mercy on human beings and to keep away all evil. They also placed various combinations of magical herbs (called "nine herbs") in their beds for protection and mixed them into their animals' food.

The smudging nights are still taken seriously in Scandinavia. This is apparent in a newspaper clipping from January 6, 2003, from Nuuk, Greenland:

Father Christmas with his pipe, his rod, and some presents, brings the fir tree from the woods, just like a wild man. (Postcard after an English Christmas decoration of the nineteenth century)

The new government of Greenland had cleansed all the governmental buildings in Nuuk from evil spirits, by an exorcist, during the time between Christmas and New Year's Eve. According to the press agency Ritzau, the exorcist Manguak Berthelsen said about the whole procedure: "My inner ear has nearly exploded from all the noise in there" (*Frankfurter Rundschau*, January 7, 2003).

Unfortunately, the author did not explain how the *neo-völva* (the exorcist, a sort of Greenlandian ghost buster) had driven out the ghosts!

Above left: Wotan and the wild hunt. (Sculpture by Johann Bossard, Bossard-Haus, Heide)

Above right: A Mexican depiction of the last supper: Skeletons dine on *Dia de los Muertos,* the Day of the Dead. (Mexican postcard)

A phallic Germanic "mushroom stone" depicting the ship of the dead for the trip to the other world, showing the mounted Wotan as an escort of souls. (Picture stone from Stenkyrka, Lillbjärs, Gotland, eighth century; from Crumlin-Pedersen and Thye 1995, 171)

Wotan and the Wild Hunt

Wodan id est furor

Adam of Bremen 1595 IV, 26

Wotan (also known as Wodan or Odin), the furious, the raving, wanderer and wild man, ancestor of the old Silesian wood- and hill-spirit Rübezahl, is the archetypical ancient German god of gods. From his name comes the Old High German words *watan* and *wuot,* from which come German words for impetuousness, wildness, and anger—but also "wishfulness" and "to wish." If we consolidate all the attributes of this god, we see he is an omnipresent force of creation and building who gives beauty to human beings as well as inanimate objects. He is the source of the art of poetry, as well as the drive for war and victory. Yet he is also a force that works for the fertility of the fields and helps people strive for the highest good and material fortune (Grimm 1968 I, VII). In his role as a mythical fulfiller of wishes, one might very well see Wotan as an ancestor of that famous bringer of presents, Santa Claus himself.

Wotan is the god who is driven to amass knowledge. He wants to know everything; he craves knowledge. For this, he travels all the lands over and—wounded by a spear—hangs himself upside down, for nine nights, on the shamanic world tree, to get to know all nine shamanic worlds and absorb all their knowledge. Then he breaks branches off of the world tree and throws them onto the Earth, where they arrange themselves into runes of beech slivers, forming letters that carry secret knowledge. Because of Wotan's self-sacrificial shedding of blood, the runes become magic. They give away their own knowledge. Wotan sacrifices one eye so that he can look into both the inner and the outer worlds. He drinks from the well of wisdom to suck up all the knowledge it contains. Every year, during the time of the smudging nights, Wotan's wild army is on the lookout for the sun, under the leadership of Wotan himself. In honor of his impetuous search in the middle of the darkest time of the year comes the folkloric name of Wotan's herb *(Heliotropium europaeum),* as well as the Latin name of a plant known variously as storm hat, Odin's hat, troll hat, and, in North America, monkshood *(Aconitum napellus)*.

Wotan, a rider on a white horse, was the ghostly rider who led the ghostly army in the storm during the twelve days around New Year's Day. At this time, midwinter, the fears of the living became focused on the community of the dead. A cultic, ecstatic connection with the dead—in fact, a special kind of honoring of the dead—is also the basis for Wotan's ability to lead the wild army. As god of the dead and the ecstasy associated with their cult, Wotan is their leader (Simek 1984, 464).

RÜBEZAHL: DESCENDANT OF WOTAN

South Tirolean legends describe a so-called "wild man" (Fink 1983, 144) as a huge and awesome woodsman with a great white beard, a wide hat, and a voice as deep as thunder. This is a legendary character of the Riesengebirge region, the Silesian mountain ghost Rübezahl, who counts beetroots in his mountain home and is often pictured smoking a pipe, just like Father Christmas.

Anyone familiar with Germanic mythology can easily see that Wotan lives on in Rübezahl. Both are described as wild men who rip up trees, determine the weather, and help the meek but harm the proud. In memory of the wild hunt led by Wotan in the southern Tirol, St. Martin can also be seen riding a white horse through the air on the evening of St. Martin's Day (November 11). On this day, the farmers finish their year of work and make an offering to St. Martin—or perhaps to Wotan? Cheese, wool, bread, and flax are considered venerable sacrificial offerings to St. Martin in the mountain regions (Fink 1983, 238). Even today, people leave hay or oats for a white horse or a donkey in

Wotan on his horse with his world spear in his hand, accompanied by his two ravens, Thought and Memory; in front of him, we see a snakelike, shamanic soul. Sky and Earth are interconnected. (Shape or figure-form picture from the time of the Vikings, from Davis 2000, 51)

Left: Rübezahl, ancestor of the smoking Father Christmas. (Woodcut from the Riesengebirge region, photograph by Widmann, before 1942, from Peuckert 1978, 97)

Right: *Rübezahl.* Painting by Moritz von Schwind (1804–1871). (Oil on canvas, Bavarian Staatsgemäldesammlung Schack-Galerie, Munich)

A Pagan Feast

Left: Trolls, Nordic wild people, also celebrate the *Julfest*. Here, on the troll's hairy, raw head, a spruce tree grows like a spiritual antenna; fly agaric mushrooms also grow there, giving spiritual nourishment. Look closely to see that the walls of the troll's house are decorated with pictures of reindeer. (Illustration from a children's book)

Below: A troll under the Christmas tree. The Old Nordic name troll means "giant, fiend, magic being" but is now taken to mean "little people" *(huldrefolk)* who play a role in stories about changelings. (Photo by Claudia Müller-Ebeling)

front of the house on St. Martin's Day. Strangely enough, the *Nigglasgehen* (Nicholas walk)—a procession of the saint and his dark helpers from house to house—was officially forbidden in the Tirol region, while the cult surrounding Ruprecht (known as Krampus in Alpine regions) remained popular (Fink 1983, 346).

FROM THE SHAMANIC WORLD TREE TO THE CHRISTMAS TREE

For a long time her [this means natura*] good deeds were hidden; and trees and woods were the highest of all gifts that were given to human beings. From these, food was taken first; their leaves made the cave-dwelling life [of the troglodytes] easier and the phloem, or bast, of the tree, served as clothing.*

PLINY THE ELDER XII

A cardboard ornament for hanging on the Christmas tree.

Up to the present day, human beings have had a special and nearly magical relationship with trees. In all times, we have realized that there is a very meaningful and multilayered symbolism in the growth of the tree—their tops look toward the heavens and their roots are anchored tightly into the Earth. Trees embody the connection between sky and Earth, especially when they grow high above all other things. There are family trees and life trees, a tree of knowledge, and world trees. World trees are symbolic of the unfolding of creation; they are shamanic staircases to other worlds. They not only provide raw materials for building and food, but in some cases they are also sources of entheogens, aphrodisiacs, and healing medicines. "I am the tree that gives human beings everything that they need for their life" (Anisimov 1991, 57). This is what defines the shamanic world tree of the Evenken, in Siberia. The world tree grows in the cosmic swamp. The sun and moon hang on its branches, and forest people live in it. Later on, the original shamanic world trees became holy trees of pagan religious worship (Caldecott 1993; Cook 1988).

Anyone who looks closely at the threshing floors of old Black Forest houses can often see magic numbers scratched upon them and may also see a tree of life, in the form of a fir or spruce branch. The same symbol can be found in some old churches. Beneath an abstract image of a Christmas tree, there are three horizontal steps, representing a shamanic staircase to the sky and the world tree, that reveal the pagan past (Schilli 1968, 34). This detail from the farming culture can easily be overlooked, yet it shows that the symbolic meaning of the fir tree has its roots deep in the past as a world tree and life tree, and only in recent history as the popular Christmas tree.

One of the first references to the fir tree in association with the Christmas tree comes from the Alsatian town of Strasbourg in 1604: "On Christmas they put fir trees in the rooms in Strasbourg, they hang red roses cut from many-colored paper, apples, offerings, gold tinsel, sugar. It is the custom to make a four-cornered frame around it" (Kronfeld 1906, 149).

Today, depending on family tradition, the tree that is taken into the house is festively decorated and is called the *jultree,* the light tree, the Christmas tree, or the Christ tree. How many are aware that this custom was for a long time reviled by the church? In the folk literature, numerous sources refer to the fact that the custom of cutting and putting up fir or spruce branches or even whole trees—*maien* or *meyen*—was despised as a heathen practice, and was explicitly forbidden by the church, and specifically because of its shamanic-pagan past: "Because of the pagan origin, and the depletion of the forest, there were numerous regulations that forbid, or put restrictions on, the cutting down of fir greens throughout the Christmas season" (Vossen 1985, 86). The record ledgers of Schlettstadt indicated that since 1521, the unauthorized cutting of *maien* had been forbidden, and emphasized the protection of the forest in the face of this "forest damage." The cutting down of Christmas *meyen* was forbidden in Freiburg, in the Breisgau, and was punishable by a fine of 10 *rappen* (Spamer 1937, 71). It was only at the beginning of the eighteenth century (one hundred years after the Strasbourg reference from 1604) that Johan David Gehard suggested tolerating the fir tree "to the degree that there was less idolatry connected with it" (Spamer 1937, 72).

Taking all of this into account, the name "Christmas tree" seems ironic. The worship of decorated May branches and May trees is still considered pagan nature-worship—and, from the Christian perspective, idolatry. In the Bible, no connection is drawn between Jesus Christ and the fir tree or any other needle-bearing tree. And it is easy to see why. Except for the pine tree, there are no needle-bearing trees in the Holy Land.

How on Earth did the pagan world tree become christened by the church as a Christmas tree? From Dorothea Forstner, choir woman of the Benedictines in St. Gabriel of Berholdstein, we learn:

> . . . the pagan origin of the May tree and maypole tree and even of the Christmas tree is a not well-known fact. You run into old superstitions having to do with the transferability of natural powers from one being onto another. By bringing branches or trees into contact with human beings, the fresh and blossoming life of nature and its fertility was transferred into them, and evil influences were warded off. Especially during the raw nights between December 25 and January 6, when evil spirits were feared most, green branches were hung, candles lit—and all these things were used as a means of defense. Later on, the *trees* themselves were used for the same purpose; and candles were hung on them. . . . The church retained these old customs, and gave them a new meaning as a symbol for Christ: the true tree of life and light of the world.*

*Forstner, Dorothea, *Die Welt der Christlichen Smbole* (Tirol: Wien, 1986), 150.

From the Shamanic
World Tree to the
Christmas Tree

Christmas Trees

The Christmas presents are underneath the Christmas tree. Weeks before,
the children had written letters to the baby Jesus and slipped them in
between the winter windows. The modern custom of giving presents
is not so very old. There was a time when the Christmas tree was
unknown in the mountainside as well.

Fɪɴᴋ 1983, 366

The market offers a Christmas tree suitable for every taste—fir, red fir, spruce—and even plastic imitations. The novelist Klaus Modick presents modern Christmas tree shoptalk concerning the selling points of various fir trees:

> The robust Northman fir, for example, originally imported from Scandinavia. . . . Or a noble spruce from the new German countries? Or something a little more conventional in the structure of the branches, but a very solid piece. The top is pronounced. The blue fir, as well, with decent color grooming in the needle lug, is always in demand. . . . Or the old and good noble fir from the Black Forest? . . . Or would you like something more spectacular? We could show you the alp fir, interbred with dwarf-pine? (Modick 2002).

On the afternoon of December 24, the family decorates the Christmas tree. (Drawing by Christian Wilhelm Albers, 1890)

The image of a tree brought into a cozy room delighted our ancestors—especially in old-fashioned, romantic times. Moritz von Schwind, Ludwig Richter, and other artists of the nineteenth century *implanted* in our collective consciousness a picture of the festively lit tree standing in the center of the room surrounded by a family with many children. The custom of bringing a tree into the room and decorating it during the time from December 24 through January 6 was a German invention. The earliest written documentation of the practice may be from the year 1419, from the baker's guild in Freiburg (Breisgau). Others claim that the oft-cited tree from Strasbourg—dating from the year 1604—was the first decorated fir tree. The first tree was illuminated there in the year 1785. An engraving after a drawing by Johann Martin Usteri (1763–1827) shows the festively lit tree as the focus of a Swiss family from Zurich in 1799. In the year 1807, the first Christmas trees came to Leipzig; in 1810, to Berlin; and in 1815, to Danzig (Fink 1983, 367). In 1848, Prince Albert of Sachsen-Coburg-Gotha, husband of Queen Victoria, brought the Christmas tree to England. In 1851, the first Christmas tree was admired in Innsbruck. Ironically, the first Christmas tree may have come to France through the German-French war, during the years 1870–1871. However, opinions on this differ. Riemerschmidt (1962, 21) cites 1837 as the date that Princess Helene von Meckleburg (Duchess of Orléans by marriage) brought the Christmas tree to Paris. Others say this occured in the year 1840.

In 1912, the first huge, lighted tree illuminated an official square in New

From the Shamanic
World Tree to the
Christmas Tree

York, on the other side of the ocean from Europe (Fink 1983, 367). Ever since, the presence of the Christmas tree may yield to religious borders, but never geographical ones. It has reached the Mediterranean countries, the New World, and the hot and humid tropics, even if (for lack of a botanical original) only as flimsy, electrically illuminated, plastic imitations. (Such substitutes originated with soldiers in battlefield service during World War I.) But even in the new millennium, the artificial, indestructible, ersatz trees cannot compete with the true wintertime evergreen. Economically speaking, artificial trees only have a fifteen to twenty percent share of the market.

Other Christmas Trees

In the New World, the Chilean evergreen *Araucaria*, commonly known as the monkey-puzzle tree *(Araucaria araucana)* has been called Christmas tree, but was rarely used as such. In southern Chile, Germans living there sometimes decorated the *Araucaria* for Christmas. Significantly, the huge, impressive tree, with its scaly bark, was worshipped as a shamanic world tree by the natives, the Araucanern or Mapuche.

Some plants are called "Christmas tree" because they are reminiscent of the fir in shape or appearance. Thus, common horsetail *(Equisetum arvense)* and purple loosestrife *(Lythrum salicaria)* are sometimes called Christmas tree or little Christmas tree. The pohutukawa from New Zealand *(Metrosideros excels,* Myrtaceae) is called New Zealand Christmas Tree in the English-speaking world.

The grape hyacinth *(Muscari* spp.)—a very popular ornamental plant—is sometimes called Christmas tree because of the shape of its blooms. It is also used in floral arrangements on New Year's Day. *Begonia* hybrids from South America and evergreen houseplants with winter blossoms remind us of decorated Christmas trees. The Rex-cultorum *Begonia* hybrids (syn. *B. rex cultorum)*

The south Chilean monkey-puzzle tree *(Araucaria araucana),* a "living fossil," can grow up to 35 meters (about 115 feet). This tree, known in Germany as Chile fir or Andean fir, can be grown as a winter-resistant ornamental tree and decorated like a Christmas tree. The Mapuche of Chile call this sacred tree *pewen* or *pehuén;* they call themselves *pewenches,* meaning "people of the Araucaria." The seeds of the tree (pine nuts) are among their most important foods.

From the Shamanic World Tree to the Christmas Tree

22

Because of its unusual flowering habit, the horse chestnut *(Aesculus hippocastanum)* is sometimes called Christmas tree or Christmas candles in the United States. And indeed, the white or red inflorescence of the horse chestnut is reminiscent of Christmas candles.

are bred from the Himalayan *Begonia rex* Putz. One variety is called "Merry Christmas." It has emerald green leaves with bright silver dots in a red center.

Because of their flowers, the bugleweed *(Ajuga reptans)* and the horse chestnut *(Aesculus hippocastanum)* are two plants that remind us of Christmas trees decorated with candles, and as a result may be called either Christmas tree* or Christmas candle. The horse chestnut comes from the Balkans (Northern Greece, Bulgaria), and was introduced to Central Europe only in the sixteenth century. Horse chestnut wood has been used to make a powder for incorporation in fireworks for New Year's Eve. Horse chestnut flour was an ingredient in Schneeberger snuff powder, the main ingredient of which is Christ rose or hellebore. The horse chestnut is considered a good luck talisman. Normally, one carries three chestnuts in a pocket.

*Christmas tree is also the black-market name for a barbiturate (Tuinal) that is sold in the form of red and green pills (Landy 1971, 50).

Holy Trees

"Wherever the tree of knowledge is—there is paradise." This is what the oldest and the youngest snakes say.
FRIEDRICH NIETZSCHE, 1886, *JENSEITS VON GUT UND BÖSE*
[BEYOND GOOD AND EVIL], SPRÜCHE UND ZWISCHENSPIELE, 152

From the Shamanic World Tree to the Christmas Tree

Whenever we decorate the evergreen tree and make it the center of the Christmas feast, we are engaging unconsciously with very ancient ideas. We

Branches in the snow: a natural work of art. (Photo by Claudia Müller-Ebeling)

From the Shamanic World Tree to the Christmas Tree

engage with the fecundity of nature, with the fact that, after all the darkness, spring comes again every year. We engage with the cyclical events in which we are bound, which are reinforced in our minds each year by the recurrent Christmas ritual. We engage with times long past, when natural events that we now take for granted were holy to human beings. Is this why we are filled with joy to see the awestruck eyes of happy children standing before the lighted tree, because we—as grown-ups—have forgotten how to be amazed by the wonders that surround us?

In the shamanic world, not only every tree, but every *being* was and is holy—because they are all imbued with the wonderful power of life, the great mystery of universal Being. "Yes, we believe that, even below heaven, the forests have their gods also, the sylvan creatures and fauns and different kinds of goddesses" (Pliny the Elder II, 3). Parents are especially holy because they are the gods that create new life. In the same way that heaven and Earth can be considered the parents of earthly life, so are parents creators of life in their own right. Everything is holy; you must only declare it holy. Holiness is a human quality projected on and reflected by the cosmic reality of all things. "Holiness is the original source of life in the human being. And it was given to the child when it was born in the truth and in the spirit" (Grönbech 1997, 119).

Every tree, like every human being, is a—or rather, is *the*—center of the universe. Big and tall, the great evergreen trees have always been considered holy. They are *helga,* "holied." Tree branches were taken into the hall during feasts. According to the *Poetic Edda,* an ancient compilation of Norse and Germanic verse and mythology, the ash tree was Yggdrasil, the world tree (Poetic Edda V, sp. 19).

Obviously, these special tree beings have a special relationship to the human spirit. Their sanctification gave them a particular sociocultural meaning. Thus, in the Christian interpretation, the tall fir tree is a Christmas tree. The recurrent, multicultural myth of the paradise tree, the tree of knowledge, and the tree of life became in Christianity the cross symbolizing the martyrdom of the sacrificed son of God. Some people in Iceland, Scandinavia, and other regions of the world still worship fir trees as the symbolic embodiment of the mythological world tree and wondrous, ever-fertile nature. In this sense, the neglect and desecration of holy trees is the manifestation of a global cultural catastrophe.

Thus, the felling of the mythical Germanic Donaroak—a tree considered sacred to the pagan gods—did not merely eliminate a physical, material being, but also a spiritual culture. It was the center of life and the focal point of the Chatten, the pagan Germanic ancestors of the Hessians. Because it was holy to them, they fought with all their strength against the sacrilege and were convinced that the bringing down of their sacred tree meant the end of the world. For them, the sacred tree represented the world tree that maintains cosmic order and insures the survival of humanity. When this tree was torn from their consciousness, their culture broke down, no longer having roots or a trunk. Understanding exactly how significant this was, the converted Aurelius Augustinus (354–430 CE), also known as the Neoplatonic Church father Augustine, came to a new conclusion about the cutting of the holy trees of the heathens. He declared: "Do not kill the heathens—just convert them; do not cut their holy trees—consecrate them to Jesus Christ" *(de civitate Dei).*

So it came to pass that the Christmas tree was cut down, but it was also brought into the home as a Christian shrine. In early times, it was holy to the gods and goddesses. When the church could not drive the tree cult out of the people, it dedicated the trees to the Christ Child.

Fir

Abies spp., Pinaceae
Abies alba Mill. (silver fir, white fir)
Abies balsamea (L.) P. Mill. (balsam fir, Canadian balsam fir, balm of Gilead fir)
Abies fraseri (Pursh) Poir. (Fraser fir)
Abies lasiocarpa (Hook.) Nutt. (alpine fir, Rocky Mountain fir)
Abies magnifica A. Murr. (red fir)
Abies procera Rehd. (noble fir, white fir, red fir)
Abies sibirica Ledeb. (Siberian fir)

Other Names

Christ tree, Christmas tree, fir tree, *kynholz* ("firewood"), noble fir, *tanne, tannenbaum, taxenbaum, weihntsbaum*

> *The fir is more warm than cold, and holds many powers within itself.*
> *And it is associated with bravery. Wherever the fir wood stands, the*
> *spirits of the air hate it, and shun it. Enchantments and magic spells have*
> *less power to effect things there, than they do in other places.*
> Hildegard von Bingen, *Physica*, III, 23

Not many people can distinguish between fir and spruce, so here are their most important features: Fir cones point up, while spruce cones point down to the ground.* Fir needles are soft and run horizontally from the branches; spruce needles are pointed and grow in a circle around the branch.

Firs can be found in many regions of the world and can grow up to 60 meters (almost 200 feet) tall. The Black Forest of Europe got its name from the

Yggdrasil (the world tree) was associated with Odin's horse (Yggr=Odin, Old Nordic for "the terrible"). The double horses are an old Germanic motif that has survived in examples like this one, depicting wooden, crossed horse heads at the end of a ridgepole. In northern Germany, they have been called "Wotan's horses" up to the present time. (Motif circa 1900)

*A large number of fir cones indicate a hard winter to come, but also point to a good harvest. "To help little children go to sleep, put a fir cone under the pillow" (Hiller 1989, 285).

From the Shamanic World Tree to the Christmas Tree

High above, in heaven, angels are pouring Christmas gifts from Christ's manger.

From the Shamanic World Tree to the Christmas Tree

26

dark, dense, needle growth of fir trees. Up to the present day, the densest fir forests are still found in this region. And it is from here that the fir conquered the living rooms of the entire world—as the classic Christmas tree. Their evergreen-needle attire is the theme of the popular Christmas song with a melody from the eighteenth century:

> *O Christmas tree, O Christmas tree*
> *how lovely are thy branches.*
> *Not only green when summer's here*
> *but in the coldest time of year . . .*

The Old High German word *tanna* not only means fir (and also, most astonishingly, oak), but—like the Middle High German *tan*—also means forest (Höfler 1990, 49). Thus, with the fir tree, you bring the forest and the wilderness itself into your house. What's more, the German name for fir, *tanne*, may be related to the word for fire, *tan*.*

In the forests of Europe, the fir has always been a holy tree. "Tacitus (I, 51) describes the holy feast *Tasana*, where people carried fir branches in their hands; and our Christmas tree also originates in this feast" (von Perger 1864, 340). Holy firs have always been worshipped in alpine countries and were considered the dwelling place, or seat, of the gods. The people believed that spirit beings lived in the firs. Even today, you can find firs in the forests that are objects of religious worship. They can be distinguished by the presence of a picture of the holy Mary, rarely because they bear a cross.

In Indo-Germanic Phrygia (Asia Minor), the fir was dedicated to the fertility goddess Cybele. Romans saw in the enclosed shape of the fir cone a symbol of virginity, and dedicated it to the goddess of the hunt and the forest, Diana. According to a legend of the Siberian Jakuten, the souls of their shamans were born in a fir on the mountain Dzokuo. And in the end, the fir became the Christmas tree of the sacred nights.

In shamanic cultures, holy trees were not to be thoughtlessly chosen and cut down, as this violated a deforestation taboo. Whoever disregarded a holy tree was punished with illness or death: "For the thieves of fir trees, it was prophesized that their arm would be cut. Whoever cut down a fir in defiance of this law was condemned to seven years of bad luck" (Hiller 1989, 285). Nevertheless, fir wood was used for ritual purposes and implements. Thus the fir tree itself, as well as its branches and the Advent wreaths made of them, had a central meaning at Christmastime.

FIR RESIN AS INCENSE

The perfume of fir resin and drying fir needles gives Advent and the whole Christmas season a characteristic, irresistible aroma.† Most firs produce a resin that is uniform in smell, consistency, and character, which explains why they have been called "resin trees." Because of its resin content, the fresh or dried wood catches fire easily and was used as kindling to start fires. This is why firs have also been called *kynholz,* meaning "firewood." In Europe, fir resin might well be the oldest incense substance of all. The use of fir for incense started long before trade in exotic resins began. In early modern times, fir resin was well known and often used as ersatz frankincense (olibanum).

Dried fir needles burn loudly and quickly. They produce a white smoke that is full of resin and smells like fir but disperses in a short time. The white or noble fir contains 0.5 percent essential oils in its needles and cones, consisting of bornyl acetate, pinene, limonene, and more. Turpentine, including so-called Strasbourg turpentine, is another product of fir. It consists of 34 percent essential oils, 72 percent resin, and some succinic acid. When turpentine is reduced to essential oil, the residue left behind is rosin.

On the trunk of this holy fir near Ruswil, Switzerland, there is a Christian cross and a memorial plate.

MAGICAL AND FOLK USE

Like many other plants with a longstanding symbolic association with Christmas, fir branches are believed to serve a guardian function and are used to ward off harmful influences. "In some places the fir branches are in front of doors and animal stalls on Christmas Eve, to prevent illnesses and epidemics. The servants are not to be paid for collecting these branches; and are therefore given cakes and clothes as a gift" (von Perger 1864, 343). In rural areas they are also used for weather forecasts. "Fir branches are used to show the weather when you balance them horizontally on a wall and their top goes up or down for an inch or so, to show if the weather turns either good or bad" (von Perger 1864, 343).

Spruce

Picea spp., Pinaceae
Picea abies (L.) Karst. (Norway spruce)
Picea engelmannii Parry ex Engelm. (Engelmann spruce)
Picea mariana P. Mill. (black spruce)

OTHER NAMES

Black fir, cross fir, *fiotha* (Old High German), forest incense, *gräne; grötzli, kynhol(t)z* ("firewood"), red spruce, red fir, resin fir, tar fir

> *As mother tree and tree of life, the spruce is symbolic of the female's nurturing and life-renewing power. Pagan German tribes venerated the Irmin pillar as a tree sanctuary (or holy tree). The sacred Irmin pillar was a spruce and later became the May tree.*
> STRASSMANN 1994, 135

Spruce trees are found in Europe, North America, and as far east as Asia. In some areas, it is a more popular Christmas tree than the fir. In western Europe, the spruce is sometimes called by the common name fir, but nobody ever seems to call fir trees "spruce."

From the Shamanic World Tree to the Christmas Tree

Magical and Folk Use

Many of the qualities mentioned above for the fir tree may also be attributed to the spruce. By using spruce, one called upon its ability to ward off evil forces: "Bringing the spruce into the room had originally to do with the worshipping of the spirits that guarded the forest" (Schöpf 1986, 86). The calming effects of spruce needle essential oil in tonic bath cures made it useful for revitalizing the nerves. "A spruce smudging has a calming effect on the body, and allows it to center itself again" (Strassmann 1994, 138).

The spruce is identified not only with the fir, but also with the pine.* Thus the Gallic Rhine Celts made offerings of pine and spruce cones to the gods associated with the sources of springs and fountains (Höfler 1911, 20). Nature-oriented people in some regions still believe that witches dance near spruces, and that blue lights seen dancing around holy spruces in the night are the souls of the dead, drawn to the trees (Fink 1983, 46).

Pine

Pinus spp., Pinaceae
Pinus sylvestris L. (Scots pine)
Pinus nigra Arnold (Austrian pine, European black pine)
Pinus palustris P. Mill. (longleaf pine, pitch pine)

Other Names

Fire tree, *föhren* ("pine bud" or "pine wood"), *heiligföhre* ("sacred pine wood"), *kienbaum*, red pine

Cultivated pine: *Pinus pumila* "Globe."

*Pine branches and pinecones were associated with the ancient god Sylvanus, god of the grove and the fields (Simon 1990, 204f).

From the Shamanic World Tree to the Christmas Tree

Witches also, yes, even the devil, are hiding in the old pine wood (föhren). In the branches of a pine wood tree in Villanders the witches played enchanting music. This is the last reminder that a human being should not come near a sacred tree!

FINK 1983, 50

Because of its shrublike growth habit, the pine was less suitable for use as a Christmas tree than the fir or spruce. Nevertheless, because of its ritual significance, it was considered a sacred tree, which can be seen easily in the name *heiligföhre* (sacred pine wood).

MAGICAL AND FOLK USE

Pines are a symbol of immortality and resurrection. The idea that lucky children could find treasure hidden under *Föhren* (pine wood) may come from the tree's long history as an object of pagan worship (Fink 1983, 50). Like fir and spruce, the perfume of pine needles and pine resin was considered "forest incense."

Larch

Larix spp., Pinaceae
Larix decidua P. Mill (European larch)
Larix occidentalis Nutt. (western larch, hackmatack, western tamarack)
Larix sibirica Ledeb. (Siberian larch)

OTHER NAMES

Hackmatack, *lärche; lärchenbaum,* tamarack

Unlike other evergreen, needle-bearing trees, the larch turns gold in autumn and loses its needles in winter. Even though the larch is different in this respect from classic evergreen needle trees, one can find larches in the Alps (for example, in Tirol or Switzerland) that are worshipped as "holy larch" or "Mother of God tree." People put offerings or votive gifts in the hollow wood of their stems, including items such as teeth, coins, and small, hollowed-out balls of turf.

> In Kaserackern, near Wolfsgruben (south Tirolia) there was a "holy" larch. In some nights it was on fire, burning to the skies; yet it was never consumed, and in its branches a human voice was sighing. The tree was considered enchanted and was worshipped. The folk belief had it that the tree was from an age, long ago, when the pagan world still reigned (Fink 1983, 48f).

Folk legends hold that angels and devils fought in the branches of larch trees. Larches were also considered dancing and resting places for forest and mountain fairies. This is why they are dedicated to the *säligen*, the forest women, and the horned animals of the forest.

Maritime pine (*Pinus pinaster*) on the Gulf of Corinth.

Larch fungi *(Fomitopsis officinalis,* syn. *Laricifomes officinalis)* on the tree's trunk suggest a shamanic ladder to heaven. There is evidence that the larch fungi was used as medicine in the time of Ötzi—the 5,300-year-old "iceman" mummy found in an Alpine glacier. (Woodcut: Tabernaemontanus, 1731)

Left: When the yew *(Taxus baccata)* bears its red berries, it looks like a decorated Christmas tree.

Right: Yew branch with red berries. Contrary to popular belief, the fruit is not poisonous; the red flesh (seed coat) has a sweet, slimy, fruity flavor. The seeds, leaves, and bark contain the strong poison taxin. The fear of yew fruit seems to have the same background as the fear of bird berries. The edible red berries were demonized because they were among the holy fruits of the druids.

Yew

Taxus spp., Taxaceae
Taxus baccata L. (English yew)
Taxus brevifolia Nutt. (Pacific yew)

OTHER NAMES

Aiw yew, common yew, yew tree, tasso

Yews grow in temperate forests in Europe, North and Central America, and parts of Asia and the South Pacific. This dark tree, with its slimy, bright red berries, can grow as tall as 18 meters (about 60 feet) and may live as long as 750 years. With a trunk diameter of 1 meter (about 3 feet), the oldest yew in Germany—the so-called Hintersteiner yew in the Allgäu, near Bärgündele—is estimated to be around two thousand years old (Hecker 1995, 168). If we could only decipher the rustle of the wind in the soft needles of its tangled branches, this veteran yew might be able to tell us much about the great changes of history.

The yew gets its name from the Gothic *aiw,* meaning "always, eternal, evergreen" (Prahn 1922, 142). This etymological root reveals several layers of meaning: knowledge of the great old age yews can reach; the Germanic interpretation of the tree as a symbol of eternity; and the use of the yew as a cemetery planting, meant to give eternal life to the dead and instill memory of the dead in the minds of the living.

MAGICAL AND FOLK USE

Its evergreen needles secure the yew a place in the ethnobotany of Christmas. It is a symbol of immortality—a plant of death and resurrection and a world

From the Shamanic World Tree to the Christmas Tree

30

tree. Carrying a piece of yew wood is supposed to ward off evil spells and fear of darkness. Its needles impart a cleansing scent.

Mountain Ash
Sorbus spp., Rosaceae
Sorbus americana Marsh. (American mountain ash)
Sorbus aucuparia L. (European mountain ash)

OTHER NAMES
Ash tree, bird berry, dogberry, dragon tree, *eberesche, moosbeerbaum*, rowan, *Thorsbjög, Thors schutz*, witchwood

Red and white bird berries (fruit of the mountain ash, *Sorbus aucuparia*) in the snow. It was a holy fruit to the pagan Germans, associated with the love goddess, Freia (=Freya), and the boar-riding fertility god, Fro (=Freyr). To the early Christians, it was a "devil berry." (Illustration by Erns Kreidolf, 1863–1956, for *A Winter Tale*)

> *If there are a lot of berries in the branches, it is considered the sign of a very hard winter. . . . If you take into consideration what good observers of nature our farmers are, you cannot believe that this is just hearsay.*
>
> MARZELL 1935, 104

The mountain ash is a shrub that can grow to a height of 15 meters (about 50 feet). It has red berries in autumn and a meaning in Christmas ethnobotany as a sacred tree. Thus country people once practiced the following custom on Christmas Eve: "All the bird berry bushes are supposed to have burning candles for the midnight hour that do not go out, even in the icy wind and in harsh snowing" (Riemerschmidt 1962, 14).

The origin of the German name *eberesche* is not clear. It may derive from *aber* in the sense that this word expresses objection. Thus, the name may indicate that this is a false ash—in other words, not a member of the genus *Fraxinus* (true ash trees). The botanist Heinrich Marzell calls it "a lively, living tree" because it is often the only deciduous tree living in the rocky desolation of the Alpine region. This observation of its nature—along with the typical color combination of white and red shown by the berries of some species—may explain its symbolic meaning in the winter Advent time.

In old Germanic times the bird berry was holy to the God Thor (=Donar) and was associated with the holy ash tree or world tree, Yggdrasil. "Our ancestors took the red berries as a sign of thunder (Donar was the god of thunder and lightning. The feathered leaves symbolized for them the clouds)" (Abraham and Thinnes 1995, 68). This explains why mountain ash branches were woven into wreaths and hung as a protection against thunder and lightning. The branches also served as divining rods. To keep animals healthy, it was customary to cut a

From the Shamanic World Tree to the Christmas Tree

branch from the mountain ash tree on St. Martin's Day (November 11)—this is the so-called "Martin's rod." The strength and endurance of the mountain ash tree was also a symbol for being able to find one's way in the dark, not only in the darkness of wintertime, but also at night. This is the origin of a specific folk belief: "Whoever was traveling at night and had a piece of bird berry wood in their mouth could never get lost" (Abraham and Thinnes 1995, 69).

According to a legend from Brandenburg, Germany, the mountain ash tree grew from the bones of Judas (Abraham and Thinnes 1995, 69). This Christian interpretation is based on the plant's role in pagan mythology. The bitterness of its fruit, which becomes edible only after the influence of frost, made the mountain ash a symbol of evil later on:

> Rooted in folk custom and folk healing art is the belief that the mountain ash is the tree of the druids, the Celts, the heathens, the witches. There is no question about it: Eating the fruits must lead to evil. And this is why the bird berry—unlike its close relatives, the rose hip and the sloe—plays only a minor part in diet and recipes. . . . The name of the bird berry is contaminated by the stain of a plant associated with witches and heathens (Pfyl and Knieriemen 1986, 6, 7).

St. Nicholas and His Little Helper, Ruprecht

> *Out from the forest I am coming*
> *I have to tell you: it's Christmas everywhere!*
> *Everywhere on the fir tops*
> *I saw golden lights glimmer . . .*
>
> *Do you have your little sack with you?*
> *I said: The little sack is here:*
> *Apples, nuts, and almonds*
> *Little children like to eat*
> THEODOR STORM, 1852, "KNECHT RUPRECHT"

Before we look at the myriad Christmas plants with which these mythical characters are connected, let us think for a minute about the appearance and origin of Santa Claus and his shadowy helper, Ruprecht.

"Tomorrow comes Santa Claus, comes with all his gifts." This, from a popular song by Hoffmann von Fallersleben, expresses the joyous anticipation of European children on the eve of December 6, St. Nicholas Day. The gifts Santa Claus generously distributed to our grandparents and great-grandparents in their tender childhoods were "apples, nuts and almonds." In Catholic regions, St. Nicholas was shown in full array with a crosier and bishop's cap (miter), striding along, full of dignity—gaining the respect of the children because of his long white beard—accompanied by his helper, Ruprecht, who carried a sack and a rod. This rod appears to be the original "rod of punishment" with which bad children might be punished during the Christmas season.

In some legends, Ruprecht is part of Wotan's wild army. The name "helper Ruprecht" comes from *hruod-peraht* (meaning "shining with glory") and identifies him with Wotan (=Odin) (Riemerschmidt 1962, 27). In Alpine regions, Ruprecht is known by the name Krampus. He is associated with the hazel wood rod, which relates to Thor (=Donar):

> The hazelnut was holy to Donar, the God of marital and animal fertility. The hazel wood rod was considered a great rod of life. With this symbol of the penis, women and animals were beaten "with gusto" in order for them to become fertile. . . . Sources can be found for this erotic pagan custom in the eighth century. Cut on St. John's Day *(Berchtentag),* a wishing rod *(penis)* is a hazel wood rod with a year-old shoot. This rod of life became a wishing rod as well in order to find hidden treasure. It was given a human face when cutting its lower part, and then given two legs (Aigremont 1987 I, 38).

Numerous postcards handed down a picture of the Christmas man who comes from the fir forest and brings presents for the children. (©Postcard Edition Andrea Gebauer, Wolfsburg)

Both the healing and harming uses of hazel wood are derived from the observation that in nature, hazel wood bushes remain untouched by lightning. On one hand, hazel wood rods were believed to ward off evil spirits, such as the "angry army," the "devil's pursuit," and the "fiery men" (Abraham and Thinnes 1995, 82). On the other, there are accounts of witches "beating on the water of a lake with a hazel wood rod, until a thundercloud appeared in the sky" (Schöpf 2001, 175). "In the Christian legend its power against thunder was shown by the fact that Mary and the baby Jesus found protection under a hazel wood bush during a violent thunderstorm" (Abraham and Thinnes 1995, 84). Like the hazel wood rod he carries, Ruprecht unites both a beneficial and a frightening side.

The Various Guises of Santa Claus

The painter Moritz von Schwind (1804–1871) passed down an image of Santa Claus in 1847 (in the *Munich Picture Book*) as a muffler-wrapped "Mr. Winter" carrying a Christmas tree into a town lit up with candles. However, he was portrayed as Sünnerklaas in a drawing from the lower Rhine; grim-faced, he rode a white horse, wore a black hood and a high-collared coat, and carried a rod and basket. He requested entry into southern German farmhouses as bishop St. Nicholas (accompanied by his horned helper, Ruprecht), rod in hand and basket on his shoulder. He is known as Samichlaus in Switzerland. In much of North

Mr. Winter, the first Christmas man. (Etching by Moritz von Schwind for the *Munich Picture Book*, 1847)

America and in Scandinavia, he drives a sleigh pulled by reindeer through the sky, and drops presents down chimneys into warm living rooms. In the Netherlands, he comes as Sinterklaas to the land via ship, accompanied by his servants, the *zwarte pieten*. Today, we see countless Santas sporting glued-on white beards and red-hooded, white-trimmed suits in advertisements and malls.

Who is this fairy-tale creature who has had different names and looks in various countries, regions, and time periods? Who or what is Nicholas, the Christmas man? Hamburg anthropologist Rüdiger Vossen believes he holds a deep and multilayered meaning: "In the end he is a compromise figure between Catholic, Protestant and pre-Christian beliefs; a mixture of childlike godfather imaginations and a child-friendly St. Nicholas, and a demonized, punishing helper, Ruprecht, with his rod and his sack" (Vossen 1985, 56). In Catholic regions, St. Nicholas worship dates back to the fourth century, to the time of the Bishop of Myra in Lycia, who was also named Nicholas.

This explains why St. Nicholas of Christmas mythology is often pictured with a bishop's crosier and a miter. St. Nicholas of Myra is believed to have been born in the harbor town of Parara, in the region formerly known as Lycia (now part of Turkey). He was ordained bishop in Myra (the present day Demre, Turkey) and died there around 342 CE. Some sources cite the day of his death as December 6, the actual date of today's St. Nicholas Day. According to legend, he performed miracles, gave away his inheritance with open hands to the poor, and helped in a time of famine with a shipload of corn. In 980 CE, his bones were taken to the Italian harbor town of Bari. From there, his cult spread to central and northern Europe, and, beginning in the sixth century, became associated with the cult surrounding a bishop of the same name: Nicholas of Sion, Bishop of Pinora. This Nicolas founded a monastery in Myra and was said to perform miracles as well. In the Eastern Church, worship of St. Nicholas dates back to the sixth century CE.

In Catholic iconography, St. Nicholas was the patron saint of children and was once considered one of the fourteen auxiliary saints, depicted with three gold bars or three golden apples. He is associated with the holiday of the innocent children and the custom of electing a child bishop in convent schools each year. Despite the fact that it was forbidden by the Church, this popular custom has persisted, but between the thirteenth century and today the date shifted from December 28 to December 6.

The legendary charity of the Bishop of Myra did not play any role in artistic representations of the Christmas St. Nicholas for many centuries. The earliest picture of St. Nicholas distributing Christmas presents dates from the fifteenth century. But in the nineteenth century, many of the atmospheric illustrations of German romantics, such as Moritz von Schwind or Ludwig Richter (1803–1884), made the holy man popular as a harbinger of the Christmas season—and one who gave presents to children. The exotic delicacies that he brought from his far away home in Asia Minor were described in a song lyric: "Ginger nuts, little apples, almonds and currants; this is what he gives to the good child."

SINTERKLAAS IN THE NETHERLANDS

In the Netherlands, according to newspaper sources, the eve of December 6 is "the only national folk feast" in honor of Sinterklaas, patron of sailors and merchants. In the second or third week of November he comes in his boat from Spain* to the Netherlands, accompanied by his black servants, the *zwarte pieten,* who dance on the boat and make jokes. Sinterklaas is dressed like a bishop. The *zwarte pieten* are dressed like medieval German mercenary soldiers, *landsknechts,* in baggy, blue-and-yellow or red-and-black pants, with pointed caps of the same colors, gloves, and shoes. Upon their arrival, the mayor welcomes them, and Sinterklaas is led through the town on a white horse while the *zwarte pieten* throw sweets and candy on the streets. In the Netherlands, the arrival of Sinterklaas is more important than Christmastime is in Germany. On December 6, Sinterklaas celebrates his birthday and vanishes again on a secret passage over Germany to Spain.

Two weeks before the arrival of Sinterklaas, Dutch children put their shoes in front of the fireplace with a little present for the white horse and sing songs, such as the following:

> *Sinterklaas, castrated cock*[†]
> *Throw something in my shoe*
> *Throw something in my boot*

Sinterklaas announces his arrival with a knock on the door and leaves a sack of presents and personal poems for each child. If he appears in person, he talks with the children about what they did during the past year. He rewards the good children with presents, the bad ones with the rod. (Most of the handmade presents given to children at this time relate ironically to the idiosyncrasies of the recipients.) On the next morning the children also find a little gift—in return for their gift to the white horse—in their shoes. Sinterklaas brings delicacies from the orient as well. Traditionally, these include marzipan, ginger nuts, oranges, and spiced biscuits *(spekulator)*. The name of this traditional

*Bari, the Italian town in which the bones of St. Nicholas of Myra are kept, once belonged to Spain.

†The description "castrated cock" refers to Sinterklaas's colorful bishop's miter.

From the Shamanic World Tree to the Christmas Tree

Christmas biscuit derives from the function of the bishop as "speculator," that is, overseer of the children.

By 1613, Calvinists were preaching in strict opposition to feasts honoring St. Nicholas, condemning them as heathen idol worship. Jacobus Sceperus (1658) wrote a 229-page indictment against Nicholas and accused him of being a papal seducer. It is interesting to note that the popular name Sinterklaas quite diplomatically does not refer to the Roman saint, who even today is considered taboo in the Protestant Netherlands.

SANTA CLAUS: THE TRANSATLANTIC CHRISTMAS MAN

> *Only in the year 1931 did the American commercial artist, Harold Sundblom, create the image of the Santa Claus that we see everywhere nowadays. Sundblom painted the Christmas man Santa for the commercials as a happy, rotund, grandfather figure, in the colors of the company that paid him to do so: Coca-Cola*
>
> APPLETON 2002, 56

The image of the Christmas man with his white-trimmed red coat and white beard—the one who flies through the air driving his reindeer sleigh, delivering presents down chimneys—was created in North America. Images from Dutch and German immigrants added a rudimentary shamanic influence. The Dutchmen Tony van Rentergehem, who immigrated to the United States in 1948, dedicated a whole book, *When Santa Claus Was a Shaman*, to the shamanic roots of the Santa Claus image.

St. Nicholas's Presents

The presents distributed by St. Nicholas are of great significance to our ethnobotanical approach to Christmas. St. Nicholas and his helper Ruprecht not only brought the hazel wood rod, but also left gifts. Typical gifts were nuts, dried fruits, chocolate, spices, biscuits, winter greens, and toys.

The presents from St. Nicholas's sack are symbolic of fertility, love, and marital good fortune. Today in Nepal, during weddings of the Newari (a people in the valley of Kathmandu who specialize in trade and arts and crafts) guests receive gifts that to a great degree resemble those from the typical European St. Nicholas's sack. One might see walnuts, almonds, pistachios, cashews, white candy sugar, cassia rinds, green and brown cardamom* fruits, cloves, chocolate, coffee candy, butter toffees, sherbet powder, popcorn, raisins, dried and salted plums, coconut flesh, betel nuts (traditional fertility symbols and love magic), *pan parag* (a betel nut snack mixture), hard dried cheese, and dried dates, apricots, and figs.

PLANTS ASSOCIATED WITH NICHOLAS AND RUPRECHT

> *The most common sort of geranium is dedicated in folklore to the holy Ruprecht, patron of the home. And it is referred to in this manner by the*

This vignette of a hazelnut bush with a nutcracker is from Franz Pocci.

*Brown cardamom fruits are from the greater cardamom (*Amomum subulatum* Roxb. Alainci), also known as ginger plant.

From the Shamanic World Tree to the Christmas Tree

botanist, who very well knows that the old Hruotperaht *means "shining glory" and that the name is as much about* Ruprecht *as it has also become* Robert . . .*

SÖHNS 1920, 159

From Ludwig Richter comes this picture of a simple lit tree and a rod on a chair, which awaited bad children on December 6.

In the German folk tradition, a number of plants are associated with Nicholas. Veronica or bird's eye speedwell *(Veronica chamaedrys)* is called by the German folk name *niklasl,* which translates in English to "eye of Christ." This plant belongs, like *königskerze* (king's candle or mullein, *Verbascum* spp.) and *niklaslbärtchen* or *niklosbärtchen* (Nicholas's beard, *Verbascum* spp.) to the group of plants known as wild tobacco—the "baccy" herbs smoked by country folk and even Santa Claus himself, as old illustrations suggest.

The plant genus name *Sanicula* (known by the German common name *sanikel*) is a contraction of "St. Nicholas." Plants in this genus are sometimes called Santa Claas or nickelweed. *Nickel* also means "goblin." Thus, in the name *sanikel,* we find St. Nicholas combined with a goblin—the helper Ruprecht!

Cranesbill *(Geranium robertianum)* is dedicated to helper Ruprecht or St. Ruprecht, the patron saint of the home. Other names for this plant include herb Robert, Herba Ruperti, Robert's herb, Ruprecht's herb, stork's beak, St. Catherine's herb, and St. Ruprecht's weed. St. Ruprecht, a missionary of the Frankish Christians, died in 717: "The saint to whom the *Geranium robertianum* is dedicated is the guardian spirit of the plant here" (Höfler 1990, 25). It is the "embodiment of the spirits of the river Elbe, who can move on the water and in the air" (Höfler 1990, 24). "It might have had an association with Thor, the god of fertility and matrimony. This is why it is also holy with St. Ruprecht, the patron of the home" (Aigremont 1987 II, 50).

In Nepal, wedding gifts for every guest symbolize long life, much like the contents of St. Nicholas's sack. (Kathmandu, Nepal, March 2003)

---

*Translators note: This is a play on the Latin species name, *Geranium robertianum.*

From the Shamanic World Tree to the Christmas Tree

The purple flower cranesbill or herb Robert *(Geranium robertianum)* is called St. Ruprecht's weed in the German vernacular.

The yellow-flowered damiana *(Turnera diffusa)* is called *hierba de San Nicolás* (herb of St. Nicholas) in Mexico.

From the Shamanic World Tree to the Christmas Tree

PLANTS ASSOCIATED WITH ST. NICOLAS IN MEXICO

The Mexican "flowers of Nicholas" remind us of the blossom miracles of the Old World. *Flor de San Nicolás, San Nicolás,* and *estrellita* (little star) are all names for *Milla biflora* (Liliaceae), known in English by the common name Mexican star. It has six-petaled, white or yellow, starlike flowers that bloom at Christmastime. People collect them on rainy days and use them as house decorations during the Christmas season. In Aztec, this petite lily plant was called *yolo-patli* (heart root) or *tlalizqui-xochitl* (white rose of the Earth). A colonial Aztec text praises its blossoms: "*Tlalizqui-xochitl:* It is perfect, outstanding, relaxing, very relaxing. Its flowers glitter, lay there glittering, they shine and glitter when it blossoms. It has a very relaxing perfume; it fills the air . . ." (Sahagun, Florentine Codex XI, 10).

The Turkish crescent (*Thevetia peruviana* [Pers.] K. Schum., Apocynaceae), which grows from Mexico to Peru, has a trumpet-like yellow flower and is considered a strong narcotic. In Aztec it was called *yoyotl* (rattle). Today, this very popular tropical plant goes by the name *San Nicolás.*

Yellow-flowering damiana (*Turnera diffusa,* Willd. ex J. A. Schultes, Turneraceae), treasured as an aphrodisiac herb, is also known as *San Nicolás* or *Hierbas de San Nicolás.* Related plants that go by the same name include *Turnera diffusa* var. *aphrodisiaca* (G. H. Ward) Urban, *Turnera pumilla* L. (*bruja,* witch), *Turnera ulmifolia* L. (*clave de oro,* golden clove). The ersatz damiana *Chrysactinia mexicana* A. Gray (Asteraceae, false damiana) can be included in this group as well.

Mexican Herbs of St. Nicholas

Hierba de San Nicolás was the Mexican name for a long list of plants:
- *Thymophylla acerosa* (DC.) Strother, Asteraceae (syn. *Dyssodia acerosa* DC.) is a smoking herb of the North American Indians.
- *Gutierrezia sarothrae* (Pursh.) Britt. & Rusby, Asteraceae, also called *pasmo, hierba del pasmo,* or broom snakeweed, is a symbolic plant for December ceremonies. It is also used as a gynecological medicine, an aromatic remedy for new mothers, and a ceremonial medicine for ailing gods. It contains aromatic volatile oils (monoterpenes, diterpenes) and flavonoids.
- *Stevia serrata* Cav., Asteraceae, is a yellow blossoming mountain plant that is also called *raíz de San Nicolás* (root of St. Nicholas) or simply *Nicolás.* The plant contains pyrrolizidine alkaloids (liver toxins) and volatile oils.
- *Tecoma stans* (L.), Juss. ex Kunth, Bignoniaceae, the trumpet tree plant, is also called *ojo de Santa Lucía* (eye of St. Lucia) in Spanish and *xkanlol* (yellow flower) in Mayan. It contains psychoactive alkaloids (indole and tryptamine).
- *Hybanthus* spp., Violaceae

Damiana has been used since prehistoric times in North America and the Mayan region as a medicine and a love potion. In his *Chronica* (1699), the Spanish missionary Jesús María de Salvatierra mentioned its use as an aphrodisiac among the North American Indians for the first time. The name damiana comes either from St. Damian, the patron saint of apothecaries, or from the name Peter Damiani, a critic of the Catholic Church who decried the lack of morals among the clerics of the eleventh century. The Austrian botanist Josef August Schultes (1773–1831) described the plant for the first time in 1820. In the nineteenth century, the herb was taken up as a tonic and an aphrodisiac in the United States; it was included in the U.S. National Formulary (1888–1947) and was in the Mexican Pharmacopoeia. In 1880, it was introduced to Europe. At the end of the 1960s, the plant gained a reputation as a legal high—an ersatz marijuana or tobacco. Today, it is the basis of a commercial baccy (herbal smoking) mixture.

Baccy Claus: The Smoking Christmas Man

The vision was putting out its wings in ecstatic flight; and there were no earthly laws anymore. With every moment the rapture was growing, and allowed an even more delicious sight in a resolution that was like incense smoke rising up from the surface of an eternal sea.

LUDLOW 2001

Illustrators of the nineteenth century, such as Thomas Nast (1840–1902), painted us a picture of a comfy, pipe-smoking Christmas man. From the jolly expression on his face, one might even be tempted to call him "Baccy Claus," as baccy is an old word for "strong tobacco." Where did this image come from? Perhaps from excavations providing clues from prehistoric times? In the area of Limburg, prehistoric pipes are occasionally unearthed. They are called *feenpipjes* and were once considered smoking tools for giants, fairies, elves, and earth sprites. "They were originally used in the ceremonial smoke offerings of the pagans even though they were used for purposes having to do with intoxication and to put oneself into another state of mind."* And this brings us back to thoughts of the shamanic origins of the Christmas man.

Baccy Claus has tobacco use in common with shamans, healers, and medicine people of all times and all worldviews. These shamans handed down to us shaman pipes, peace pipes, and baccy pipes of all kinds. In the Grimm fairy tale *The Blue Light,* the hero—a soldier—always meets a helpful, mysterious, magic being, a little man, a mandrake sprite, whenever he lights his pipe.

The oldest European pipe used for smoking opium was found in Cyprus, on the island of Aphrodite. In Kítion, an old Phoenician settlement on Cyprus, there was a very important temple in which the great goddess was worshipped under her Phoenician name, Astarte. Inside the sanctuary, a three-thousand-year-old carved ivory opium pipe dating from the Bronze Age was found

*Kappell, F., In *Zeitschrift des Vereins für rheinische und westfälische Volkskunde,* 1907 (quoted in Golowin 1985, 122).

From the Shamanic World Tree to the Christmas Tree

SHE IS FAT AND CHUNKY BUT YOU WILL LIKE HER

Christmas tobacco label: "Mrs. Jack Frost" is not only a fat cigar, but is also dressed like a royal fly agaric mushroom female; notice her helping spirits bringing her winter greens in the form of a holly twig.

during excavations (Karageorghis, 1976). Numerous antique smoking pipes from the time of the Roman Empire have been found in Europe (Golowin 1985, 121). The dairymen pipes of the Alps, the Nordic and Irish fairy pipes, Danish pipes, and baccy pipes were so popular in their day that one cannot imagine the Christmas man without one. "The long pipe is a safeguard of fidelity" says a popular poem of the nineteenth century. The pipe projects a homey, comfy atmosphere that suits the charitable Christmas man well.

Baccy is, of course, not normal tobacco, but "strong tobacco"—often containing hemp *(Cannabis)*. Etymologically, *baccy* means "bad-smelling tobacco." In Germany, beginning around 1700, baccy was described by the word *knaster*. This is an abbreviation for *kanaster-tobac* or *knastertobak*, words originally used to indicate a high-quality blend of tobacco sold in cane baskets. *Knaster* is believed to be derived from the Greek word *kánna*—meaning "cane"—which in turn goes back to the noun *kánastron*, "a basket made from cane." (The Greek *kanna* is also the root word for *kannabion*, "hemp!"). By way of the Spanish *canasto* and the Dutch *knaster*, it came into the German language (according to the German dictionary, *Duden*).

The German word *knaster* describes a sound with a dark tone; *knister*, in contrast, is a noise with a light tone. For example, the sound of a fire is described as *knistert*, the sound of tobacco as *knastert*. Of course, true tobacco makes no noise when one smokes it. But when the pipe is fed with *Cannabis* flowers containing seeds, then the exploding hemp seeds make little popping sounds: hemp *knastert!*

A useful definition of strong tobacco can be found in the *Encyclopedia of All Folk Medicine* of 1843, one of the most important home medical reference books of the nineteenth century:

> Unscrupulous manufacturers adulterate the smoking tobacco blend by adding to the mix *Ledum palustre* (wild rosemary), henbane, thorn apple—even opium—in order to make the tobacco stronger and more intoxicating. For people who have not developed resistance to it through frequent use, it causes nausea, vomiting, dizziness, intoxication, etc. (Most 1843, 586).

The comfy Father Christmas with his long pipe. (Woodcut by Thomas Nast, circa 1865)

The name "smoke weed" *(rauchkraut)* was applied to *erdrauch,* "earthsmoke" *(Fumaria officinalis,* also called savior weed) as well as common juniper *(Juniperus communis).* Both belonged to the family of "weed" that farmers

40

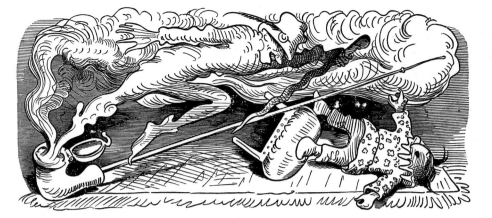

loved to put in their Sunday pipes (carved from juniper wood), blended with a mixture of coltsfoot (*Tussilago farfara,* so named because it looks like a horse's hoof) and dried veronica (*Veronica* spp.).

Baccy Ingredients

> *It is the lovely veronica that brings to us the greetings of our god. Just look into its beautiful eye: it carries the color of fidelity. There is nothing false in it.*
>
> ZIMMERER 1896, 237

Veronica *(Veronica officinalis)* is a strong yet subtly stimulating folk medicine, and is therefore known by many vivid names: basic salvation, *grindheil, grossbatengel,* little heaven flower, men's fidelity, salvation of all damages, snake weed, speedwell, *thunderbesom,* thunder flower, world salvation, and others.

Farmer's tobacco *(Nicotiana rustica)* comes from the New World. When it was introduced to Europe, it was considered a kind of henbane *("Hyoscyamus Peruvianus")* and was smoked in the baccy pipe. Farmer's tobacco is not used as commercial smoking tobacco, but it does contain a high concentration of nicotine: usually 6 percent to 9 percent, though sometimes as much as 16 percent or even 18 percent. It has been called "bad tobacco" because of its status as a weed that could very well cause intoxication.

Strong Tobacco

"In the age of witchcraft the use of hemp was very popular in Europe. And the aphrodisiac effect of the substances that were in the hemp plant was very well known. Hans Ulrich Megerle, better known as Abraham of Santa Clara (1644–1709) preached against the 'farmers that fill themselves up on hemp like the Turks on opium.' After the introduction of coffee and tobacco in the sixteenth and seventeenth centuries, hemp lost its former significance and became a 'poor person's weed.' As a drug of pleasure and ingredient for tobacco, it was of almost no value anymore. Yet, as late as 1925, hemp-tobacco blends were still sold everywhere in Europe, and a pipe with tobacco and hemp was called *Sunday pipe* in Gotthelf's* times" (Lussi 1996, 134).

---

*Translator's note: This is the pseudonym of Albert Bitzius (1797–1854), Swiss pastor and Swiss-German writer.

The night of wrapped packages has arrived.

Baccy Claus brings the presents: pre-rolled Christmas cigarettes. (Christmas card from the magazine *Hanfblatt*, 1999)

Below left: Dried leaves of coltsfoot *(Tussilago farfara)* are an important baccy ingredient. (Woodcut from Brunfels, 1532)

Below right: Hazelwort or European wild ginger *(Asarum europaeum)* contains asarone, a hallucinogenic substance. Hazelwort is among the traditional European incense and baccy substances. (Woodcut from Brunfels, 1532)

---

*Nearly all of these plants are also called "witches' weed" in the folk vernacular.

From the Shamanic World Tree to the Christmas Tree

42

In England, this plant has names specifically related to the ethnobotany of Christmas: European mistletoe, mistletoe, and golden bough (not to be confused with true mistletoe, *Viscum album*). It is also called Sylvester flower (Arends 1935, 263). The dried herb contains a volatile oil and flavonoids.

In the nineteenth century at Christmastime, Christmas herbs were added to baccy blends to give aroma to the smoke: anise, benzoin, cassia flower, cardamom, cinnamon, cascarilla (sweet wood bark), cloves, coriander, gum mastic, iris roots (orris), lemon rind, rose blossoms, star anise, storax, and valerian. In the nineteenth century there was a brand-named tobacco, The Three Magi, that contained baccy ingredients. It was called "preacher baccy" and "hell baccy," and gave smoking products a Christian dualism, just right for the upside-down world of the raw nights! Even today, smoking tobaccos are blended with Christmas spices: vanilla, cocoa, and so on. The Indonesian *kretek* cigarettes are famous; they contain a big portion of cloves.

Many other medicinal and food herbs also served as smoking or baccy weeds. In the folk vernacular these were sometimes called "wild tobacco" or "tobacco flowers": arnica *(Arnica montana)*, burdock *(Arctium lappa)*, belladonna *(Atropa belladonna)*, broadleaf or bitter dock *(Rumex obtusifolius)*, clematis *(Clematis recta)*, coltsfoot *(Tussilago farfara)*, corn flower *(Centaurea cyanus)*, henbane *(Hyoscyamus niger)*, male fern *(Dryopteris filixmas)*, mullein *(Verbascum spp.)*, lavender *(Lavandula spp.)*, lily-of-the-valley *(Convallaria majalis)*, sweet woodruff *(Galium odoratum)*, and yellow sweet clover *(Melilotus officinalis)*.*

❦

Baccy Recipes

The following recipes are mentioned as cultural and historical curiosities and are not intended to suggest actual use. Farmer recipes almost never provide exact quantities, so the dosage of active ingredients can be a problem. Of course, the use of illegal substances as ingredients can also present a problem. Please take into consideration that only Baccy Claus himself is above the law!

Farmer Baccy
Equal parts veronica *(Veronica officinalis)*, coltsfoot *(Tussilago farfara)*, blackberry leaf *(Rubus fruticosus)*, hemp (weed, marijuana, hashish, *Cannabis* spp.), and tobacco *(Nicotiana tabacum* or *N. rustica)*

Stimulant Baccy
Henbane *(Hyoscyamus niger)* or belladonna *(Atropa belladonna)*, baccy weed or hemp *(Cannabis* spp.), dried fly agaric mushroom *(Amanita muscaria)*, and tobacco *(Nicotiana tabacum* or *N. rustica)*

Alexandrian Baccy
Tobacco leaves *(Nicotiana tabacum* or *N. rustica)*, hemp leaves *(Cannabis* spp.), hashish *(Cannabis* spp.), opium poppy latex *(Papaver somniferum)*, mace *(Myristica fragrans,* the seed coat of the nutmeg), cloves *(Syzygium aromaticum)*

Medicinal Baccy (after a recipe from Berlin from the year 1816)
5 parts hemp leaves *(Cannabis sativa)*, 1 part thorn apple seeds *(Datura* spp.)

Christmas Baccy
Leaves of arnica *(Arnica montana)*, veronica *(Veronica* spp.), coltsfoot *(Tussilago farfara)*, sorrel *(Rumex acetosa)*

Herbal Baccy
Mugwort *(Artemisia vulgaris)*, sweet woodruff *(Galium odoratum* [syn. *Asperula odorata])*, yarrow *(Achillea* spp.), great goose grass leaf *(Galium aparine)*, bilberry leaf *(Vaccinium myrtillus)*

Left: The dried leaves of beetroot *(Beta vulgaris)* were used as ersatz tobacco and a baccy ingredient. The German name for beetroot, *mangold,* means "fair." The plant was used—especially by men—as a stimulant. (Prahn 1922, 151)

Center: The winter-resistant leaves of the forest blackberry *(Rubus fruticosus* L., Rosaceae) are a basic ingredient of old baccy mixtures. (Hamburg, February 2003)

Right: The flowers of the female hemp plant *(Cannabis* spp.) produce a baccy commonly known as marijuana or "grass." In earlier times, hemp seeds ("bird food") were cooked in a Christmas mush. In the last years of the twentieth century, many elderly people could still recall how they or their parents sometimes smoked a pipe of "strong tobacco" containing hemp after church, in the morning at a pub, comfortably at home, or on a bench in the garden.

From the Shamanic
World Tree to the
Christmas Tree

Left: A hemp-smoking snowman in the Christmas forest. (Postcard: PsykoMan snowman, © Psykoman 2000)

Center: *Waiting for the Snowman!* (Christmas cigar box label)

Right: St. Peter with his key to heaven, in the garb of Father Christmas, smokes his baccy pipe. With it, he spreads "the perfume of the heavens." (Envelope of an exhibition of the Museum in Altona, Hamburg; Hinrichsen 1994)

From the Shamanic World Tree to the Christmas Tree

Other baccy plants included hawkweed (*Hieracium* spp.), yarrow (*Achillea* spp.), mugwort *(Artemisia vulgaris)*, hazelwort *(Asarum europaeum)*, Roman chamomile *(Chamaemelum nobile)*, as well as leaves of the walnut tree (*Juglans* spp.), wild rosemary *(Ledum palustre)*, potato *(Solanum tuberosum)*, lime or linden tree (*Tilia* spp.), stone clover *(Trifolium arvense)*, witches' weed, bilberry, or huckleberry (*Vaccinium* spp.), rose (*Rosa* spp.), wild cherry (*Prunus serotina)*, sunflower (*Helianthus* spp.), beech (*Fagus* spp.), hawthorn (*Crataegus* spp.), blackberry *(Rubus fruticosus)*, sage *(Salvia officinalis)*, elder (*Sambucus* spp.), and rhubarb (*Rheum* spp.). In the older literature, walnut tree roots, potato roots, and the leaves of the common beet (*Beta vulgaris*) were also listed as baccy ingredients.

In the nineteenth century, hemp (*Cannabis*), thorn apple (*Datura stramonium*, also called smoke apple, raw apple, witches' weed, witches' cumin, and jimsonweed), henbane *(Hyoscyamus niger),* and belladonna *(Atropa belladonna)* were all considered smoking weeds because of their distinctive psychoactive effects. *Cannabis* (hemp, also called raw hemp and smoke hemp) was not only a baccy ingredient, but was also used in the smoking mixture known as Alexandrian. In the eighteenth century, Alexandrian tobacco (or Smyrna powder) consisted of real tobacco (*Nicotiana tabacum*) blended with hemp and hashish (*Cannabis* spp.), opium *(Papaver somniferum)*, mace, and cloves.

The baccy smoker can find everything he or she needs in the woods and the meadows. A basic recipe for baccy mixtures is three equal parts of coltsfoot *(Tussilago farfara)*, veronica *(Veronica officinalis)*, and blackberry *(Rubus fruticosus)*. One can, of course, also add some "weed" (*Cannabis*) and homegrown tobacco (*Nicotiana tabacum* or *N. rustica*).

Today, baccy is commercially available again in the form of herbal mixtures for rolling one's own herbal cigarettes. These traditional mixtures contain coltsfoot (*Tussilago farfara*), speedwell (*Veronica* spp.), mint (*Mentha* spp.), and other historical European baccy herbs. Very often they are based on damiana *(Turnera diffusa)*, the Mexican herb of St. Nicholas.

Smoking can be considered a sort of incense burning. Some modern baccy factories market their products as "herbal mixtures to purify the air in the room." Smoking concentrates and delivers pharmacologically active compounds to the body more effectively than incense, though, because it brings active ingredients into more direct contact with sensitive mucous membranes. Incense burning provides its own aromatherapy and neuropsychological effects. However, smoking is more efficient when one's goal is to effect an immediate change in state of mind or consciousness by inhaling bioactive ingredients.

A gingerbread man, with his baccy pipe and fir greens, in a red and white St. Nicholas boot—a modern throwback to "St. Baccy Claus." (Christmas sticker, 1998)

Father Christmas: An Anthropomorphic Fly Agaric Mushroom?

Perceptive people have associated St. Nicholas with the fly agaric mushroom that, in former times, was eaten during the winter solstice in northern Europe—and which made it possible to fly through other worlds.

NAUWALD 2002, 37F

Among the many aspects of the modern Christmas ritual that have their origin in pagan customs is the figure of Santa Claus or Father Christmas himself. At close inspection, the red-and-white dressed Father Christmas can be seen as another version of Wotan or a secret shaman. As we shall see, even his flight through the sky in his reindeer sleigh has shamanic origins. But most astonishingly, he might even be seen as an anthropomorphic fly agaric mushroom! A scandalous claim? Perhaps. But first, let us look more closely at his connection with the shamanic fly agaric mushroom.

Old Nordic Shamanism was associated closely with Odin (Wotan) and resembled the shamanism of the Lapps and the ancient Finnish peoples. In many mythologies, storm and thunderstorm gods are associated with the fly agaric mushroom, perhaps because the thunder and lightning of the outer world can be triggered by the agaric mushroom flight through the inner world.

The Germanic thunder and fertility god, Donar or Thor, drives his goat cart through the air. He causes thunder and lightning when he throws his hammer in the clouds. Then thunder stones (belemnite fossils) begin falling and hitting

A modern fly agaric female shaman wishes us good luck. (Postcard circa 2001; illustration by Hans-Christian Sanladerer)

The Fly Agaric Mushroom *(Amanita muscaria)*

The characteristic red mushroom with its white dots is the Nordic shamanic drug par excellence. Most shamans of the Northern Hemisphere ate it ritually. Its shamanic use can be traced to the Lapps, the Siberian nomadic peoples (for example, the Samojeden, Ostjaken, Tungusen, and Jakuten), and the North American Indians.

A red and white mushroom goblin. (Garden decoration, Germany, 1998)

Fly agaric spirits and Christmas goblins under the fir tree.

*The ravens' names, Hugin and Munin, reflect the flighty aspects of the human mind: thought and memory.

From the Shamanic World Tree to the Christmas Tree

46

The "Soul Flight" of Father Christmas

"According to many researchers, the wonderful voyage of Father Christmas in his reindeer sleigh through the midwinter night sky is another surprising remnant of the shamanic flight of the soul that has been retained over the years in Anglo-Saxon countries. It was said that this image comes from the shamanism of reindeer-breeding tribes of arctic Europe and Siberia. These people experienced their soul flight with the help of the hallucinogenic fly agaric mushroom *(Amanita muscaria)*, which has a characteristic red and white hood—the same colors that we find in the clothing of Father Christmas!" (Dévereux 2000, 131f).

the earth. Where they inseminate the ground, mushrooms grow, especially fly agarics.

Mythology recorded in modern times contains some stories in which Wotan (Wodan or Odin), the shamanic god of ecstasy and knowledge, was associated with the fly agaric mushroom. According to legend, the fly agaric mushroom grows where Wotan rides on his horse through the clouds with his followers, the members of the wild hunt, in the dark nights around the time of the winter solstice. Wherever the froth of Wotan's horse fell to the ground, the ground would become "pregnant" nine months later with sprouting fly agaric mushrooms, at the time of the autumn equinox. The story sometimes says that the fly agaric mushrooms grow from of a mixture of the blood (red) and froth (white) of Wotan's white horse. The wild hunt is drawn to the mushroom, calmed and put in a good mood with incense. In the smoke columns of the incense, and wherever it finds nourishment, the wild hunt army becomes guardian of house and farm.

In the folk vernacular, fly agaric mushrooms are called "raven's bread." Ravens are not only age-old shamanic power animals, they are also messengers of Odin, also known as *Hrafnöss*, "raven god." In Skaldic poetry, fly agaric is called *munins tugga* "food of the raven *(munin)*" *(Gísli* 31, 4). Could it be that the fly agaric mushroom has a direct connection with Odin's ravens, Hugin and Munin? Are the mushrooms food for the two ravens, who carry his thoughts and memories during their flights?*

In Kamchatka (a peninsula in the far northeast of Siberia) the raven *(kutch)* is still a sacred animal for the shamans who live there. In the mythology of the Korjaken, the fly agaric mushroom, or *muchomor*, grew from the saliva of the Creator where he spat on the Earth. Great Raven, the cultural hero and animal helper of the Korjaken, first spied the strange sprout and ate it at once. Suddenly he began to feel funny, started dancing, and became clairvoyant. Great Raven said: "Let the fly agaric mushroom live forever on the Earth; and let my children see what it has to show them."

The ethnic cultures that live in the north of Kamchatka, especially the Tschuktschen and Korjaken, live as reindeer nomads and wander with their flocks in the vast plains of that country. They and other north Siberian shamans ritually ingest the fly agaric mushroom, especially when they want to communicate with the souls of their ancestors* or make contact with the spirits for divination and to heal the sick.

Liberty Caps and Fly Agaric Mushrooms

Hallucinogenic mushrooms are as spread out all over the world as the image of Father Christmas.

SIEGEL 1995, 72F

Like dwarfs, brownies, and goblins, the famous Father Christmas wears a pointed red hat. It resembles the helmets we see worn by Viking warriors and by Wotan in the few pictures of him that may be seen in Scandinavian museums. Their typical outline resembles mushrooms; they are often called liberty caps.

Mushrooms are neither plants nor animals; they are in a category of their own called fungi. In the Alpine region they are known as "little sponges." Some knowledge is needed to distinguish the poisonous from the edible; even biologists are wary of mushrooms, as are the majority of collectors. Whoever loses this fear and gains knowledge of mushrooms can find treasure in the kingdom of fungi, including delicious meals, healing remedies, and kindling to light fires, as well as coloring and fermenting agents. For example, without yeast, a kind of fungus, there would be no alcohol to drink.

Emphasizing the similarity between the hat of Father Christmas and the hat of the mushroom is not as far-fetched as it might seem. Even Homer considered mushrooms "a connection between heaven and Earth." Porphyrius called mushrooms "children of the gods," and poets of ancient times called them

Left: These liberty caps, also commonly called dwarf hat or goblin hat, are *Psilocybe semilanceata*—mushrooms that grow in middle Europe. Ingested, they create colorful hallucinations and open the doors to the goblin world. (Postcard, Psychedelic Shop)

Right: Thunder god Thor or Donar flies with his goat cart through the air, creating thunder and lightning. (Illustration by Lucian Zabel for a brochure for the company Minimax, Berlin)

---

*Fly agaric mushrooms are known for stimulating auditory hallucinations. Such acoustic manifestations and changes can be interpreted as messages from distant worlds. Or maybe these are not hallucinations at all, but instead are extraordinary perceptions of reality?

*St. Veit, Latin Svantovitus, also known as Santevit, Svantjevit, or Svantjewit.

†"On June 15, St. Veit rides on his blind horse through the woods of the old world and lets mushrooms grow. Their strange forms and unreal colors (some are even fluorescent) and the fact that some of them are poisonous, are considered sure signs that this must be the devil's semen" (Frond and Lee, 1979).

From the Shamanic World Tree to the Christmas Tree

48

The Origin of the Fly Agaric Mushroom

"God Wotan was riding his horse at Christmastime, and suddenly he was followed by devils. The horse started galloping, and red-dotted foam was running down from its mouth. Wherever the foam fell, the next year the well-known white-dotted red hats of the fly agaric mushroom started to come up" (Pursey 1977, 80).

"children of the Earth" (Lonicerus 1679, 160). Their Greek godfather, Zeus, the lightning-thrower, was considered father of the mushrooms. His most important symbol was the thunderbolt, which fertilized the Earth and made the mushrooms grow (Wasson 1986). The same image can be found in Germanic mythology, as described earlier.

This universal relationship between mushrooms and gods, attributed in shamanic cultures to natural forces, has also been linked with Christian saints. On the island of Rügen on the Baltic Sea, the former Slavic war god St. Veit* was worshipped as the patron saint of mushrooms. "The Slav said that he was accompanied by good goblins that let mushrooms grow" (Frond and Lee 1979). St. Veit is considered the protector of the fields. He carries a cornucopia and, like Wotan, rides on a white horse: "From his horse's foam all the mushrooms grow" (Müller-Ebeling et al. 1998, 20).†

In Europe, fly agaric mushrooms are considered a symbol of good luck. This is why they are so popular for New Year's and other holiday greeting cards. Fly agaric mushroom spirits appear in glossy pictures and on Christmas decorations during the Christmas season. One can find all kinds of items decorated in a fly agaric motif, from plastic figurines of "smurfs" holding fly agaric mushrooms to "lucky mushroom" fireworks for New Year's Eve parties. The mushrooms also appear on Easter cakes, chocolates, and marzipan.

Reindeer, Sleighs, and Shamans

The feeling of flying that occurs after consumption [of fly agaric mushrooms] is an effect that could be the origin of the Scandinavian and English version of Father Christmas, who flies through the air on his reindeer sleigh.

BREMNESS 1994, 286

The idea of a great variety of reindeer sleighs flying through the air at Christmastime seems to be pervasive in cultures that celebrate Christmas. A laughing, red-and-white Father Christmas sits in his sleigh with his sack, his

rod, and the presents. Every year this ancient shaman comes down to Earth in his reindeer sleigh and lands on numerous roofs—the very image of a great, twinkling, lit-up, Christmas decoration. "Father Christmas is a pagan shaman from the gray mist of a distant European past. This might seem strange to a lot of people in our day; they may even think that this is an extremely far-fetched claim. Can you prove something like that?" (Appleton 2002, 53).

Siberian mythology describes a "heavenly hunt" similar to the Germanic wild hunt. The Siberian shamans ride on reindeer sleighs through the air, up to the clouds. The world tree is their goal; this is where the magic reindeers live. The Siberian Tschutschuken say that the moon is a man on a sleigh that is pulled by two reindeer to Earth and can fly back up to heaven—just like Father Christmas (Guter 1978, 57ff).

The association of reindeer and shamanism is ancient. In the caves of the Ardèche are wall paintings of reindeer that are around thirty thousand years old. As early as the Old Stone Age, reindeer were sunk in moors as sacrificial offerings—for example, in the Hamburg steppe of Meiendorf and Stellmoor (Pohlhausen 1953). This is the ritual context of cultic poles or stakes crowned with anthropomorphic mushrooms with dwarf caps. Sometimes, reindeer skulls were even placed on top of such sacrificial stakes. These often-neglected details may be early associations of the reindeer with the godly mushrooms, just as the mushroom-topped ritual poles may be early ancestors of the Christmas tree. So the red and white Father Christmas, riding on his reindeer sleigh through the air, is nothing less than an anthropomorphic fly agaric mushroom, a modern version of a fly agaric mushroom shaman.

It has often been observed that reindeer get "high" on fly agaric mushrooms and even search for them in the snow. Many travelers have observed that reindeer are even keen on the urine of people who have taken fly agarics.

It is well-known that the urine of human beings who eat fly agaric mushrooms is also hallucinogenic. Among the Siberian peoples, it was a common custom to collect the urine of those who got high on fly agarics and

Above left: Father Christmas on a fly agaric trip. (Illustration by Pablo Bruera, *Érase una vez Papa Noel*. © 2001 from *Cáñamo*, Especial 2001)

Above right: Father Christmas and a shaman meet in a Finnish children's book entitled *Father Christmas in Search of His Own Origin*. (Illustration from Kunnas, Mauri. *Zauberspuk beim Weinachtsmann*, 1996. (Hamburg: Verlag Friedrich Oetinger)

Fly agaric spirits appear to those in the visionary state of mind, looking blue-skinned like smurfs (relatives of goblins). The fly agaric mushroom is the scepter of a king, maybe even a symbol of the three magi from the orient. ("Smurf" figure under a Mexican papier-mâché fly agaric umbrella, twentieth century)

A flying fly agaric mushroom hanging from a fly agaric "umbrella"—what a perfectly shamanic Christmas decoration! (Wood figure from Käthe-Wohlfahrt-Vertrieb, Germany, 2001)

*These woods were cut down at a frightening pace. A map of the Roman Empire as it was in the fourth century shows the Black Forest and the Vosges as one whole area of woods. The picture of a primeval forest on a plate in the Lorenzhof in the open-air museum Vogtsbauernhof in Gutarch depicts a threatening, "horrible wilderness," which is the way the Black Forest was seen for a very long time (Schilli 1968, 69).

From the Shamanic World Tree to the Christmas Tree

50

drink it in order to achieve yet another state of mind—one said to be even more intense than the one that was caused by the fly agaric itself (Samorini 2002, 54).

Christmas Tree Decorations

How beautiful is the Christmas tree right there before us, its top crowned by an angel! It represents Christ's family tree, of which the Lord himself is the crown. How brightly shine its many lights! They express the enlightenment that came to people through Christ's birth. How tempting the red apples are! They seem to be laughing! They remind us of the expulsion from Paradise . . .

FRIEDRICH NIETZSCHE, *AUTOBIOGRAPHY FROM THE YEARS 1856 TO 1869,*
SCHLECHTA INDEX III, 33

Modern people adorn the Christmas tree with a purely decorative point of view. As with many long-standing traditions, we do not know much about the origin of the activity in which we are engaging when we decorate the tree—and, in fact, we don't really care much about it. All that matters is that the tree looks good and that the colors match the decor of the house. But the decoration of trees is actually an age-old custom practiced throughout the world. Everywhere—in the shamanic world, in pagan cultures, and in religious customs—holy trees are decorated with pieces of cloth, pictures of saints, and offerings.

The tree decoration of the Christian religion has roots in old celebrations of the Christmas feast: "On Christmas Eve there was a desire to stimulate the fertility of the trees by making a ritual offering of Christmas Eve supper leftovers and even putting cake on the leaves" (Spamer 1937, 16). Shamans decorate juniper bushes with red and white pieces of cloth in the Himalaya region. Pliny (23–79 CE) wrote sensitively on pagan tree worship: "Forests were the temples of higher powers; and even today, a very beautiful tree is still dedicated to the god, in an age old custom on the countryside" (Pliny the Elder XII, 3).

During the same period, the Roman historian Publius Cornelius Tacitus (circa 55–120 CE) became acquainted with the customs of Germanic tribes living in the deep forests that covered wide areas of the land.* Like Pliny, he noticed the nature worship practiced by the "barbarian peoples" in the "sacred groves":

They think it incompatible with the sublimity of the heavenly, to lock up the gods behind walls and to somehow imitate them with human faces. They dedicated clearings and groves to them; and invoked them with the godly name of their secretive being that only they can see—from within their state of awe (Tacitus, *Germania* IX).

Like the North American Indians, our Germanic ancestors knew the Great

Spirit in the beings of nature, and they treasured this elemental basis of life. The great forests were plundered in the Greco-Roman Age for the building of warships. "In their ambition to build their civilization, the Greeks and Romans thoughtlessly deforested the Mediterranean region. By the fourth century BCE, Plato already sentimentally recollected a time when wide areas of Attica were still covered with forests" (Pogue 1992, 75).

In the fourth century CE, the Roman Emperor Theodosius the Great (347–395) forbade pagan rituals, and, most important of all, the custom of decorating holy trees:

> If someone burns incense in front of images of man-made idols, they are damned; or if such a person worships idolatrous images by decorating a tree with ribbons, or if he sets up an altar outside—he is guilty of blasphemy and of a sacrilege—even if he is making religious observance (quoted in Fillipetti 1979, 30).

The forest was the temple; the trees were the gods and goddesses. The incense offering was the contact between the pagans and the *numinosum*—the religious experience. (Arnold Böcklin [1827–1901], *Holy Grove*, 1886. Oil on mahogany wood, Hamburg Kunsthalle)

Nevertheless, the custom has survived to the present day—even if the symbolic meaning of decoration as a ritual invocation having to do with fertility has been forgotten. Yet this is what the decoration of the Christmas tree is really all about.

> On a branch she hung little reticules cut from colored paper, and each reticule was filled with sweets. Golden apples and walnuts hung down as if they had grown from the tree. Hundreds of red, blue and white small lights were put firmly on the branches. Little dolls that looked like human beings . . . were hovering in the green; and, high above in the treetop, a star made of gold foil was attached. This was splendid, extraordinary and splendid! (Hans Christian Andersen, 1845).

A rolling fly agaric mushroom man. (Toy, Germany, 1999)

Selecting festive decorations for the Christmas tree is a popular hobby these days. In the nineteenth century, the glass balls and wood figures manufactured in a cottage industry in poor areas of Germany, such as the Erzgebirge and the Thuringian forest in Eastern Germany, as well as the lower Bavarian forest, ensured the survival of whole regions. Today, Christmas romanticism ensures the survival of whole marketing chains (such as Käthe-Wohlfahrt-Vertrieb in Rothenburg), as well as industrial subsidiaries that locate their production in Asian countries where labor is cheap. But the flood of Christmas products—from the artsy to the kitschy, from the folkloric to the commercial—is not our subject. Let us concentrate instead on natural tree ornaments that come from the plant kingdom, made from materials that are "refined" in the oven. The human imagination knew no boundaries when it came to decorating the Christmas tree,

Left: North American Indians of the plains region hung pieces of cloth, feathers, dream catchers, tobacco-filled cloth balls, and prairie sage bushes *(Artemisia ludoviciana)* on pines and junipers as ritual offerings for inspiration in their vision quests. (Devil's Tower, Montana, U.S.A., May 2001)

Right: The ancient custom of decorating sacred trees growing near temples in order to worship them has persisted to the present day in Cyprus. This tree, decorated for the love goddess, grows beside a Christian chapel. (1992)

From the Shamanic World Tree to the Christmas Tree

52

Advent wreaths, doors, and the table with the bounty of mother nature, brought to the home from near and far. There were straw stars, red berries, and dried ground cherry capsules from local sources as well as exotic cinnamon canes, lotus fruit capsules, eucalyptus branches, and more from faraway places.

- **Fly agaric mushrooms,** their shamanic origins, and their meaning as a good-luck charm at Christmastime and on New Year's Eve have already been described. Next to birch trees, fir trees are the favorite host of the fly agaric (Heinrich 1998, 73). However, real fly agaric mushrooms are not used for decorating the tree, only imitations made of sundry materials.

- **Apples**—real red fruits or imitations made out of glossy, red-gold paper—have been a symbol of fertility for ages. In the context of Christianity, as fruit of life, apples are associated with the tree of paradise. The pale side of the apple, the one not exposed to light, was considered to be dying or perishing; the red side was seen as alive and growing. "The late Middle Ages seems to have considered the blossoming and fruit bearing trees always as apple trees" said the Bishop of Bamberg in 1426 about these "miracle apple trees" (Spamer 1937, 74). Since apples do not keep long, glass Christmas balls took on the role of the apple later on—representing, as the imperial orb, the worldly and religious power of the Savior.

- **Christmas balls** reflect the brightness of candles and were supposed to multiply luck, wealth, and the fruitfulness of human striving. Thuringia, especially the town Lauscha, famous for its glassworks and blown glass, contributed a bounty of colorful balls. These shimmering, artificial creations serve as modern substitutes for natural fertility symbols, and today can be found in all colors and shapes.

- **Pomegranate, oranges, dried orange slices, and lemons** from the Mediterranean served a purpose similar to that of apples as fertility symbols, but were not as often used as tree decorations. In their home climate, they were the first fruits of the year, so their appearance heralded a good harvest in the coming year.*

- **Nuts**—for example, hazelnuts—have always been considered a symbol of life and fertility. In wintertime, they helped people survive periods of extreme cold and deprivation, because they are easily stored and are rich in fats, minerals, and vitamins. The Germanic peoples dedicated nuts to Iduna, the goddess of the resplendent green. Around 400 CE, church father Augustine gave them a Christ-related meaning: "As a symbol of Christ, the shell is the flesh of Christ that has tasted the passion; and the fruit is the sweet inwardness of the god that gives food, and through the oil it gives light—the shell is the wood of the cross" (Vossen 1985, 102). Hazelnuts with little feathers glued on to them were placed on the Christmas tree to symbolize little angels. Even in the year 1795, a description of the Nuremberg Christmas tree tells us that the tree decorations included hazelnuts painted with gold and hung on cords.†

- **Walnuts** *(Juglans regia)* were in ancient times the holy tree of Dionysus and of Artemis; Caryatis, the pre-classical Greek goddess of the walnut tree (*karya*=walnut) was later considered an erotic form of Artemis. Walnuts were also associated with Jupiter, explaining why the Romans called them *Jovis glans*, meaning "Jupiter's glans." (The botanical name *Juglans* comes from "Jovis" and "glans.") Walnuts were a symbol not only of fertility, but also of immortality. In addition to their use as Christmas tree decorations, the Alemannic tribes put walnuts into the graves of the dead.‡

- **Tinsel** (paper strips, gold foil, golden nuts, apples made of gold foil, rose and fairy decorations; in short, all that glitters): These things are not only reminiscent of the glittering snow, ice cones, and the otherworldly shimmer of golden-locked angels' hair, but also recall the age-old custom of putting metal plates, coins, pieces of cloth, and other eye-catching items on holy trees in order to sanctify them. Golden, shimmering things were thought to have a magic that could ward off demons—and they promised purity and health. Even in old Mesopotamia, angels were depicted hovering around the tree of the world. When angels were hung on the Christmas tree, incense was burned for the heavenly flock as if the figurines on the tree were really hovering invisibly in the ether.

- **Shaped breads** of all kinds, including Christmas cookies and gingerbread, often are decorated or shaped according to Christian motifs—St. Nicholas, angels, the baby Jesus. Worldly motifs are also popular: nutcrackers, rocking horses, stars, suns, trees, patterns, and so on. Decorating Christmas trees with shaped breads is a very old custom. The ancient Greeks believed that breads bearing blessings would bring good luck and—because they were dedicated to the Greek healing god

Red and white goblins decorate a snowy fir tree in the forest with candles, red apples, and spices. (Christmas card from a picture by Fritz Baumgarten, Germany, circa 1999)

---

*This is why they served in Cairo as shop amulets (Seligmann 1996, 35).

†In *Der Simplizianische Wundergeschichts-Calender auf das Jahr 1795*, from Riemerschmidt 1962, 17.

‡In early modern times, the walnut was incorporated as an ingredient in love potions and was considered a special aphrodisiac. In ancient medicine systems, the walnut was seen as a visual representation of the brain and was therefore believed to be a brain tonic.

Left: A Christmas tree, decorated all over with fly agaric mushrooms, from the Käthe-Wohlfahrt-Vertrieb shop in Rothenburg. In this very popular tourist shop, it is Christmas all year round, twenty-four hours a day. (Photograph by Claudia Müller-Ebeling, October 2001)

Right: At Lucky Mushroom in the Magic Forest, a Käthe-Wohlfahrt-Vertrieb chain store, Father Christmas sits under a fly agaric mushroom in the shop window. (Photograph by Claudia Müller-Ebeling, October 2001)

From the Shamanic World Tree to the Christmas Tree

54

Asclepius—good health in the coming year. The Romans sent each other shaped breads as New Year's gifts (Seligmann 1996, 45). In medieval convent bakeries, all manner of spices and a great amount of honey were used to make gingerbread, a means of sacrificing everything the world had to offer to honor Jesus Christ. Apart from these specific meanings, calorie-rich sweets promised everyone who ate them health, long life, and an abundance of food on the table in the new year.

- *Springerle* are anise cookies, baked hard and crisp and frosted with a white icing. Their name (meaning "little jumpers") comes from a traditional equestrian motif, known from chess figurines but possibly dating back to the amulets used to ward off the ghost army of the wild hunt. In the Erzgebirge region of Germany, the bread baked during the Christmas week was considered magic.

- **Sugarwheels**—chocolate biscuits and sweets wrapped in shiny paper and tied with little ribbons to facilitate hanging on the Christmas tree—succeeded the shaped bread and tinsel used as tree decorations in the eighteenth century. In 1797, Jean Paul wrote, "Fruit and sugar trees with candle-lit branches, silver fruits, golden tassels of apples, nut and fruit ribbons, and also hanging sugar." Sugar was "not only the sign of plenty, but also the sign of the charity of God" (Riemenschmidt 1962, 24).

- **Poppy seedpods and pinecones** (gilded or natural) are age-old symbols of fertility because of the plentiful seed they produce. Dried, they keep forever, and thus also connote eternal life and the resurrection of the

Angel's Smoke Incense

Ingredients

    60 g benzoin resin *(Styrax benzoin)*

    60 g storax resin *(Liquidambar orientalis)*

    30 g white sandalwood *(Santalum album)*

    8 g cloves *(Syzygium aromaticum)*

    2 or 3 pieces of orris root *(Iris germanica)*

    2 nutmegs *(Myristica fragrans)*

    A small amount of fresh lemon rind

    A splash of rose water

Grind the nutmegs, cloves, orris root, and sandalwood. Crush the benzoin and storax resins with a mortar and pestle. Thoroughly mix these ingredients together. Grate fresh lemon rind over the mixture, splash with rose water, and knead to blend. Place the incense on the smoking coal in small portions.

A little red devil serves as a Christmas ornament. (Germany, 2001)

dead in a Christian sense. Miniature pieces of art consisting of a manger in a poppy seed capsule fall into this category of Christmas decoration. To the ancient Greeks, poppy seeds and grains were among the attributes of the great Earth goddess Demeter (=Ceres), whose blessings insured a good harvest.

- **Straw stars** became popular relatively recently. But those possessed by straw-star fever during the 1950s may not have known that the use of the material goes back to ancient field cults and resurrection rituals that utilized straw figures. An example of this was observed by the folklorist K. Ritter von Perger in Schlesien (von Perger 1864, 343). There, a fir tree bound with straw chains was carried around during the so-called *todaustragen*, the ritual "carrying out of the dead" performed during Lent to protect the living during the coming year.*

A typical Christmas ornament: Dried orange slices remind us of the sun wheels of Helios. (Photograph by Claudia Müller-Ebeling)

- **Candles** made of tallow are presumably of Etruscan or old Italian origin and played a central role in the worship of gods and goddesses as well as in burial rituals. During Saturnalia, candles and clay dolls —"life lights" and "clay men"—were exchanged as presents. The glow of candles symbolizes the return of the sun and the light of life. Christianity took over this custom on dates on which it was practiced in the past, especially February 2, Candlemas—forty days after the birth of the Son of God. "Many know the shining beauty of gold and silver, and the even brighter glitter of gemstones. But nothing compares to the beauty and the brightness of a candle." The physicist and chemist Michael Faraday (1791–1867) thus summarized the fascination with this form of light in a speech to his pupils entitled "the natural history of the candle"

---

*"The grain comes from the dead!" (Hippocrates, Vict. 4, 92; VI 658 L).

From the Shamanic World Tree to the Christmas Tree

Left: Pinecones in the Christmas arrangement.

Right: A Christmas tree candle in the form of Father Christmas. (Photograph by Claudia Müller-Ebeling)

The dried fruits of the Japanese lantern flower *(Physalis alkekengi),* also known as ground cherry, are used as an ornament for Advent arrangements, wreaths, and dried bouquets. The orange-red "lanterns" are the red berries surrounded by the blown-up, orange-red calyces (the outer portion of the flower). They are also called "devil's cherries" or "devil's dolls." Like tobacco, mandrake, and henbane, this popular garden plant is a member of the nightshade family (Solanaceae). In the United States, the ground cherry is cometimes called Christmas cherry.

(Riemerschmidt 1962, 20). In addition to good old beeswax candles and products made of paraffin and stearin, another raw material for candles is a wax that comes from trees. Until the end of the fifteenth century, a wax toll was among the taxes paid by the faithful in order to buy the necessary quantity of raw wax for liturgical candles. The successor of the Christmas candle is the electric Christmas bulb—thanks to the invention of light bulbs by the American inventor, Thomas Edison.

The Golden Apples

. . . the scaly dragon with its fierce look, the guardian
Golden shine of the apples in the Hesperide's garden
That entwine the tree stems with huge rings
LUCRETIUS, ON THE NATURE OF THINGS, V, 32FF

Apples have always played an important role in cultural history. We know them from the Germanic myth of the apples of immortality, wherein the love goddess Freia (=Freya) presents the race of gods with apples. In Wagner's *Rhinegold,* the fire god Loge comments: "Old and weak they become, if they happen to miss Freia's fruits." Similarly, the Icelandic goddess Idun—whose Icelandic name means "the renewer" or "the rejuvenator"—provides golden apples for the gods to eat so they will not age.

As the fruit of life, apples confer everlasting youth. As a symbol of the sun, they belong to the cult of the sun god Apollo. In Delphi, apples were one of the prizes for winners at the Pythian games. Eve picked the apple as a forbidden fruit from the tree of knowledge, and this is why we hear about "love apples" in connection with the Garden of Eden.

No surprise then that baked apples are a traditional Advent-time treat,

reminiscent of the apples in St. Nicholas's sack. Red apple decorations hang on the Christmas tree and appear in gift boxes, baskets, and platters. Even pomanders, the aromatic clove-studded oranges traditionally made and given as Christmas gifts, get their name from *pomme*, the French word for apple.

In Europe, the apple tree (*Malus sylvestris* P. Mill., Rosaceae) has been part of human culture since the Early Stone Age. In the Holy Land, it did not exist: "Even though there is a widespread belief that the forbidden fruit in the Garden

Left: Flower blossom miracle on the apple tree: In late autumn, the fruit-bearing tree sometimes grows some flowers. This is a good example of a Christmas Eve flower blossom miracle. (Fruit tree, Berne, near Hamburg, Germany, 1999)

Right: Apple rings with chocolate coating on the Christmas tree: sweet, cocoa-coated apples of Idun.

of Eden were apples, they are not called by that name in the story" (Zohary 1986, 70). "It is very strange that, in the midnight hour of Christmas Eve, apple trees are supposed to blossom and bear fruit, just because they played such an important part in the fall of man for our ancestors in paradise" (von Perger 1864, 57).

Apples are still on every Christmas tree, and the custom of exchanging presents dates far back, to pagan times. The old image of Wotan was an evergreen tree, and even spirit-beings were giving presents on the Holy Night. When Saxo Grammatikus Haddin sat at the table on Christmas Eve, a female Earth-sprite stuck her head out of the ground and gave him a fresh mandrake herb. On Christmas, a poor citizen of Budissin was welcomed by a little man with a big round hat and given apples and nuts that turned into gold [Idun]. On Christmas Eve, bread was shaken from the trees and pretzels were shaken from the bushes . . . (von Perger 1864, 58).

When it comes to understanding the meaning of religious feasts, we often find that certain customs that at first appear to be exclusively tied to magical beliefs are discovered to actually have origins in observations of nature. For example: "When you tie wet straw bands around the trees on Christmas Eve, they become fertile. This is because these bands keep away the white frost that freezes the blossom [frost giants]" (von Perger 1864, 58).

The custom of letting the last apple hang on the tree comes from the old practice of making an offering for the apple tree goblin or the tree nymphs of the ancient world. The Meliads were the nymphs of the apple trees. They were naturally associated with Aphrodite, the Cypriot love goddess, whose temple was in the Tasmanian field in the region now known as Cyprus. There, "in the middle of the plains, a tree is shimmering, red, and full of leaves—red-gold is

From the Shamanic World Tree to the Christmas Tree

rustling in its leaves" (Ovid, *Metamorphoses* X, 647f). And there, Aphrodite picked her famous golden apples.

Pomegranate
Punica granatum L., Punicaceae

OTHER NAMES
Love apple

> *So the pomegranate is the symbol of the secret in the body of the woman, and also of the entry to it. It belonged to Aphrodite and to any other goddess of fertility and sexuality. The pomegranate, Hera's symbol of marriage, was also a fruit of Demeter.*
> GRIGSON 1978, 190

The dried pomegranate makes a beautiful Christmas decoration. It dries hard as stone and almost resembles a Christmas ball. The pomegranate is also one of the golden apples of Aphrodite. After the Cypriot legend, Aphrodite—who came from the eastern world herself—planted the first pomegranate tree in Cyprus. Why is this fruit so dear to the love goddess? If you inspect the bud just before it opens, you might see an almost lifelike, dark-red model of a well-formed penis.

Often the love goddess is pictured with a pomegranate in one hand and a pomegranate blossom in the other. Fruit and blossom embody both poles of sexuality, male and female, which are unified by the goddess. The pomegranate has also been regarded as a "tree of life" or "tree of knowledge" (Muthmann

Pomegranates are among the most important wedding gifts in the wedding rituals of the Newari, a Nepali people who make a living trading arts and crafts. (Kathmandu, Nepal, March 2003)

From the Shamanic World Tree to the Christmas Tree

1982). According to some interpretations, the famous apple from the tree of knowledge, the forbidden fruit of the Garden of Eden, is not the apple but the pomegranate.

Pomegranates play an important role in the feast honoring Aphrodite as well as weddings. Even today, pomegranates are thrown in front of houses of newly wed couples in Cyprus so that the house will be blessed with fertility. The more seeds that fall out of the bursting fruit, the greater the blessing of children will be. Aphrodite is still worshipped under the Catholic cloak as "holy virgin of the mountain of the golden pomegranate," in the Convent of Chrysorogiatissa near Pano Panayia.

MIRACLE BLOSSOMS FOR THE WINTER SOLSTICE

I want to show you how a flower can shine in the middle of
darkness. The blossoms will open before your eyes even
though it is fall, even though it will be winter soon.

SCHENK 1943A, 218

As important as evergreens in the ethnobotany of Christmas are flowers that "miraculously" bloom in the dead of winter, when all is cold and dreary. We are accustomed to seeing plants turn green and flower in the spring and fade in autumn. This is why we value evergreen bushes and trees during the winter. But we are especially awed by plants that put forth flowers during the time of ice and snow. In truth, every single flower on Earth is a miracle—a miracle that few modern human beings perceive, acknowledge, or even admire. Whether we realize it or not, Christmas flowers that bloom in wintertime—indoors or out—remind us of this ongoing miracle.

Why do certain bushes and trees remain green in winter, and why do the tender flowers of some plants defy the snow and ice? These "unnatural" phenomena have always commanded interest among the peoples of Europe, and even today, such botanical miracles hold a special fascination, particularly at Christmastime. Year after year, even those who have never considered the origins of ethnobotanical customs want blossoming potted plants in midwinter and fir greens for their Advent wreaths.

The artists of former epochs arranged the sequence of human life stages figuratively, in terms of vegetation life cycles. Many sayings relate the miracle of flowering in nature to the nature of the human being. We talk about the budding of childhood and youth, of the bloom on a child's cheeks, of the flowerlike beauty of a young girl. As young adults, we are in the flowering stage of life; in old age, we consider what we have harvested during our lives. Our fantasy flowers; the heart flowers with love; our consciousness gives us flowers of knowledge. As human beings, we consider ourselves the flower and crown of all creation.

During all time periods, human beings have explained the wonders of nature in ways that fit with their own cultural, mythical, religious, and scientific beliefs. The ancients attibuted the growth of plants, the variety of colors and blossom forms, and the effects of plants on human beings to gods and goddesses and handed down these ideas as their myths. Christian authors consider creation a book written by the hand of God, and have made allegories of the many legends surrounding the life and deeds of Jesus Christ and the saints—many of which draw analogies with the nature and appearance of plants. To the present day, pagan peoples and shamanic tribal cultures believe that the actions of plant souls play a role in human life, and this is expressed in their own mythical explanations of the nature of reality.

The sight of evergreen and flowering plants in winter gave people of the pagan world hope for a return of the light and the renewing power of goddess nature. Christians interpreted these astonishing phenomena as a sign of the almighty power of the Creator and his son, whose birth redeemed them from the powers of darkness. Plants that opened their buds at Christmastime were therefore baptized with Christ's name in honor of his birth, and believers explained the winter flower blossom miracles with Christian legends.

To the ancients, the fir tree that became the Christmas tree represented the male element, the spear, and the phallus—the life-sustaining world tree or world axis. The flower-blossom wonder is the female element of the universe: the well of wisdom, the blossoming, the birthing, the unfolding, the grail, the vulva.

> Carnations, hog's fennel, pennyroyal, saffron, hellebore, mandrake and the cherry tree: all flower on Christmas Eve. Also, the so-called rose of Jericho *(Anastatica heirochuntica)*, which seems dead and dry throughout the whole year, unfolds and has a most delicious scent. This is why it is also called the "resurrection flower," and is dedicated to the Savior (von Perger 1864, 56f).

St. Barbara's Boughs

St. Barbara's Bough is a harbinger of spring, in its freshness even winter cannot harm it; it embodies the constantly reawakening life. Its power of life is transferred to human beings. They bear good luck and blessings into the following year. But if the branch is dying—then the owner is facing bad luck.

MARZELL 1935, 147

The custom of creating Barbara's boughs—putting bare winter branches in a vase so that they are green and flowering for Christmas—has roots in old Roman practices. On the winter solstice and at the beginning of the new year, the Romans gave each other evergreen branches from needle-bearing trees, boxwoods, rosemary, and mistletoe. In the old Roman calendar, the year began on March 1, only later on January 1. *Etrennes*, the gifts traditionally exchanged by the French for New Year's, also hark back to these Roman customs.

Barbara's boughs are traditionally cut on December 4, the day of St. Barbara. The decision as to which trees are the best for this Christmastime greening and blossoming miracle differs from region to region. The Munich Food Market does not consider fruit tree branches suitable. However, in some rural regions, branches from the sour cherry (*Prunus cerasus* L., Rosaceae) are very popular for this purpose.

If branches kept in a warm place bloomed on time, it indicated a good fruit harvest for the coming year. If blooming did not start on time, a bad harvest was foretold. It is interesting to note that this custom was based not on magic and superstition, but on observation of nature. In 1864, K. Ritter von Perger already recognized the natural facts behind the belief. According to von Perger, "because the [leaf and blossom] buds for the next year are already formed in autumn, one can make a judgment about the future from the appearance of a higher or lower number of those with more or less fruit" (von Perger 1864, 53).

In lower Austria and the Swabian region around Ellwangen, it was customary to put up a branch for each member of the family. Whoever was associated with the branch that developed best was to have the best luck in the following year. For family members with branches whose buds did not open, bad luck or even death was predicted. In Silesia (now part of Poland), girls of marriageable age set aside a branch for each of their suitors. The adorer whose branch bloomed first was said to have the best chance. Martin Greif wrote a poem about this:

> *On St. Barbara's Day I took*
> *Three branches from the cherry tree*
> *I put them in a vase*
> *I said three wishes in my dream*
> *The first that one would court me*
> *The second that he is still young*
> *The third that he had money enough.*
> *Christmas Eve before church*
> *I saw that two branches were in bloom*
> *I know a poor boy*
> *I take him the way he is.*

Christ Rose or Hellebore

The black hellebore is warm and dry and a little humid,
but it has a special greening power that is useful.
HILDEGARD VON BINGEN, *PHYSICA,* 152

Helleborus spp. L., Ranunculaceae
Helleborus niger L. (black hellebore)
Helleborus viridis L. (green hellebore)

The plant soul of the hellebore *(Helleborus niger)* is cold in the snow: "The winter's dress is its cradle blanket" (Söhns 1920, 35). (Book cover: Bohatta, Ida, *Little Flower in the Winter* [Munich: Ars Edition 2000])

---

*The stinking hellebore *(Helleborus foetidus)* is also called "wild Christ root," as is bitter vetch *(Lathyrus linifolius)* (von Chamisso 1987, 24, 99).

Miracle Blossoms for the Winter Solstice

OTHER NAMES

The Christ rose or black hellebore is popular under many names in many different languages: *alröschen, brandwurz, Christbaumwurzel, Christblume, Christiana,* Christmas flower, Christmas herb, Christmas rose, Christ rose, *Christrosenwurzel, Christröslein, Christwurtz,* * *eisbluem, ellébore noir* (French), *feurwurz, frangekraut, gillwurz, hainwurz, helleborische nieswurz, helleboros* (Greek), *herbe de feu* (French), *herrgottsrose, himmelswurz, isaia* (Arabic), *leüsskraut, niesswurzel, nyesewurtz, rose d'hiver* (French), *rose de Noel* (French), *schneeberger, schneeblumen, schneekaderl, schneekalt, schneekatzen, schneekönigin, schneerose, schneerosenwurz, schwarze nieswurz, weinachtsblume, weihnachtsrose, weinblume, winterblume, winterkind,* and winter rose.

There are around fifteen species in the genus *Helleborus* in Europe and western Asia. The plants are frost-resistant and the blossoms long-lasting. In the wild, hellebores grow in the Alps of Berchtesgarden and in Tirol, where their white petals start to appear shortly after the snow melts. In mild winters they are punctual, arriving right in time for Christmas. Cultivated varieties are very popular in the city, as are Christmas cards depicting their white blossoms. Hellebores are considered the "Christmas rose," especially in England, where they are taken in pots into the house and used everywhere as decorations.

The poet Agnes Franz praised the beauty of the hellebore's white petals (Söhns 1920, 35f):

> *Like a starry sky it is glimmering*
> *Deep in its emerald wreath of leaves*
> *And whoever sees it and whoever takes it*
> *Congratulates himself and says:*
> *Praise the Lord! The time has come*
> *When earth and heaven are at peace!*
> *The sun is shining peacefully*
> *The day grows longer, the night shorter*
> *Christ rose blossom, you star light!*
> *Praised be the feast of the Lord!*

The botanist Otto Brunfels (1489–1543) offers the first interpretation of the name Christ's root in the sixteenth century:

> It is called *Christ's root* because it blossoms on Christmas Eve, and its flower is all green. That is where this name comes from. I have seen it myself—you

The Christ rose or black hellebore *(Helleborus niger)* contain the digitalis-like cardiac glycosides helleborin and helleborein.

may jest about it all you want. It is called "sneezing root" because, in the form of a powder, it makes one sneeze (Brunfels 1532, 62).*

MAGICAL AND FOLK USE

Because the white flowers and green leaves of the Christmas rose are resistant to the cold, they were thought to have magic powers. Numerous protection and divination enchantments sprang from this idea. For example, country people believed that planting hellebore near a stall or putting a bouquet on a tall door would protect animals from epidemics. Others saw it as an oracle for the coming harvest year, because its flowering represented the beginning of a new growing cycle.

The Gauls put hellebore juice on spears and arrows, believing that this would make the meat of the dead animal much more tender. But they cut out the flesh around the wound. While digging out the hellebore, one had to draw a circle around the plant, then get up before morning to pray. If an eagle showed itself, the one who dug the root would die in the following year. Digging out hellebore causes a heaviness in the head; because of that, in former times one was required to eat garlic and drink a glass of unwatered wine for protection. Hellebore was dedicated to the planet Saturn. It protected against many illnesses, and whoever carried it along with them could become very old (von Perger 1864, 184).

The human longing for flowering messengers of spring in the dark, cold

*Otto Brunfels seems to be describing the green hellebore *(Helleborus viridis* L., also known as wild Christmas rose), which has green flowers.

Miracle Blossoms for
the Winter Solstice

The Christ Rose as Oracular Flower

In the Zurich Oberland, twelve Christmas rose buds were dropped in water on Christmas. Then the people noted which one opened. The one that opened first indicated good weather in the month corresponding to its number; the ones that remained closed meant bad weather in those months. (For example: If the sixth bud opened, it meant good weather in the haying month, and so on.)

In the canton of Zurich, it is considered a good sign for the coming wine year if the Christ rose turns reddish (instead of brownish) while fading. In Rhineland Palatinate, hellebore was called the wineflower because the wine-growers say that it is going to be a good harvest when they bloom a lot (Marzell 1935, 167).

Christmas season explains the continued popularity of the Christ rose in December. Its reputation as a magical and health-promoting plant persisted until the recent past:

> In the winter of 1932–1934, the Christ rose was very popular as a symbol of sacrifice with the winter hardship services institution that existed during the German Reich. A number of German cities had a "Christ Rose Day" during Advent, during which Christ roses made of white cloth were sold and collections taken up in the streets and pubs to help poor compatriots suffering in winter (Marzell 1935, 166).

Another reason for the belief in the magic powers of the hellebore lies with the root of the plant. The powder made out of the root induces sneezing. The Roman name for black hellebore, *veratrum,* comes from *verus,* or true—"because the powdered root causes sneezing, which is considered a proof of the truth" (Söhns 1920, 35).

Every day in Germany, people say "good health" *(Gesundheit)* when someone sneezes. (*Gesundheit* is the German equivalent of the English "God bless you.") Behind this spontaneous exclamation is a magic formula not known to many people. Even less is known about the historical background of the blessing and the particular plant to which it refers—hellebore.

Normally, we consider sneezing a symptom of a cold and say *Gesundheit* because we don't want the person who is sneezing to get sick. However, the ancient Greek physician Hippocrates considered sneezing a sign of a fortunate *avoidance* of illness. Other ancient sources interpret strong sneezes as the sign of the exorcism of an illness demon. Because sneezing can be stimulated with the help of sneezing powder, several drugs made from different kinds of hellebore were very popular for this purpose with the early Greeks. In fact, in ancient times, hellebore was the most famous medicine of the Greek materia medica. The plants that were grouped together under the Greek name *helleborors* were used frequently and in many different situations to ward off illness. In old Egypt, sneezing was believed to be caused by demonic influence and was considered a sign of the presence of illness-causing demons or of evil forces that needed to exit the body. Just as in Greece, helpful sneezing was provoked with sneezing powder made from powdered hellebore root.

Frost-hardened hellebore roots were especially popular with herbalists. While digging for black hellebore (also known as *melampodion,* or "plant of Melampus") one had to be careful not to agitate the plant spirit, which could appear in the form of an eagle:

> You are supposed to draw a circle around the black hellebore. And you should say prayers facing the east. You are supposed to keep an eye out for an eagle coming from either the right side or the left side. And if an eagle does come close, this is very ominous for the cutter. He will die in the course of a year (Theophrast, *Geschichte der Pflanzen* IX, 1).

Hellebore root contains a poisonous chemical compound, helleborin, that causes vomiting and diarrhea and was in earlier times considered a purgative for "people with a strong constitution" (Marzell 1935, 167). To escape the dark moods that could occur during the long, dark winter, folk healers and homeopaths prescribed hellebore tincture to prevent melancholy, heart weakness, madness, and epilepsy.

In the pagan tradition, *Helleborus niger* was considered a magic plant and a plant of Saturn; it was believed to have the power to cure madness. Concoctions made with the powdered root were demonized by Christian as a witches' herb. In order to become invisible in preparation for the Sabbath flight, witches are supposed to have powdered themselves with it (Emboden 1974, 66).

Bornemann offers the following explanation for hellebore's reputation as an aphrodisiac and psychoactive plant:

> Christ rose is considered the Lord's penis, and is therefore a potency-triggering medium. It contains a substance that increases circulation, the glycoside helleborin . . . Christmas rose [is a] consciousness-altering aphrodisiac . . . (Bornemann 1974, 52).

The hellebore *(Helleborus)*. The root makes those "who are out of control, are melancholic, or are crazy, healthy again." (Illustration from Brunfels 1532, 62)

Miracle Blossoms for
the Winter Solstice

"Real Schneeberger sneezing powder, Adler pharmacy, Schneeberg."

Apothecary package of Schneeberger sneezing powder (1981). (From Martinetz 1994, 126)

Miracle Blossoms for the Winter Solstice

A PINCH OF GLACIER: A MOUNTAIN OF SNOW TO SNUFF

It is called black hellebore because, in earlier times, the powder of the black root was used as snuff tobacco.

VORNARBURG 2002A, 66

The famous German Schneeberger tobacco is named after the town of Schneeberg in the Saxon Erzgebirge, where it was once produced. Schneeberger means "snow mountain," an appropriate name for a product that once contained substantial amounts of hellebore. However, tobacco is not an accurate name for the Schneeberger product, which in earlier times was a sneezing powder (snuff) made from hellebore, liverwort, and medicinal soap. Today, though it is made with a different recipe and is no longer produced in the Erzgebirge, Schneeberger snuff can be found again in the form of peppermint powder (Hartel 1977, 52).

The two main ingredients of Schneeberger "snuff tobacco" were black hellebore *(Helleborus niger)* and white hellebore *(Veratrum album),* both of which are now illegal ingredients.* Another ingredient, also now forbidden for use in commercial products, was hazelwort or European wild ginger *(Asarum europaeum* L., Aristolochiaceae). The poison hazelwort "was a contribution to the witches' herbal, because it was seen as part of the herbs of Bacchus, like ivy and hellebore (Christ rose)" (Beckmann and Beckmann 1990, 165).

In addition to these primary ingredients, numerous other plants found their way into the famous snuff powder over time. One is arnica *(Arnica montana),* a plant with specific meanings of its own in the ethnobotany of Christmas. In the vernacular, arnica is sometimes even called Schneeberger flower or snuff tobacco flower, demonstrating the plant's association with Schneeberger snuff powder (Arends 1935, 239). The lovely, delicious-smelling lily-of-the-valley *(Convallaria majalis)* is also associated with the legendary snuff powder; its

Pulvis Sternatutoris Schneebergensis

Here is a recipe for Schneeberger snuff tobacco (Schneeberger Prime) from *Hager's Handbook of the Pharmaceutical Practice* (Frerichs et al. 1938, 591).

20 g hazelwort herb *(Asarum europaeum)*

5 g lily-of-thevalley flower blossoms *(Convallaria majalis)*

2 g hellebore root *(Helleborus niger)*

50 g orris root *(Iris germanica)*

15 drops bergamot essential oil *(Citrus bergamia)*

Cut up raw plant material and sprinkle with bergamot essential oil. When it is dry, grind the mixture very finely. It is said that soap powder can be used as a substitute for the poisonous hellebore. *Gesundheit!*

dried and pulverized blossoms were once an important ingredient. This is why the plant has been called "little tobacco flower" and, in Alsace, "little sneezing flower" (Marzell 1935, 37). The folk names "snuff tobacco clover" (yellow sweet clover, *Melilotus officinalis*) and "snuff tobacco herb" (salsify, *Tragopogon pratensis*) tell us that these two plants were also once incorporated into snuff. In English, yarrow *(Achillea millefolium)* is still sometimes called "sneezewort."

Horse chestnut flour *(Aesculus hippocastanum)* was another primary ingredient of Schneeberger snuff powder

Modern Schneeberger snuff powder contains only a pinch of dextrose. It is no longer made in the Erzgebirge region. The bottles pictured here are souvenirs from Garmisch-Partenkirchen, purchased in 2001.

Other Christ Roses and Roots

Pheasant's eye (*Adonis vernalis* L., Ranunculaceae) is also known as Bohemian Christ root or Bohemian hellebore (Schoen 1963, 51). In the Latin apothecary and in the vernacular, it is known both as Christ root herb and devil's eye. The plant has been treasured and feared since antiquity as a strong pharmacological agent with healing—but also potentially fatal—powers.

Yellow dock (*Rumex crispus* L., Polygonaceae) is another plant commonly called Christ rose. The legendary medieval abbess Hildegard von Bingen suggests, "if a man loses his sense or his mind because an illness or weakness plagues his head, so that he becomes senseless, you administer Christ rose, and add a little quendel [wild thyme]" (Hildegard von Bingen *Physica*, 129). In ancient times, dock was an ingredient of the legendary Egyptian incense, kyphi. The incense ingredient later on became a smoking herb, called "wild tobacco" in the vernacular: "The country people, not infrequently, smoked its dried leaves as tobacco" (von Chamisso 1987, 144). *Rumex crispus* (yellow dock) was used by the North American Indians in a similar manner. The Iroquois considered dock a love medicine and love magic; it was used as a panacea and a tonic, a substance that strengthens. The Ojibwa made a hunting medicine from dried dock leaves mixed with kinnikinnik (*Arctostaphylos uva-ursi*) that was smoked as "Indian Baccy" to attract wild animals (Moerman 1998, 496).

Arnica (*Arnica montana* L., Asteraceae), also called Mary's herb, motherwort, wolf's eye, St. Lucy flower, and St. Lucian herb, has golden-yellow ray flowers. It is "a little sun" that is "a reflection of the heavenly light that is covering the carpet of vegetation . . . and reveals to us, in this manner, that the light of the creator always shines through the plant world—even if the eye of a human being is very often too cloudy to see it" (Zimmerer 1896, 254f). The Wends, a Slavic people of the Lausitz region of eastern Germany, described arnica roots as "Christ's roots" (Seligmann 1996, 82). In the region of the Nahe River, the yellow-flowering greater celandine (*Chelidonium majus* L., Papaveraceae) is also known as "Christ's root" (Söhns 1920, 95).

Miracle Blossoms for the Winter Solstice

The red rose (*Rosa* spp.) is a symbol of love and a pure heart, a holy plant.

(de Vries 1989, 167). In addition to liverwort *(Hepatica nobilis)*, nontoxic herbs such as marjoram *(Origanum marjorana)*, lavender *(Lavendula angustifolia)*, sage *(Salvia officinalis)*, and rosemary *(Rosmarinus officinalis)* were used to round out the formulation.

Christmas Roses

Eros was leading the dance at the feast of the gods; and with his wing he pushed against a cup of nectar. . . . So it was that the drops of nectar fell down to the earth and changed white roses to red.

GRIGSON 1978, 181

"Lo how a rose e'er blooming" is the beginning of a very popular Christmas song. The melody was composed in 1599 in Cologne; Michael Praetorius set lyrics to the music in 1609.* In both verses, Praetorius tied an image of the rose's roots to the family tree of Jesus. The "flow'ret bright . . . amid the cold of winter," refers to the newborn baby Jesus, who drives away the darkness with his bright light. The song also celebrates Mary "the Virgin Mother kind," who brought us the little flower. Even though roses develop their beauty and splendor not in winter but in summer and autumn, similar allegorical comparisons between the holy family and roses of all kinds have been woven into the Christmas story. In turn, they inspired a whole folklore of plant names and customs referring to Mary, Jesus, and the holy night.

The little flowers of the bushy, wild, thorny hedge rose are white, like snow. The rose hips sometimes survive the autumn to glow red against the winter snow. In the Nahe River region they are called Mary's rose or Mother of God rose; in the Swabian area, ladythorn; on the Swabian Alb, little Lord's rose or Savior rose; and in Thuringia, herb of Jesus. Christian legend offers an explanation for its white blossoms and their delicate smell. During their flight from Herod into Egypt, Mary dried the newborn Jesus's diapers or his scarf on a wild rose bush. The next morning the bush bloomed with white roses that had a lovely, delicate fragrance.

In the Allgäu region, rose hips were used to foretell the severity of the coming winter. If the rose hips were plump in the fall, the winter would be very cold; if the rose hips were long, the winter would be long as well.

"For centuries," the rose has been a symbol "of the highest honors of the church," wrote Walahfrid Strabo in the ninth century in his *Hortulus*, the most important record of the early history of agriculture in Germany. Strabo was the abbot of Reichenau Island in Lake Constance. Tourists still go there every year because of the bountiful richness of its flowers and blossoms. Strabo's contemporaries saw the Virgin Mary as a mystical rose, a symbol of

*As in this case, lyrics for popular melodies were often written much later than the music.

Miracle Blossoms for the Winter Solstice

chastity, virginity, and love free from desires of the flesh. Also associated with Mary is the following Christmas folk custom: "If a girl cuts a rose on the summer solstice and wears it to church on Christmas day, her future husband will show himself when he takes the rose instead of the girl" (Hiller 1989, 233).

The association of roses with the love of beautiful women was handed down to us from the ancient Greeks. One Greek myth tells us that the rose fell out of the hair of Aurora, goddess of the dawn. In another myth, roses bloomed under the steps of the love goddess, Aphrodite. "In the moment the young goddess was created from the sperm of Uranus in the sea, a new bush was growing on earth. The holy assembly of gods sprinkled drops of nectar on the branches, and every drop became a rose" (Grigson 1978, 179).

The Lesbian poet Sappho (sixth century BCE), who worshipped Aphrodite all her life, described the rose as "queen of all flowers." Achilleus Tatios (second century BCE), the Alexandrian poet who became famous for his romance *Leukippe and Kleitophon,* honored not only love, but also the rose:

> It is the ornament of the earth, the pride of the plant kingdom, the crown of the flowers, the purple of the meadows, the reflection of beauty. It is full of love in the service of Aphrodite, it shows its perfumed petals, is dancing on moving leaves, is happy with the smiling Zephyrus.

The wild roses *(Rosa canina)* that grew from the tears of Aphrodite when she wept for Adonis carry the perfume of the love goddess. Thus the Romans, who in effect credited the smile of Eros with the creation of roses, perceived in wild roses the scent of Venus. Ancient Germans worshipped the blossoms and fragrance of the wild rose as holy to the love goddess, Freia.

Many cultures see the red or white rose blossom as a mystical, holy, feminine symbol of love. The use of rose water in Christmas baking and Christmas incense comes from this tradition. The ancients tell us that "The rose is the fragrance of the gods" (Grigson 1978, 180).

Many aromatherapists associate the changing symbolism of the rose and its vast number of beneficial effects—as numerous as the petals of its flower*— with the range of different intensities of love caused by Eros, from chastity to burning love:

> The rose smells like purity and virginity. Yet it is also an aphrodisiac, a substance that stimulates sensuality. Historians write that the Romans, in their most decadent times, used large quantities of roses to decorate halls, streets and sleeping rooms meters high (Fischer-Rizzi 1989 [reissued 2002], 142).

*Cultivated rose varieties have been known in Germany since medieval times. One of the oldest garden varieties is the cabbage rose, *Rosa x centifolia,* whose species name comes from the root word for hundred. This "hundred petals rose" might be the result of a cross between the apothecary's rose *(R. gallica x officinalis)* and the wild species known as dog rose *(R. canina).*

Miracle Blossoms for the Winter Solstice

The flowering rhododendron tree *(Rhododendron arboreum)* of the Himalayas. (Dhulikhel, Nepal, March 2003)

*Perhaps the best known "living fossil" of the plant kingdom is *Ginkgo biloba,* which dates back to the geological times before flowering plants came into existence. Flowering plants started developing in the Cretaceous period. They experienced an evolutionary explosion when dinosaurs, cuttlefish, and ammonites were dying out.

Miracle Blossoms for the Winter Solstice

Rhododendron, Christmas Rose of the Himalayas

Rhododendron spp. L., Ericaceae (rhododendron)
Rhododendron arboreum Sm.
Rhododendron giganteum Forrest

The name *Rhododendron* was introduced by Carl von Linné. It was taken from the Greek *rhodos* (rose) and *dendron* (tree) and thus translates literally as "rose tree." *Rhododendron* is a member of the heather family (Ericaceae), which dates back to the time of the earliest known flowering plants of the Cretaceous period. The plant developed at least one million years ago.*

The first rhododendrons came from the area that is now Yünnan, Szechuan, and Tibet. Nearly all of today's rhododendrons, including all species and varieties, may be derived from the Chinese species *Rhododendron giganteum,* a tree that can grow up to 25 meters (about 80 feet) tall (de Milleville 2002, 2). Thus the rhododendron is a gift from the Himalayas to the whole world. The Himalayas of today were once under the Sea of Thetys. During the continental shift, when the Himalayan mountains were rising up to the skies, *Rhododendron arboreum* was growing in Sikkim, Darjeeling, and Nepal. The plant thought so well of itself sitting there on the throne of the gods—on the roof of the world—that it became the floral emblem of Nepal. About thirty kinds of rhododendron may have ethnobotanical meaning to the Nepalis. The people carve everyday tools as well as ritual objects from its wood, commonly known as rosewood. Many species have medicinal applications and are used in healing incenses and beverage infusions (teas). The red-flowering *Rhododendron arboreum,* called "beautiful woman" in Nepali, is of particular ethnobotanical importance (de Milleville 2002, 59).

Like the poinsettia, the red and green rhododendron is radiant with traditional Christmas colors. No wonder then that the Yeti—the legendary Himalayan snowman—is associated in his home region with Father Christmas. This idea is not at all far-fetched. Because the Christmas feast is such an important ritual to them, the Nepalis logically identify the Yeti with Father Christmas. Conversely, for westerners, the Yeti is the best-known figure from the legends of the Himalayas. When Reinhold Messner searched for the Yeti in 1998, was he actually trying to follow a childhood dream and see Father Christmas face to face?

Yeti, the Snow Being

Of course, the Yeti is not a physical animal,* as believed by Reinhold Messner, the mountaineer and conqueror of the Himalayas (1998). It is a shamanic being. It is the *ban jhankri*, the wild man or forest shaman: a figure from the shamanic universe, a spiritual being, a shamanic spirit (Müller-Ebeling et al., 2000).

---

*The Yeti is pictured and described in the *Tibetan-Mongolian Anatomical Dictionary for Recognizing Numerous Illnesses* (Vlček 1959): "The Wild Man is a being from the bear family, who lives in the vicinity of the mountains and looks very much like a man. He has great powers. His flesh is a good medicine against evil spirits that cause illness" (Vlček et al. 1960, 153). Bear flesh is considered aphrodisiac (Rätsch and Müller-Ebeling 2003).

Yeti, disguised as Father Christmas, climbs to the heights of the Himalayas. (Christmas card from Kathmandu, Nepal, 2002)

A MULTICULTURAL FATHER CHRISTMAS

The Tibetan Father Christmas sits in a wheelbarrow pulled by a white horse. He spins the Lamaistic prayer wheel, sending the blessing *Om mani padme hum* (the jewel in the lotus blossom) whirling in all directions. Instead of Christmas tree fairies, Christmas balls, and gold foil, Tibetans decorate the Vajarayan fir tree with prayer flags. The wind is supposed to scatter the prayers throughout the whole world to reach all compassionate beings.

The Christmas tree does not care about the religion, worldview, or ideology of the perspective from which it is adored. The main thing is that the tree is adored! The gesture of contemplation in the presence of the tree is what is important. If Christmas really is the feast of love, then all people are free to take their share of the feast. The form this takes—whether festive, satirical, comedic, or contemplative—does not matter.

Tibetans' prayer wheels mark the pulse and the music of life, making the jewel in the lotus blossom shine and sparkle. *Om* is the beginning, and *hum* is the end and the beginning of *om*. All is cyclical. Christmas is the most prominent manifestation of the eternal return of the beautiful life that we all share. This is why all over the world, Christmas symbolizes the end of one year-long cycle and the awakening of a new year-long cycle.

On this note, we encounter a Father Christmas born of a westernized, Asian-Buddhist perspective. It is an amusing example of Tibetans "going native" with the image of Father Christmas, down to the typical traditional Bhotya dress of the highland Tibetans who live in Nepal. It is obvious from the symbol on his fur coat that this Father Christmas is no Christian believer. He wears the famous Buddhist sign of luck, long associated with the Tibetan region and culture. In English, such good luck symbols are described as auspicious, a word that comes from the Latin *auspicium,* meaning "observation of the sights." One of the sights in Nepal is that of bearers carrying two baskets full of goods through the narrow, winding streets. These goods should be for

Miracle Blossoms for
the Winter Solstice

73

Left: Tibetan prayer flags flying in the wind. (Swayambunath, Kathmandu, Nepal, March 2003)

Right top: Father Christmas dances with a Tibetan couple. (Christmas card from Kathmandu, Nepal, 2002)

Right center: The Tibetan Father Christmas brings the holy tree on a horse-drawn wheelbarrow. (Christmas card from Kathmandu, Nepal, 2002)

Right below: A Buddhist bearer of goods dressed as Father Christmas. (Christmas card from Kathmandu, Nepal, 2002)

sale, but Father Christmas makes an exception, or he would not be the mythical bringer of presents.

Whether you worship Father Christmas as the charitable bishop St. Nicholas, Sinterklaas, Santa Claus, helper Ruprecht from Wotan's wild army, or, as we suggest here, a Buddha figure bearing presents, this is an intercultural spiritual concept that comes from a common foundation. It is an obvious, age-old pattern that has been programmed into the genes of the human being. Whoever worships nature will receive many gifts, especially love. "Love life!" was the way my father Paul Rätsch addressed these great questions—he whom, in my childhood, dressed as Father Christmas to delight the children.

Rose of Jericho
Anastatica hierochuntica L., Brassicaceae
Selaginella lepidophylla (Hook. & Grev.) Spring, Selaginellaceae

A Psychedelic Christmas Flower

In Mexico, a snow-white flowering bindweed known as Christmas vine or Christmas flower (*Turbina corymbosa*, L. Raf., Convolvulaceae) was ritually used as an entheogen since pre-Spanish times by Mazatec, Zapotec, and Mayan shamans. In Aztec, it was called *ololiuqui* (that which causes spinning) and in Mayan, *xtabentun* (jewel cord). After ingesting the seeds, which contain a molecule similar to LSD, shamans can travel or fly in an alternative reality to find the cause of their patients' illnesses and a way to heal them (Rätsch 1998a, 513ff).

In contemporary Mexico, this bindweed is used to induce trance. Strangely enough, in Spanish it known as *flor de pascua*, meaning Christmas flower, just like the poinsettia, *Euphorbia pulcherrima*, which is also called *pascua, santa*, and *Santa Catarina*. Does the Christmas flower bindweed open the way to Santa Claus?

Other names for this plant include *bejuco de San Pedro* (tendril of holy Peter), *flor de la virgen* (flower of the virgin) and *hierba María* (Mary's herb).

Christmas flower *(Turbina corymbosa).* Known as jewel cord by the Maya, this bindwind serves as a psychedelic tunnel that connects the shaman with the cosmos. It is an umbilical cord connected with the birth of a new world. This is why in Mexico, the bindweeds are associated with the miracle of birth. Whoever tastes of the jewels of the cosmic umbilical cord sees a wonderful, fantastic world: the mystery of being, which includes the poles of life and death and exists only because of them.

OTHER NAMES

Auferstehungsblume, chérites panagiás (Greek, "hand of God's mother"), Christ rose, *doradilla* (Mexican), *id fatma bint e nabi* (Algerian, "Fatima's hand"), Jericho rose, *kaff maryam* (Arabic, "ball of Mary's thumb"), *Marienrose, rosa della Madonna, rosa di egitto* (Italian), *rose de Marie, rose hydrométrique* (French), *weihnachtsrose, weinrose*

> *The crusaders considered this plant a symbol of the*
> *resurrection . . . because of its ability to shrivel up its dead*
> *husk and grow afresh from the wet seed.*
>
> GERMER 1986, 50

No Central European Christmas market would be complete without a stand selling examples of Christmas plants. Recently, the rose of Jericho has reappeared in old-time markets for customers who have a sense of reverence for the plant. This plant—an excellent example of a Christmas blossom miracle—is sold in the form of a dry nodule which, after being placed in water, quickly rewards one with a flower. The true rose of Jericho is a desert plant, *Anastatica hierochuntica*. The rose of Jericho offered at Christmas markets of today, however, is from an entirely different species of plant, *Selaginella lepidophylla*. This is a club moss from Mexico that is botanically unrelated to the true rose of Jericho, but provides a satisfactory blossom miracle in lieu of the original.

Rose of Jericho *(Anastatica hierochuntica)* grows in the desert regions of Morocco, southern Iran, and Egypt.* This strange desert being is unrelated to true roses, but has much in common with their symbolic and mystical qualities.

*Not to be confused with the Jericho tomato or gray solanum (*Solanum incanum* L.), whose narcotic fruits were sometimes identified as the apples of Sodom! Rose of Jericho is also a common name for *Asteriscus pygmaeus* Coss. et Kral. (Asteraceae), another desert plant.

Miracle Blossoms for the Winter Solstice

Left: The "Rose from Jericho" *(Rosa Hierichuntis)* (Woodcut from Lonicerus 1679: 501)

Center: The three sexes of the roses of Jericho *(Rosa Hierichuntina)* (Woodcut from Tabernaemontanus 1731: 835)

Right: In the early modern era the ominous herb *Amomum* was regarded as belonging to the "Roses of Jericho." The woodcut in the herb book of Tabernaemontanus (1731: 1336) is hard to define botanically.

The stem—perfectly adapted to the desert climate—shrinks during drought to an ugly, dry nodule as big as a fist. This ball can be carried by the wind through the desert, just like a Texas tumbleweed. But as soon as it is put into water, it quickly becomes green and puts forth little white blossoms. Botanists describe this moisture-induced flowering as hygrochastic.

In earlier times, the rose of Jericho was the center of an important Christmas miracle blossom ritual. On Christmas Eve, people would put an inconspicuous rose of Jericho nodule (a dried stem) in a basin of water beneath the Christmas tree. After it flowered, before New Year's Eve, it was put back in a box to dry so that it could be enjoyed again the next year, with another miraculous flowering. Over time this famous Christmas miracle was forgotten.

Christian interpretations saw in the rose of Jericho a link to the Eucharist (the symbolic presence of the son of God in the consecrated bread and wine taken during the Communion sacrament). Accordingly, they saw the greening of the plant as the resurrection of Christ: "The so-called Rose of Jericho *(Anastatica hierochuntica)* that looks the whole year as though it were dead and dry unfolds out and has this delicious perfume, which is why it is also called the resurrection flower and is dedicated first of all to the Savior" (von Perger 1864, 56f).

The Coptic Christians of Egypt took this symbol for their own when they placed a rose of Jericho in the hands of a mummy, found in a grave dating from the fourth century CE at Antinoe. Crusaders and medieval pilgrims brought the strange botanical rarity from Jerusalem to Europe. They saw a clear analogy between the flowering of the rose of Jericho and Christmas, because "with Christ's birth, the flower blossomed, during his crucifixion it closed its petals, and for the resurrection it opened its blossoms again" (Mercatante 1980, 121). There are numerous legends connecting the Virgin Mary with this plant's emergence and indestructible constitution. The plant was purported to have sprung from a footprint left by the holy family on its flight to Egypt. Mary was believed to have blessed the plant and thus given it eternal life.

The first modern "fathers of botany" had the infamous rose of Jericho as a subject. It was first described by Lonicerus in 1679. Tabernaemontanus wrote about the "three generations" of the rose of Jericho: "The old women think a

Miracle Blossoms for the Winter Solstice

lot about this rose: And they get it/ that it takes all year/ outside of Christ night/ when in certain hours it opens/ if it is put in fresh water/ and then they have their intuition and their sense of it/ like later many things will happen/ which is wrong/ because put in the water/ it goes up every hour" (Tabernaemontanus 1731, 836).

MAGICAL AND FOLK USE

The use of the rose of Jericho in folk medicine goes back to the birth of Jesus:

> . . . because when Holy Mary was climbing up in the dense darkness to the skull hill Golgotha, wherever she left a print of her hand, the rose of Jericho grew. While she was in labor, her suffering made her face and her lips moist with sweat, which was blessed with the rose of Jericho so it was easier to get through the hard hour (Seligmann 1996, 137f).

Muslims had a particular woman in mind when they named this plant. In various languages, its name means "hand of the blessed Fatima," in honor of Fatima,* the youngest daughter of the prophet Muhammed. From the nature of its miraculous blossoming, pregnant women read prophecies concerning delivery and birth, and special magic rituals were handed down. For an easy birth and faster healing, for example, a pregnant woman should drink the water in which the flower is blossoming. "The blossoming of the rose during the end period of the pregnancy [foretells] a happy birth. If it does not open, though, it is a bad augury for the woman who is giving birth" (Fabich 1991, 116f).

FALSE ROSES OF JERICHO

The roses of Jericho sold today in our Christmas markets come from a Mexican plant, *Selaginella lepidophylla*, which is a member of the club moss plant family

Above: *Texochitl yamanqui.* The first botanical drawing of false rose of Jericho (*Selaginella lepidophylla*), a club moss from Mexico. (Illustration from Martín de la Cruz, *Libellus de Medicinalibus Indorum Herbis;* Aztec manuscript from 1552)

Left: The "rose of Jericho" offered for sale in modern Germany is a dried but live plant from Mexico (*Selaginella lepidophylla*).

Right: A living *Selaginella* with wide-spread leaves (Shimbé, Peru). This plant is used as a magical plant by Peruvian *curanderos* (healers) and shamans during nighttime rituals.

*Fatima was born around 610 CE and died in 632 CE. Thus, according to historic sources, she was only 22 years old at the time of her death.

Miracle Blossoms for the Winter Solstice

The poinsettia *(Euphorbia pulcherrima)* is originally from Central America but quickly spread to South America. The inconspicuous flowers, which can be found in the middle of the bright red sepals (leaflike structures) that attract the eye, are actually very small and unattractive.

Miracle Blossoms for the Winter Solstice

(Selaginellaceae). In contemporary Mexico, the plant is called *doradilla,* "little gold-leafed one." Other common names for the plant translate to "resurrection plant." This plant, which can be found growing from Texas to El Salvador, is related to the northern fir moss or club moss (*Lycopodium* spp.). It was first described in an Aztec manuscript from 1552, which was translated into Latin by Juan Badiano. It appears with a picture under the name *texochitl yamanqui* (soft blossom that is born in the stone). This document noted that the plant "arouses sexual things" (de La Cruz 1996).

In the eighteenth century, folk healers prescribed *yamanquitexocitl* for illnesses of the liver and kidneys and "melancholic hypochondria." In contemporary Mexican folk medicine, it is used for relief of temporary impotence and to treat *tabaquismo,* chronic nicotine overdose. Applied topically in powdered form, *Selaginella* can be rubbed on painful body parts as a protection against illnesses caused by bewitchment. Kidney ailments are treated with a tea, *doradilla y cola de caballo,* made from *Selaginella* and horsetail (*Equisetum* spp.)—a combination of Christmas rose and Christmas tree!

Selaginella is best collected in October. In the Mexican state of Puebla, the plant is offered up on *Dia de los Muertos,* the Day of the Dead (November 1). On Christmas Eve, the baby Jesus *(el niño Dios)* can be found nestled in those flowers, and the people make a Christmas tea from *doradilla* and *cabellos de elote* (sweet corn flat cakes).

Christmas Stars

Many flower blossoms remind us of radiant stars in appearance and color. Poets wrote lyrically about "blossom stars," and star-shaped flowers and pointed seeds gave rise to folk names such as star herb, a common name for woodruff *(Galium odoratum).* A popular star-shaped Christmas baking spice is called star anise *(Illicium verum).* Such comparisons of flowers and other plant parts with stars lead ultimately to the Christmas star or star of Bethlehem, a natural conclusion from the Christian point of view that dominated even science until at least the end of the nineteenth century.

Poinsettia: The Christmas Star
Euphorbia pulcherrima Willd. ex Klotzsch, Euphorbiaceae

OTHER NAMES
Adventsstern (Advent star), *alwa' akal ch'ohool'* (Huaxtec, Christmas plant), *bandera* (Spanish, flag), *bebeta, catalina* ("little dung-heap"), Christmas bush, Christmas flower, *Christstern* ("Christ star"),* *cuitlaxochitl* (Nahuatl, "yellow Christmas flower"), *estrella federal* (Spanish, "federal star"), *feuerblume* ("fire flower"), *flor de navidad* (Spanish, "flower of the holy birth"), *flor de nochebuena* (Spanish, "flower of the holy night"), *flor de Santa Catalina, hirtenrose* ("shepherd's rose"), *lalupate* or *lalupati* (Nepali, "red leaf"), *lalu pati dhupa*

("incense of the red flower"), *liebesstern* ("love star"), *listoncillo,* Mexican flame leaf, *noche buena, pascuaxochitl* (Nahuatl, *flor de pascua,*[†] "Christmas flower"), *poinsette, poinsettia, Weihnachtsblume* ("Christmas flower"), *Weihnachtsstern* ("Christmas star")

The poinsettia's tall red sepals attract attention. They shine like a floral illusion on the stem. This flower blossom miracle is an obvious sign that the time of the holy feast is upon us. In its native country, the evergreen poinsettia shrub grows to a height of 3 to 4 meters (about 13 feet). Its big, jagged leaves form a starlike pattern. Its wild form—seeming rather a poor relation today—can be seen in the tropical rain forest of the Mexican state of Chiapas, especially near the splendid Mayan ruins of Palenque.

Why has poinsettia—a plant from the tropics—become such a popular symbol for Advent? This is a plant from the New World, not from the cold winter woods of the north, where the Yule feast originated, or the arid deserts of the Middle East, where the stable of Bethlehem stood. Where did the poinsettia get its start in botanical history? Strangely enough, this is an early example of a classic marketing success story! In 1828, Dr. Joel Roberts Poinsett, an American from South Carolina, "discovered" the ever-popular Christmas star in Mexico and began to propagate it in the United States. His report on the plant and his translation of the Mexican name as "flower of the holy night" secured for the ornamental shrub an important place in the Christmas botany of Europe and North America. During the Christmas season, we see potted poinsettias everywhere in supermarkets and flower shops. They decorate shop windows, public buildings, and private homes. Their red leaves send an obvious message: *Attention! Christmas is at the door. Be ready! Buy me, and with me, buy the promise of tropical blossom splendor!*

MAGICAL AND FOLK USE
Mexican folk nomenclature and usage of the plant harks back to old gods and saints and the long-standing role of the plant in Christmas rituals. Many

Left: The "blossoms" (sepals) of the poinsettia. The gruesome Hindu witch goddess, Kali, loves this flower the most. After the red rhododendron, *lalupate* is the most important flower for ritual offerings to Kali.

Right: *Lalupate,* "red-leaf star incense," or *lalu pati dhupa,* "red flower incense" are Nepali names for the dried raw material, which consists of flowers, fruits, and the bright red poinsettia "blossoms" (sepals). (Kathmandu, Nepal, March 2003)

Miracle Blossoms for the Winter Solstice

The goddess Kali. (Relief in a Tantric shrine in Kathmandu, Nepal)

---

*This milky latex contains diterpenes and esters. They produce symptoms of poisoning, such as "shaking, vomiting, diarrhea, sleepiness, drowsiness" (Roth et al. 1994, 344).

†As in Mexico, Nepali women make a tea from poinsettia sepals to stimulate milk flow (Manandhar 2002, 228). In Nepali folk medicine, the latex is used to treat boils and sores. Up to the present day in Mexico, women practice a folk magic involving poinsettia to prevent a venereal disease named after the plant: *cuitlaxochitl* or *cuitlasuchil* ("bastard flower" or "dung flower" in Aztec). It is believed that a woman can ward off this disease by stepping over poinsettia flowers or the "high leaves of the plant."

‡In Byzantine art, the image of the mother of God giving the breast to the baby Jesus is called *panajia glaktotrophoúsa*, meaning "the one who nourishes with milk."

Indians in Chiapas use the chili pepper–red leaf stars as offerings and dedication gifts for ancient pagan gods or pre-Catholic saints. The Tonotaken, a people from the land of vanilla (Central America) who were suppressed by the Aztecs, decorate their altars for Christmas with the red and green leaves.

For Hindus in India and Nepal, the red color of the "false illusion" petals of the poinsettia symbolize the female life force (Majupuria and Joshi 1988, 223). Europeans associated it with the red garb of Father Christmas.

The Aztec name *cuitlaxochitl* (bastard flower of the gods) refers to the plant category of *xochitl*, "flower." However, in Aztec, *xochitl* does not merely mean flower. Rather, the meaning amounts to something like "plant that makes consciousness blossom." These "flowers of the Earth" are magic, shamanic plants (for example, peyote cactus) with psychoactive effects that can give human beings "blossoming dreams." The word *xochitl* also has a sexual connotation. The vulva is the blossom of a woman, because out of it blooms a new human being—a flesh-and-blood blossom miracle. The star of Christmas (poinsettia) is not psychoactive, but through its symbolism, does stimulate the power of fantasy.

The whole plant contains a milky latex.* The Florentine Codex, an Aztec source from the sixteenth century, stated that the people considered this latex a galactogogue, meaning that it was used to stimulate milk production in nursing women.† Christian missionaries associated this folk custom with the nourishing mother of God, and made the indigenous people worship the plant in honor of the birth of Christ.‡ The Huaxtec, who live near the Gulf of Mexico and whose language is related to Mayan, have called the poinsettia *alwa' akal ch'ohool* (Christmas plant) since the time they were Christianized. They make a tea from the shoots in order to read and sing more easily and to become wiser (Alcorn 1984, 648, 650).

In Nepal, where the poinsettia grows splendidly, the plant is called *lalupate*, "red-leaf star incense," or *lalu pati dhupa*, "incense of the red flower." This name refers to its starlike bud and the use of its seeds, buds, and fruits as ingredients for incense for shamanic rituals (Müller-Ebeling et al. 2000, 54, 151). It is also used to make "witch smoke" *(bokshi dhup)*, an incense mixture for warding off the dangerous influence of witches and demons—much like the smudging performed during the raw nights in old Germany.

Lalupate (or *lalupati*) is the favorite flower for sacrificial offerings to the Hindu goddess Kali. Kali is simultaneously the embodiment of both the destructive and creative aspects of the loving goddess Parvati. Europeans considered Kali the Indian sister of the Greek magic goddess, Hecate, who originated in Asia Minor. Some scholars of witchcraft believe the German word for witch *(hexe)* is derived from her name.

For the Newari, who live in the valley of Kathmandu in Nepal and work as craftsmen and merchants, the poinsettia is the traditional flower of marriage, serving a purpose similar to that of Barbara's boughs for our ancestors. On her wedding day, a Newari bride becomes Kali, recognizing the necessary destruction of old bonds to make way for new things (Mookerjee 1988). It is only on her wedding day that a woman finally leaves her parents' home to become a part of her husband's household. During this drastic rearrangement of the social order, *lalupati* symbolizes fertility, the blossoming of new life, the flower blossom miracle of the holy wedding night, and the bride's farewell to her parents' home.

On the wedding day, two copper or brass jugs are placed next to the entry to the bride's home. They are filled with water that represents godly *soma* (also called *amrita* or nectar) and topped with an earthenware bowl filled with yogurt. The white color and source of the yogurt remind the Nepalis of the holy white cow and its nourishing power, just as Christians see white snow as a symbol of the innocence and the immaculate conception of Mary. The yogurt is decorated with the sign of the swastika, created with a sprinkling of red *tika* powder.* Red poinsettia blossoms surround the jugs.

The sight of the swastika is utterly appalling to most Americans and Europeans, especially Germans. But this symbol has been known since prehistoric times in practically all cultures. It represents the wheel of life, the sun and the course of the Earth around it, the four seasons, the cyclical nature of existence, the five elements, shamanic power, and the pre-Lamaistic Bon religion of Tibet. The word *swastika* comes from the Sanskrit and translates literally as "from good luck." The swastika is the holy cross of Kali. A swastika turning to the left represents autumn and winter and is considered female; turning to the right indicates male power and symbolizes spring and summer. The swastika is also dedicated to the snake gods and the elephant-headed Hindu god Ganesha. In Asia, his sign on temples and houses protects human beings from the evil eye (Stutley 1985, 139).

The amrita wedding jug by the door of a Newari house in Kathmandu. Decorated with poinsettias and swastikas, the jug is a lucky charm for the new marriage. (Photo by Claudia Müller-Ebeling, Nepal, March 2003)

Star of Bethlehem
Ornithogalum umbellatum L., Liliaceae

OTHER NAMES
Doldiger milchstern, dove's dung, *drudenzwiebel*, *gemeine vogelmiclh*, *milchstern* ("milk star"), star of Bethlehem, *stern der heiligen drei könige*, *sternchen*, *sternchengucker*, *sternkraut*, *sterntaler*, *weisse sternchen*

This lily plant, native to the eastern Mediterranean, is distributed widely across Europe today. There are around eighty species. The leaves are green in winter; the mostly white and sometimes yellow blossoms develop May through June.

The name star of Bethlehem refers not only to the plant's starlike, white blossoms, but also to its hope-inspiring ability to become green during winter,

*The sacred red color of the *tika* with which Hindu women decorate their foreheads originally came from natural vermilion pigment. Now the color comes from a synthetic substitute.

Miracle Blossoms for the Winter Solstice

Star of Bethlehem (Ornithogalum umbellatum) is a white-flowered lily plant. The bulb contains the digitalis-like poison convallatoxin, which is also found in lily-of-the-valley (Convallaria majalis). (Woodcut from Tabernaemontanus 1731, 1020)

Miracle Blossoms for the Winter Solstice

82

around the time of the birth of the son of God in the stable of Bethlehem. The white color of the flower and its botanical origin in the lily family reinforce its symbolic association with Mary's immaculate conception of Jesus. Older Greek sources associate the plant—originally from Cyprus—with the love goddess, Aphrodite:

> Here on the hard ground, above sand and stones, the tender little white flower called the star of Bethlehem (Ornithogalum tonuifolium) is growing— a spring flower whose origin is on Cyprus. The Cypriots say that the white flower first grew under the naked foot of the newborn Aphrodite. Aphrodite stepped on the ground, and flowers, roses, were born (Grigson 1978, 32f).

Since the earliest days of recorded history, victors of war have imposed their own ideas and value systems on the defeated. They destroyed or demonized what was important and holy to the defeated culture or assimilated their holidays and rituals into their own customs. This has been true also for plants and their common names. Some plants holy to pagans were demonized as "devil's weed"; others came to be associated with the story of Jesus, the symbolism of Mary, and the traditions of Christmas. The Christian renaming of milk star (Milchstern), holy to the Greek love goddess Aphrodite, as "star of Bethlehem" provides a good example of this.

Bedstraw
Galium spp., Rubiaceae
Galium aparine L.
Galium odoratum L.
Galium verum L.

OTHER NAMES
Cleavers, goose grass, Mary's bundle, our dear lady's bedstraw, sweet woodruff, true bedstraw, woodruff

In the folk tradition, a number of other starlike flowers and plants are associated with Christmas events. One is bedstraw, also known as woodruff. From the Christian vernacular come the unusual names "our dear lady's bedstraw" and "Mary's bundle" for bedstraw *(Galium verum)* (Söhns 1920, 38ff). Behind this changeable name and its association with Mary and Christ's birth is an old custom of the Germanic pagans. The practice was to put a bundle of bedstraw in a pregnant woman's bed to help ensure a good birth and a plentiful flow of milk. The plant was originally holy to the love goddess Freia, protector of fertility, marriage, and love. In 734 CE, when the Council of Leptinae put the Christian curse on such heathen customs, the associations survived under new auspices. The former pagan heathens, now recently sanctified Christians, justified their old customs by connecting them with the birth of Jesus.

Exotic Christmas Flowers

From cultures around the world come still more flowers with important roles in the ethnobotany of Christmas. Even cacti from the deserts of North, Central, and South America have been incorporated into Christmas rituals by local peoples.

Brunfelsia: A Brazilian "Christmas Flower"
Brunfelsia spp., Solanaceae
Brunfelsia hopeana (Hook.) Benthe.
Brunfelsia uniflora Pohl. D. Don

OTHER NAMES
Blossom of Lent, *borracheras* (Spanish, "drunkmaker"), Christmas flower, *flor de Natal* (Portuguese, "Christmas flower"), good night, lady of the night, manaca, *manacá jeratacaca*, raintree, Santa Maria, white tree

Brunfelsia, a member of the nightshade family (Solanceae) is well known to plant lovers as a decorative plant from tropical South America and the Caribbean. The genus contains forty to forty-five species. Some species have

The characteristic blossoms of *Brunfelsia (Brunfelsia pauciflora* var. *calycina),* the Brazilian Christmas flower. Because of their beauty, most species enjoy widespread use as ornamental plants in tropical areas. *Brunfelsia* is also cultivated successfully in frost-free areas of the Mediterranean.

applications as healing remedies, some are known as ornamental plants, and some are used as ingredients in psychoactive preparations (Plowman 1977, 290ff). In Germany, *Brunfelsia* is a folk remedy called manaca, long valued for the healing properties of its root. In the vernacular, many species are called *borracheras* (drunkmaker) and serve as ingredients for the shamanic intoxicant known as ayahuasca.

The *Brunfelsia* genus was named after Otto Brunfels (1489–1543), a German doctor, botanist, and theologist. When the Portuguese came to north Brazil, they observed how the Indians used *Brunfelsia uniflora*. The inhabitants of the Amazon region made poison for arrows from extracts of the plant's roots. The *payés,* or shamans, used the root for healing and for performing magic (Plowman 1977, 290f). The variety known as manaca sometimes is recommended as an aphrodisiac in Brazil.

In Brazil, *Brunfelsia* is part of both urban and rural Christmas ethnobotany. Its flower blossoms, which may be both white and violet on the same plant, symbolize the blossom miracle—creation beginning anew. Brazilians not only call the plant *manacá jeratacaca* (snakebite medicine) and *umburapuama* (medicine tree), but also *flor de Natal* (Christmas flower). In English, it is called Christmas flower, Santa Maria, white tree, good night, and blossom of Lent.

Christmas Cacti
Schlumbergera spp., Cactaceae
Schlumbergera x *buckleyi* (T. Moore) Tjaden (Christmas cactus)
Schlumbergera truncata (Haw.) Moran (false Christmas cactus)

OTHER NAMES
Christ cactus, holiday cactus, limb cactus, lobster claw, false Christmas cactus

Miracle Blossoms for the Winter Solstice

The Christmas cactus (*Schlumbergera* spp.) develops its fiery red blossoms in time for the feast. (Photo by Bruno Vornarburg)

*Cacti are considered a lucky charm because they can only
survive with luck in the deserts where they originate.*

HILLER 1989, 148

Cacti are strange, fleshy, spiky beings from the deserts of North, Central, and South America. They are popular collectibles with plant growers. Their spikes are treated with respect, their flower blossoms with joy. The hybrid most widely known as Christmas cactus, *Schlumbergera* x *buckleyi,* is a popular indoor ornamental that puts forth vivid red blossoms in winter. Other cacti provide food and medicine, and some are worshipped in shamanic cultures as entheogens. These are psychoactive plants celebrated as incarnations of the gods and eaten in the search for visions. The psychoactive substances in peyote *(Lophophora williamsii),* called phenethlyamines, are also found in other cacti—for example, bishop's cap or hat of St. Nicholas *(Astrophytum myriostigma),* which the native people call wild peyote.

In pre-Spanish times, psychoactive cacti were especially popular for rituals. The Mexican Huichol Indians gave peyote—known in Germany only as "drug cactus"—a central role in their lives and their universe. This little nodule, a desert inhabitant with no spines, is a shamanic being that provides insight into paradisiacal worlds, gives humans mystical vision, and reveals to them something of the great mystery of being. In South America, the huge *Trichocereus pachanoi,* originally called *achuma,* is widely known today by its Christianized name, San Pedro cactus. The San Pedro cactus is named after St. Peter—the saint who holds the key to heaven—and contains, like peyote, the vision-inducing substance mescaline.

Because of their bloom times, certain cacti are associated with ritual dates and family feasts. In addition to Christmas cactus (*Schlumbergera* spp.), we are familiar with Mother's Day cactus (*Mammillaria* spp.) and Easter cactus

Miracle Blossoms for
the Winter Solstice

The giant saguaro *(Carnegiea gigantea)* is known in Europe through "Western" movies. It is native to Arizona and northern Mexico. (Tucson, Arizona, February 1992)

(Rhipsalidopsis gaertneri). The so-called true Christmas cactus found in flower shops is a hybrid: *Schlumbergera* x *buckleyi,* a cross between *S. russelliana* and *S. truncata.* The limb cactus *(S. truncata)* is originally from the Organ Mountains near Rio de Janeiro, Brazil, where it grows on tree crowns up to 50 meters (about 165 feet) above ground. Here, in the tropical Yucatán, the region of South America where the Mayans settled, this cactus finds an arid climate that suits its needs. This plant is an epiphyte—one that absorbs moisture and nutrients directly from the air—and in South America is pollinated by hummingbirds. If properly cared for, the Christmas cactus will overflow with bright, carmine-red flowers year after year.

The giant saguaro, another cactus from the New World, is widely known by its characteristic silhouette. The saguaro plays a role in the Christmas festivities for some local people: "In some parts of Mexico, the huge *Carnegiea gigantea* serves as a Christmas tree. It is decorated festively and presents are put underneath it. But the cactus is not transferred into the house; it stays outside" (Berger 2002b, 51).

This cactus can grow up to 12 meters (about 40 feet) and has a main stem and eight to twelve secondary branches. The white blossoms, which have bright yellow stamens and pistils, emerge from green, scaly buds at the tips of the stem and branches. The cactus blooms for the first time at fifty to seventy-five years of age (Bruhn 1971, 323). Its fruit can be as large 6 to 9 centimeters (about $2^{1}/_{2}$ to $3^{1}/_{2}$ inches) around and produces more than two thousand seeds. The saguaro can live 150 to 175 years and weigh 6 to 10 tons at maturity. The Indians of the southwest made a wine from its fruit that was drunk for the purpose of ritual intoxication and as an aphrodisiac.

The Tohono O'odham (=Papago), an Indian tribe of Arizona, worship the saguaro cactus as a holy tree. They say that it grew from sweat drops condensed into pearls that fell from the eyebrows of I'itoi, the older brother in the family of gods of the tribe. In another myth of origin, the cactus is an enchanted boy. When his mother was not paying attention, he got lost in the desert and fell into a tarantula's hole. He came back up again as a cactus. This may explain the folk custom of burying the placenta next to a saguaro so the newborn child will have a long life. At the time of the spring equinox, the O'odham sang special songs all night long to insure that the saguaro cacti would bear fruit (Hodge 1991, 47). The Serí Indians, who live in the Sonoran desert of Mexico, also believe that the saugaro was originally a human being. They share the O'odham custom of burying the placenta next to the root so that the newborn will rejoice in a long life.

Miracle Blossoms for the Winter Solstice

CHRISTMAS GREENS

Green is the sacred color of the plant cults.

GOLOWIN 1985, 139

Not only is there a meteorological white Christmas, there is also a botanical green Christmas. "If there is no snow on Christmas, then expect snow on Easter, according to the saying 'green Christmas, white Easter'" (Hiller 1989, 322). We are accustomed to the fact that, in our climate, the plant world reflects the course of the year. Nevertheless, in the northern European evergreen forests, some green is always evident in the bare, snowed-in woods. This hope-inspiring winter green is also expressed by other plants all over the world, especially such seasonally important greens as mistletoe, holly, laurel, and ivy.

Even city people, living in comfort and far removed from nature, feel depressed when leaves begin falling off the trees in autumn, when the flowers and greenery wither and the days grow shorter, colder, and misty-gray. Our ancestors felt the same way. They feared that when winter set in, nature might die forever, that the sun might never rise above the horizon again after the bow of its arc flattened and the temperature fell.

Of course, our experience shows us that autumn does not result in a great death of trees, but is only a natural event in the course the year. Year after year, nature withdraws in November and December, and we envy the bears—the early shamanic gods of our ancestors—their winter sleep. With the last falling leaves, we begin already to anticipate spring, the time when the trees wake up to "new life," herbs start growing again, and flowers bloom. Spring is the great flower blossom miracle. Like the legendary plants that blossom in the winter, most needle-bearing trees survive on the "dying Earth" as carriers of hope, and they send their green shimmering through the fog and the snowy forests. This winter green gives comfort and inspires belief in the reawakening of nature that sustains us through the dark time. This belief runs like a green thread through the period of ice and cold. No wonder our ancestors saw evergreens as mysterious, holy plants. No wonder either that we take this eternal green into our homes during the darkest time to remind us of the greening power of nature.

The pagans saw divinity in the world of plants. Green was the divine juice of life. This is why evergreen plants were especially holy, divinely full of soul. In the first century CE, the Roman naturalist Pliny wrote, "Yes, we believe that even down below the heavens, the forests also have their deity, their sylvans, fauns, and (various) kinds of goddesses" (Pliny the Elder XII, 3).

Our ancestors took evergreen branches in pre-Christian times into their houses and huts. . . . The faithful green was supposed to give shelter to

Wintergreen (*Pyrola* spp.). "The kinds of species of *Pyrola* that can be found in the sorry shadows of our deepest pine forests, in humid and mossy places that a plant lover really likes, are low shrubs with tender white and open flowers. They do no harm to us, and exist only for our appreciation" (von Chamisso 1987, 172). (Woodcut from Brunfels 1532, 188)

The evergreen box tree (*Buxus sempervirens* L., Buxaceae), one of the evergreens of Christmas, also has a connection with Barbara's boughs. It "stops craziness or anger of the brain. To sleep or rest underneath the box tree diminishes the reason because the smell of it is repugnant to nature." (Woodcut from Lonicerus 1679, 72)

the friendly forest spirits during winter time, and as a symbol of the eternal life force, it was supposed to keep away bad spirits (Kluge 1988, 123).

Christmas has always served as a reminder of the cycle of nature, of our obvious connection to the natural order. This is why there are European sayings such as "green is hope" or "to have a little house in the green." The calming and relaxing effect of the color green is familiar to practically everyone. What's more, green is the complement of red, its direct opposite on the color wheel. Those who are color-blind cannot see the red and green colors of Christmas, only dead gray.

Red and white gnome children bring Christmas greens: mistletoe and holly. (Picture from *Mistletoe* by Mili Weber, 1891–1978)

The Old Ones of the Woods

"Old one of the woods" is a name for female plant spirits or souls. These beings teach humans about the powers of plants. "The old one" is the pagan winter goddess. Her lover is the "green man," the winter god. They are Frau Holle and Wotan. To them holly, ivy, mistletoe, and green winter palms were holy. "At one time the decorating of evergreen plants for Christmas was forbidden as 'heathen' but it is again 'en vogue'" (Storl 2000b, 330).

Whoever makes a place in the garden for plants of the genus *Vinca* will become well acquainted with an "old one of the woods." In the vernacular and in fairy tales, *Vinca* is called by many different names, including forest woman, wild woman, moss woman, *Frau Holle,* and grandmother evergreen (Golowin 1985, 81). These common names are also applied to other forest plants. For example, musk yarrow *(Achillea sochata)* is also called forest miss and wild miss; elder *(Sambucus nigra)* is called *Frau Holler* or simply *Holler;* false mandrake or victory onion *(Allium victorialis)* goes by *fräulein* (miss); and black horehound *(Ballota nigra)* is known as old woman.

We know Frau Holle from the Grimm brothers' fairy tale "Goldmary and

Pitchmary." In old Germanic times, she was worshipped as the Earth and fertility goddess Hludana (Hlodyn, Hlödin), and as the mythical mother of Thor (Donar), the thunder god. Frau Holle and her son Donar are associated with virtually all the evergreen plants important in the ethnobotany of Christmas, especially holly and mistletoe.

Frau Holle led the *Hollen* or *Hulden,* a demonic flock of spirits that were counted among the members of Wotan's wild hunt. In the legend, she and her son Donar lived within the plants known as wintergreen, periwinkle, and everlasting. Holle was a being from the other world, and her nature was perceived as ambivalent, both friendly and punishing. In her underworld empire down below, she received the souls of the dead and released the souls of the newborn. Around 1000 CE, Bishop Burchard of Worms identified Frau Holle with the Latin goddess of the forest and the hunt, Diana. Both were witch goddesses, as far as the Catholics were concerned.

The thick-leaved plant called hens and chicks or houseleek (*Sempervivum tectorum* L., Crassulaceae) in English is known in Europe not only as wintergreen, but also by the folk names thunder beard, thunder flower, thunder herb, *Jovis barba* or Jupiter's beard (Jupiter=Donar, the thunder god). "The old one" is also encountered in various species of the genus *Pyrola* (Pyrolaceae), widely known in English as wintergreen. *Wintergrün* is the German name for *Pyrola media* as well as *Pyrola rotundifolia,* which is also called *winterpflanze* (winter plant). In the German vernacular, the related plant *Chimaphila umbellata* (pipsissewa or prince's pine, formerly *Pyrola umbellata*) is called *winterlieb* (winter dear), *wintergrün* (winter green), and *waldmangold* (forest-man gold). *Polygala paucifolia* (Polygalaceae) is called flowering wintergreen.

Left: Creeping myrtle (*Vinca minor* L., Apocynaceae) contains idole alkaloids. Its five-petaled flower looks like a pentagram, the "druid's mark." This is why it was considered a plant of witches and sorcerers. "While collecting the evergreen, all who picked it had to be free from any impurity" (Bourke 1913, 409). (Kathmandu, Nepal, March 2003)

Right: Periwinkle (*Vinca major* L., Apocynaceae) is also called *singrün* or sorcerer's violet. It was considered a magical protection against the so-called *kehrhexen,* dangerous beings from an upside-down world: "These witches mostly walk around with their heads on upside down, but you can't see them. Whoever is curious to see an upside-down witch only needs to put three sprigs of periwinkle above the door through which the witch is walking, and he will see at once that her head is upside down" (Söhns 1920, 45).

Christmas Greens

Mistletoe: Winter Woods Green

Mistletoe opens the doors to the underworld and provides protection in the face of magic and illness. . . . The Germanic peoples needed it for every magic potion.

SCHÖPF 1986, 115

Viscum album L., Viscaceae (European mistletoe)*

OTHER NAMES

All-heal (Old English), *Donarbesen* ("Thor's broom"), *Donnerbesen* ("thunder broom," *drudenfuss* (Tirol), *gui* (French), *Hexenbesen* ("witches' broom"), *knister* ("crackling"), *knisterholz* ("crackling wood"), *marentacken* (Schleswig-Holstein, "branch against nightmares"), *maretak* (Dutch), *mistlestein*, pentagram, *vischio comune* (Italian), *wintergrün* ("wintergreen"), *Wintergrünholz* ("winter green wood")

Mistletoe is like a key that opens the door to Christmastime. When the green nests of the mistletoe with their mother-of-pearl berries are shining, high up in the crown of poplars or fruit trees in the pale winter sun, the plant appears for sale in the Advent-time markets. In England and in France, mistletoe is a popular Christmas decoration with a longer tradition even than the Christmas tree.[†] In Germany and the United States, we bring mistletoe into the house and joyfully place it over a door. Why? We do it because mistletoe is decorative, traditional, and brings good luck—especially if a couple kisses while standing beneath the "kissing bough." We somehow simply *know* about this from the past. But what lies behind this Christmas custom and its symbolism?

As we so often discover, the key to a better understanding of these old, almost subconscious rituals may be found in long-standing traditions of careful observation of nature. Our ancestors had plenty of time for that. Thus they discovered that the European mistletoe is strange in many ways. It does not grow on the earth, but instead sprouts in the crown of trees, especially poplar, apple, and pear trees, but also on firs and sometimes even on stone oaks *(Steineiche).*[‡] The mistletoe develops from all sides into a ball shape and keeps its leathery green leaves all year long. Its pearly white berries are slimy inside and emerge late, in November and December. In short, this plant "seems to have emancipated itself from the yearly rhythm of the sun" and behaves "as if the seasons did not concern it," as the ethnobotanist Wolf-Dieter Storl aptly stated (Storl 2000b, 247). Today we have a scientific explanation for this botanical peculiarity. We now know that mistletoe is parasitic and takes water and mineral salts from its tree host. Thus its growth is not dependent on the process of photosynthesis or the energy of light.

Our ancestors drew mythical and symbolic conclusions from their observations of nature and handed these down to us. The Celts, whose British

*Phoradendron spp. (Viscaceae), especially *Phoradendron leucarpum* (common leafy mistletoe), are used as Christmas mistletoe in the United States. The American Indians associate the plant with magic.

†Beginning in the sixteenth century, in the Alsatian region, church law forbid the custom of placing fir branches and sprigs of mistletoe on the walls at Christmastime.

‡Firs and oaks were counted among the world trees by the ancients.

Christmas Greens

descendants are responsible for enriched the ethnobotany of Christmas with mistletoe, associated the airy growth habit of the plant with the cosmic powers of heaven, especially when seen growing in an oak (which still very seldom happens). The Celts called the oak *duir,* "oak king." It represented the solstice, the time of transition from one half of the year to the other. According to Pliny, mistletoe was the most important magical plant of the Celtic druids and served as a symbol for the winter solstice. The druids, like the popular Father Christmas, wore white robes and red cloaks. They cut mistletoe from the crowns of oaks with golden sickles and concocted magic potions with it (like Miraculix in the world-famous comic *Asterix and Obelix*).

Drastic love under the mistletoe. ("Vampire Santa" illustration by Michael Kanarek. Postcard © Rockshots, Inc. New York, 1980)

The Celts believed that the slimy berries were drops of semen from the cosmic bull that impregnated the fecund goddess Earth, a horned god who symbolized the power of the divine lightning-thrower or thunder god. This explains the Celtic belief that putting mistletoe on the roof affords protection against thunder and lightning.

The Germanic god Donar gets his onomatopoeic name from the sound of thunder,* and the legendary Hessian Donaroak[†] has cultic meaning as a tree of life or world tree. Like the oak, mistletoe was dedicated to Donar, the rainmaking thunder god of vegetation (von Perger 1864, 65). In German, it was called thunder broom *(Donnerbesen),* which is echoed in the English thunder besom. The plant was demonized in early Christian times as *hexennest* (witch nest) or *teufelbesen* (devil's broom). Nevertheless, the custom of putting up mistletoe at Christmastime persisted.

European mistletoe is distributed from Europe to Asia and northwest Africa but does not occur in Ireland, Iceland, or Scandinavia. This geographically limited distribution explains why mistletoe is portrayed in a Germanic myth as the arrow of death of the sun god Balder. The Germanic people living in Scandinavia had no idea what mistletoe looked like and thus had no knowledge of its "greening power." Some authors write accurately of the non-Germanic origin of mistletoe.[‡] How mistletoe came to be included in the *Poetic Edda*[§] (a compilation of ancient Norse mythology in verse) has not yet been adequately explained by folklorists, the science of comparative religions, or the mythology of science.

*The words *thunder* and *thor* are also onomatopoeic in English.

†The famous Hessian Donaroak suffered the same fate as other sacred trees and groves of the ancient Germanic people. After an order from Pope Gregor, St. Bonifacius allowed them to be felled in 723 CE.

‡See Becker, Hans and Helga Schmoll, *Mistel: Arzneipflanze, Brauchtum, Kunstmotiv im Jugendstil* [Mistletoe: Medicinal Plant, Customs, and Art Motifs in Art Deco] (Stuttgart: Wissenschaftliche Verlagsgesellschaft 1986).

§In the thirteenth century, Snorri Sturluson of Iceland composed the so-called *Younger Edda* and thus transcribed the last few remaining Nordic god legends, adding an overlay of Christianity. Many of the older *Poetic Edda* verses are believed to date back to the ninth century CE.

MAGICAL AND FOLK USE

The symbolism of the evergreen mistletoe, which bears its fruit in winter, is related to the importance of fertility in folk tradition. In the Swabian region of Germany, the people bound mistletoe to fruit trees during the winter in hopes of ensuring a good harvest of fruit (von Perger 1804, 229). In Austria, the people placed mistletoe in the bedroom to help encourage the conception of a child. In the French-speaking part of Switzerland, mistletoe in the bridal bouquet meant a good marriage. In Wales, folk healers made a remedy from dried mistletoe to prevent infertility (Seligmann 1996, 217). The familiar tradition that allows a boy to kiss any girl standing beneath the mistletoe further demonstrates the long-standing association of mistletoe with fertility.

Other customs portray the mistletoe as a key to vitality and good luck and a defense against bad influences. In Scandinavia, mistletoe branches were used as "wishing rods" or "spring roots" that were supposed to enable one to open treasure boxes. In many regions, mistletoe served as a protective barrier against witches and sorcerers.

WITCHES' EXCURSIONS: BROOMSTICKS AND RODS

Witches' broom: Branches of holy mistletoe resembling broomsticks were used to drive out witches.

PRAHN 1922, 147

The rod of St. Nicholas or Father Christmas is nothing other than the infamous witches' broomstick, the basic vehicle for a shamanic or witch flight. Mistletoe was not only called "witches'-broom" in the vernacular, it was actually considered a vehicle for the witches' flight. Mistletoe found growing in birches was seen as especially important for this purpose (Höfler 1990, 40). In pagan times, the birch broom was a ritual object used for cleaning in preparation for new beginnings. With it, one swept out impure spirits of house and yard. Spirits nesting in the body of a human being could be driven out with birch broom beatings.

Two well-known elements of the Christmas custom—helper Ruprecht's rod and the chimney down which Father Christmas throws the presents—are also attributes of witches. "Most of the time a witch rides on a broom[*] out of the chimney, and comes back the same way. If she is not back before the next morning's bells, she will fall down the chimney" (Schöpf 2001, 169). "If you put a broomstick on the floor behind a door . . . a witch could not enter" (Hiller 1989, 125). And it is easy to associate the following belief with the concept of Father Christmas coming down the chimney: "Three brooms should be put in the chimney if you want visitors to come" (Hiller 1989, 29).

"Witches'-broom" is a folk name for a thick-branched growth of fungal origin that affects many different types of plants. In fir trees this abnormal phenomenon is called "fir cancer" and is caused by an infection with the fir broom rust fungus, *Melampsorella caryophyllacearum*.

In old Europe, "life rods" were made of branches from evergreen box tree, juniper, rosemary, and holly:

Not so long ago, in some parts of Schleswig-Holstein, children were still going house to house with their rods, threatening to strike the inhabitants

---

[*]In England, witches' broomsticks were traditionally made out of hemp (*Cannabis* spp.).

Christmas Greens

92

Witches'-brooms

"The so-called witches'-brooms or thunder brooms are associated with thunder and lightning. They are nest-like, normally caused by a parasitical fungus proliferating on white firs, birches, and cherry trees. In earlier times, they were put on roofs to protect houses from lightning and fire. Just as these malignant plant growths were connected with the witch's broomstick, the folk belief also makes an association with lightning: The 'broom' is a symbol of the lightning itself, purifying the air and sky. In combination with storm clouds, lightning very often resembles brooms brushing the sky. Sailors call the west wind 'sky broom'" (Engel 1978, 60).

and receiving hot buns and sweets as "protection payment." . . . The rod, which has a life-affirming function in the Germanic peoples' belief system, has been associated in the Christian value system with the opposite attributes. The rod made of brushwood in the hands of Father Christmas remains a sign of that (Rust 1983, 39).

As many examples in folk literature show, the rod and the broomstick also have a close symbolic relationship to fertility rituals and protection magic. They were used to invoke life and to both inflict and ward off bad weather and bad luck.

The hazelnut was dedicated to Donar, the god of marital and animal fertility. The hazel rod was a very good rod of life, and with this symbol of the *penis*, women were beaten like animals or "nutted" so that they would become fertile. . . . Through old records, this erotic pagan custom has been proven to have been practiced all the way back to the eighth century. The

Above: Helper Ruprecht with his rod. The rod of St. Nicholas or Father Christmas is nothing other than the suspicious witches' broomstick, the vehicle of the shamanic witch flight. (Feather drawing circa 1840, by Franz Graf von Pocci, 1807–1876)

Below left: A witches'-broom growth on a weeping birch (*Betula pendula* Roth., Betulaceae), a tree called witches' birch in the vernacular. It is said that witches sit and dance on its hanging branches on witches' nights. No wonder the fly agaric mushroom grows under these trees.

Below right: Birch-branch broomsticks. Birch branches served as both life rods and witches' broomsticks—a sure sign of pagan nature worship. "The witches' brooms that were made out of birch rods were used as offerings to cure boils in Higher Bavaria" (Aigremont 1987 I, 30).

Christmas Greens

wishing rod *(penis),* which was cut on St. John's Day, is a hazel rod with a year-old shoot. This life rod became a wishing rod because it was also used to find hidden treasures. It could be given a human appearance by cutting the bottom into the shape of two legs (Aigremont 1987 I, 38).

Today in Nepal, one can still come face to face with the shamanic roots of the witches' broomstick. The Kirati shaman Parvati Rai has informed us many times that when she is in trance, she sees witches riding on brooms through the air. Much to our amazement, she and other *jhankris* (shamans) told us that they know of a kind of witch Sabbath and that the *bokshis* (witches) ride on broomsticks. According to Parvati Rai:

> *Bokshis* keep every kind of broom between their legs, but not the *kucho* broom. In blue moon nights they dance around the pipal tree and wish for power for their negative intentions. We *jhankris* also do that. Our brooms are made out of *kucho* from the holy *amlisau* grass. We ask for power to heal illnesses. This dance reminds us of the original quarrel between *jhankris* and *bokshis,* and of our duty to use our powers for positive purposes and the ever-changing game that is played between illness and health.

The *jhankris* use brooms to treat the ill. They whisper mantras (magic formulas and sayings), blow on the patients, and brush away strange beings, germs, and negative energies from their bodies. Shamans use the broomstick to heal, whereas witches use it to fly and to perform harmful magic. The tool is the same, but the means and intention of the user are different.

Holly: Frau Holle's Holy Tree

Of all the trees that are in the wood, the holly wears the crown!
ENGLISH CHRISTMAS SONG

Ilex aquifolium L., Aquifoliaceae (holly)*

OTHER NAMES
Agrifolio, alloro spinoso, aquifolio, aquifolius balme, bat's wings, *buk, Christdorn,* Christ's thorn, *füe, gaispalme, holegen* (Old Greek), holly, hollywood star, *holm, holst,* holy tree, *hülse, hülsebusch, hülseholz, hulis* (Old High German), *hulm, hulst,* hulver bush, *hurlebusch, igelstechpalme, kolleno* (Celtic), *leidendorn, myrtendorn, palma, palmdorn, palmendistel, padnore, quacke, schradlbaum, schwabedorn, schwarze eiche, spiselhölzli, stächlaub, stechblacka, stechdorn, secheichen, stecholder, stechlaub, stechwiederl, tinne, wachslaub, walddistel, walddistelstrauch*

Wild holly branch *(Ilex aquifolium)* in a Nordic forest.

---

*The name *Ilex* comes from an unknown old Mediterranean language!

Christmas Greens

94

With its shiny green, spiky leaves,* and red berries, the holly tree in the snow looks like a Christmas tree decorated with red balls. In Scandinavia, celebrants put up holly for the *jul* feast, believing they will bring luck to the house. In England, holly is a popular Christmas decoration and often used for Christmas cards and wrapping paper. In German-speaking areas, holly is sold during winter in the form of potted plants and branches.

Unlike other evergreen plants that grow in Central Europe, the holly is only partly frost tolerant. It grows primarily in moderate climate zones, especially in England, which is blessed with the influence of the Gulf Stream. There, the Celtic druids once worshipped the holly tree. They cut the spiky branches as rods of life. The red berries embodied female energy, just as white mistletoe berries symbolized male semen. United in the ritual performed for the summer solstice, these two plants became "mythical parents" and played the vital role of guaranteeing renewed life in springtime.

In the Roman Bacchus cult, holly was the female counterpart to the male ivy, and this is why doors of houses were decorated with wreaths from both plants during Saturnalia. The doctor of the church, Quintus Tertullian, forbade this practice as a heathen custom in the second century CE. Church authorities were helpless in the face of the ongoing popularity of the holly rituals, however, and eventually reinterpreted the practice in Christian terms: "In the legend, every palm that greeted the Savior Jesus during his entry into Jerusalem received thorns as a reminder of the ordeal that Christ was put through" (Schöpf 1986, 146). Thus the spiky leaves of the holly became a Christian symbol of the thorny crown and its red berries became the blood of Christ.

Today, *Ilex* is a protected plant in Germany. The extensive use of holly branches for Advent and Palm Sunday endangered natural tree populations in many parts of the country. In the German Teutoburger Forest, for example, the extinction of *Ilex* trees around the sacred Extern Stones† was prevented by a nature-conservation treaty at the beginning of the twentieth century. In the British Isles, the holly forests that remain ("The Hollies") are considered a botanical treasure by plant-lovers.

Nomen est Omen — TRACING THE PLANT NAME

The meaning of holly as a symbol of eternal life and wise foresight is mirrored in its English name, holly, which is related to the word holy. In the Celtic holly day ritual performed the night before the winter solstice, holly branches were collected and put up in the house as a protection against sorcery, lightning,

Father Christmas and the holly. (Motif circa 1900)

---

*This thorny appearance is reflected in the Latin name, *Aquifoliaceae*, which means "spiky leaves."

†Translator's note: The Extern Stones are natural limestone formations that have played an important role in cultic worship. Some are as tall as 125 feet (38 meters) and bear large, possibly man-made, carvings. Some people think these represent not only the stars and constellations, but also the original gods of the German pantheon.

Christmas Greens

The holly fairy, a form of Frau Holle. (Postcard: *The Holly Fairy*, Flower Fairies™, © The Estate of Cicely Mary Barker, 2000)

and death. From this comes the term "holy day," later demoted profanely to "holiday"! The Celts collected branches with red berries in solitude in the dark of the midnight hour, deep in the middle of the woods. To properly cut them from the trees, a drop of blood was considered essential, but red wine was supposed to do the job as well. The red drops stood for the "oldest and most powerful god of the land [England]" (Hyslop and Ratcliffe 1989, 17).

Germanic tribes worshipped the spiky evergreen tree as an embodiment of the love goddess, Freia, the Great Mother (Ströter-Bender, 1994). Her holy day was Friday (free day). The German name Hülse, which comes from the Old High German *huls* or *hulis,* is related etymologically to the English plant name holly and mythologically to Frau Holle (also Holde, Holda), who belonged to the flock of spirits in the wild army and is the mother of Thor (Donar). She is the heir, in folklore, of the Germanic love goddess Freia, and thus the circle back to Freia is completed. (For more on Frau Holle, see "The Old Ones of the Woods.")

The legendary Christmas plant is also called "hollywood star" and "star of the holy wood," names that found new meaning in the New World. Supporters of English Christmas customs brought holly and its symbolism to North America and a new Hollywood: the heart of the American film industry. "British Immigrants to the U.S. established holly plantations so they would not have to live without the Christmas spirit" (Storl 2000b, 294). The fact that the legendary American Hollywood inherited this ancient name is not mere coincidence.

MAGICAL AND FOLK USE

Like other evergreen plants, the jagged, thorny leaves of the *Ilex* were believed to both protect against and attract dangerous powers: "It was the belief of the people that there were signs that the witches needed the red berries of the holly to brew thunderstorms. The berries were an important ingredient of witches' ointment and incense" (Weustenfeld 1996, 111).

They were used in magic as protection from nightmares, incubi and other demons, and lightning.

Planted near a house, holly keeps away evil magic. Pythagoras writes that the power of their blossoms changes water into ice. He also says that when a holly branch stick is flung at an animal without enough force to reach it and is about to land a little short of the animal, the stick will make itself

Christmas Greens

come nearer by a cubit through its own magic, such a great power is in this tree (Pliny the Elder XXIV, 116).

Folk sources also discuss the symbolic erotic and fertility power of this evergreen rod of life. An old Latin document states "that the dresses of women were lifted, and they were beaten on their naked behinds with it. A remnant of an age-old ritual that involved beating women on their genitals with the life rod" (Aigremont 1987 I, 51).

As with other plants important in the ethnobotany of Christmas, folk customs connected with the *Ilex* point to the chimney as the entry portal for spirits and other legendary beings, such as St. Nicholas.

> The chimney was considered the entry and exit for ghosts or spirits and ancestors. In order to keep this door clean, and to drive out the bad spirits that were kept in the soot in the dark, a magic broom was needed. Up to the present time, the chimney is decorated with boughs of holly so that the Christmas Spirit or Old St. Nick can come in at the midnight hour and bless the inhabitants. It is considered bad luck to bring holly into the house before Christmas Eve (Storl 2000b, 294).

With this multilayered background of symbolism, the popular holly tree truly deserves its reputation as the crown jewel of evergreen life. This is why the Green Man wears a crown of holly leaves. He is descended from the pagan vegetation gods with anthropomorphic bodies and masks made of leaves that appear on Roman doorways. The tradition continues today with the holly wreaths that we hang on doors, mantles, and walls at Christmastime.

Laurel: The Sun God's Plant

. . . nothing burns in the world with such a horrendous crackle as the flames of the tree that is dedicated to the Delphic Phoebus.
LUKREZ, *VON DER NATUR* VI, 154F.

Laurus nobilis L., Lauraceae (bay laurel)

OTHER NAMES
True laurel, sweet bay

We know the bay laurel as a spice for hearty winter potlucks and as a crown for glorious heroes, for whom the evergreen leaves of this aromatic plant symbolized perpetual commemoration, even beyond death. The evergreen leaves of the bay laurel evoke the yearly, springtime return of green after the dark and frosty winter days.

The laurel's long history as a symbol of perpetual life in Mediterranean

culture secured it a major role in the European ethnobotany of Christmas. As far north as Scandinavia, where the sunbeams do not even reach the horizon in winter, homes were decorated with laurel branches for the *Jul* feast. As a holy plant of the Greek sun gods Helios, Apollo, and Phoebus, the evergreen branches of the laurel brought the sun into wintry, dark houses.

The evergreen laurel was holy to the ancient Greeks and Romans. The aromatic tree was dedicated to Apollo, the god of spiritual ecstasy. According to myth, a beautiful woman or nymph hid behind it:

> Daphne . . . was the name of the nymph that Apollo loved. She was a beautiful, wild virgin, and when Apollo lusted after her, she fled to her mother Gaia, who changed her into a laurel tree. Since then, the laurel is dedicated to Apollo, and inspires him with its hearty, aromatic scent, which is also used as a medium for purification. So the legend says that Apollo washed himself, after killing the dragon Python in the valley of the temples in Delphi, which is still overgrown with

Daphne is transformed into a laurel bush right before Apollo's eyes. (Illustration from *Cod. Guelf.* 277.4 extrav. Fifteenth century. Herzog-August-Library, Wolfenbüttel)

laurel. And then he entered Delphi, crowned with laurel, as a purified victor. This is why the laurel is a sign of victory, glory, and honor. The oldest sanctuary of Apollo was supposed to be built out of laurel branches (Pausanias 10.5.9).

The first temple in the ancient, legendary town of Delphi was built out of laurel wood. The oracle of this temple, which was dedicated to Apollo, was announced with "the rustling of the laurel." The prophetic priestesses of the temple, called Pythia, slept on laurel, inhaled laurel, and chewed laurel before they fell into trance. On the altar of Apollo, laurel wood was burned. Only laurel brooms could be used to sweep the court of the sanctuary.

Christmas Greens

Smudge Recipes

Apollo Smudge
Ingredients

    4 parts frankincense (olibanum, *Boswellia sacra*)

    2 parts myrrh *(Commiphora molmol, C. myrrha)*

    2 parts cinnamon *(Cinnamomum verum)* or cassia *(C. aromaticum)*

    1 part laurel leaves *(Laurus nobilis)*

Grind and mix all ingredients. Place by spoonfuls on the smudging coals.

Protection Smudge
Ingredients

    2 parts laurel leaves

    1 part thyme *(Thymus vulgaris)*

    3 parts frankincense (olibanum, *Boswellia sacra*)

Grind all ingredients into coarse pieces and mix. Place by spoonfuls on the smudging coals.

Laurel and other aromatic plants were important ingredients in protection smudges. "A fast and deep purification from negative influences is induced with a smudging smoke mixed of thyme and frankincense burned together" (Belledame 1990, 89).

In the same way that Apollo and Dionysus were associated with one another, their botanical attributes were tied together as winter greens: Laurel was dedicated to Apollo and ivy to Dionysus.

Ivy: Tendrils of the Maenads

The snakes that the Maenads had cast upon the tree stumps coiled around it and transformed themselves into ivy tendrils.

Nonnos, Dionysiaca

Hedera helix L., Araliaceae (ivy)

OTHER NAMES

Abheukraut, English ivy, *eppic, ifenkraut, waldeppich, wintergrün* ("winter green"), *winterpflanze* ("winter plant")

Like other evergreen plants, ivy was important at Christmastime, especially as a symbol of everlasting life. Shiny, dark-green ivy leaves appear on all sorts of holiday cards, reminding us that the dormant vegetative forces of nature will be revived with the arrival of springtime. In Christian symbolism, ivy represents eternal life and the resurrection of the son of God.

The evergreen ivy is neither an herb nor a tree, but a vine or liana. It grows at first on the earth, but then crawls in a spiral up the nearest tree; this is the origin of the species name *helix* (meaning "spiral") in Greek. The ivy vine is a snake spirit that brings about a connection with Mother Earth; it is a shamanic "ladder to heaven" (Storl 2000b, 327). Ivy winding around a tree trunk can overwhelm and kill the tree, burying it under ivy leaves.

Ivy was dedicated to the Egyptian vegetation god, Osiris. In many cultures, the plant served as a symbol of immortality:

The long-haired, ivy-crowned wild man, dressed in winter greens, is a folkloric reminder of the pagan gods Wotan, Dionysus, and the Green Man and a relative or ancestor of Father Christmas. In this picture, he carries a club over his shoulder instead of a rod or staff. In other pictures, he carries a fir tree. *(Carnival Games.* Woodcut by Pieter Bruegel the Elder, sixteenth century)

The belief in immortality adheres to the evergreen, her eternal leaves and her winter green. It is the wood mother *(Silva Mater)* who lovingly embraces the trees. In folklore, her leaves and her wood had the power to prolong life and give the weak a renewed life force (Höfler 1990, 55).

Ivy was one of the favorite plants of the Greek god of ecstatic intoxication, Dionysus (who also was called *Kisso,* or "ivy god") because it had such chthonic,* earthy qualities and brought to mind the cult of snake worship. Ivy was considered a sure sign of the presence of Dionysus. From Europe throughout the region conquered by Alexander the Great, it was believed that ivy tendrils sprang up wherever the god had fertilized the ground with his feet.

The Maenads ("the fury" or "the raging") were women dedicated to Dionysus who ritually underwent a state of temporary insanity (mania). They screamed wildly and ran through the forest naked or dressed only in ivy tendrils; they killed and ate animals and ate the flesh of human beings. However, in this state, they had the gift of transcendence and prophecy: "The Maenads were returning to the original state of creative chaos, in the middle of which all order disappears, so everything can start anew" (Bosse 1990, 110). The Maenads clearly had a potion that put them into a state of Dionysian frenzy or ecstasy. The potion was a kind of pine beer or mead with ivy leaves mixed into it.

Folk belief held that ivy could make people impotent and bring on a kind of madness. Plutarch said that ivy contained a brutal spirit that could produce mad outbursts and cramps. Ivy could bring on intoxication even without drinking wine and bring out madness in those who had a natural propensity for ecstasy. When mixed with wine, ivy caused delirium and a madness of the sort normally seen only with henbane (Plutarch, "The Roman Questions," 112). But at the same time, ivy wreaths were believed to prevent drunkenness!

Chthonic means of or related to the underworld.

Christmas Greens

100

THE AROMAS OF CHRISTMAS: A SHOWER OF PHEROMONES

In the aroma of the plant, the universe, the world soul,
communicates with us and other creatures . . . scents are
always the expression of the soul beings.

STORL 1996A, 99

A fairy, a being from the otherworld, climbs out of the smoke. (Etching by Moritz von Schwind in the *Album of Smoking and Drinking*, 1844)

The sense of smell is closely connected with emotion and memory. Smell has a potent ability to evoke vivid memories and sensations, a phenomenon that is difficult to explain but is now known to have a basis in scientific fact. A smell "awakens feelings, kindles emotions, directs thoughts and wishes, spirit, and matter on a surreal level" (Rovesti 1995, 45). Nearly everyone is familiar with the power of smell to bring long-lost memories back into consciousness. In this sense, it is not at all far-fetched to claim that smells can generate psychoactive reactions!

In all cultures, throughout history, special scents have been associated with important rituals. These aromas are intended to awaken past memories of the rituals and signal the olfactory nerves in the brain that the holy time has come again. Thus the smells that we associate with Christmas from our childhoods remind us of the holy feast as long as we live.

Natural fragrances have a significant impact on the nervous system. They not only influence memory, thinking, and emotions, but also sexual behavior. Today, we have a better understanding of the nature of the chemical messengers known as pheromones, substances secreted by humans and animals to influence the behavior of other members of the species. Scientific research has shown that pheromones seem to have an even bigger impact on our choice of sexual partner than physical appearance. In the world of botany, we now know that many plants generate chemical compounds that are quite similar to human hormones and pheromones. Certain plant aromas appear to have effects similar to those of pheromones. Many love potions, incense ingredients, and perfumes contain such alluring messenger substances. These are chemicals that can induce a euphoric state, heighten enthusiasm and mood, and entice our readiness for love. "Pheromones, like smells, make us open up and become curious about things we are yet to encounter; they make us ready, on a subconscious level, for a sensual experience, even if it is not actually going to happen" (Wieshammer 1995, 65).

Typical Christmas aromas provide us with a true shower of pheromones!

NOSTALGIA

WOODLAND

"Nostalgia Woodland" scent pouch: Christmas oak-wood block, pinecone, and greens from pine, larch, and holly— a real gathering of Christmas ethnobotany. (From England, around 2001)

Nearly all incense resins and balsams (for example, frank-incense and myrrh) contain phytosterols. Pine resin *(Pinus sylvestris)* contains substances much like the male hormone testosterone and its chemical precursor, androstenedione. Myrrh contains a testosterone-like substance too. The chemicals zingiberone and zingiberol in ginger essential oil can act as pheromones, and the violet-scented dried orris root *(Iris pallida)* contains the pheromone-like compound α-irone. Coconuts, walnuts, and hazelnuts contain γ-nonalactone. Other plants substances that can act like pheromones include myristicin from nutmeg *(Myristica fragrans)*; cuminaldehyde from cumin *(Cuminum cyminum)*; asarone from calamus oil *(Acorus calamus)* and hazelwort *(Asarum europaeum)*; safranal from saffron *(Crocus sativus)*; α- and β-santalol from sandalwood *(Santalum album)*; cinnamaldehyde, benzaldehyde, and cuminaldehyde from cinnamon *(Cinnamomum verum)*; anethol from anise *(Pimpinella anisum)*; and vanillin and benzaldehyde from vanilla *(Vanilla planifolia)*. Like cinnamon and vanilla, bitter almond *(Prunus dulcis)* also contains benzaldehyde: "During the Christmas season the scent of bitter almond essence is one of the most popular baking ingredients, found nearly everywhere" (Wieshammer 1995, 87).

The aromas we associate with Christmas come from Christmas evergreens and the Christmas tree, Christmas spices, Christmas incense, and special scent-producers (pomanders, oil lamps, scented candles, and so on). Little aromatic pouches and potpourris are especially popular in the United Kingdom. These contain what amount to aromatic *drugs* (a word that comes from an old Dutch term referring to dried plants). These so-called "designer drugs" in the form of dried plant parts are included in potpourris, tea blends, and smoking mixtures partly for aesthetic reasons, but also because of their symbolism.

In England, little scented pouches are fabricated for every imaginable purpose, including Christmas. On the European continent, we decorate oranges—"the golden apples of the Hesperiden"—with whole cloves *(Syzygium aromaticum)* to make scented balls or pomanders. German names for cloves—*gewürznelken* and *nelken*—refer to the nails used to hang Jesus on the cross. Both words are derived from the diminutive form of *nage*, meaning "nail."

In ancient China, clove-studded oranges were used to freshen the air in rooms. To make a scented Christmas pomander ball, simply poke cloves into the peel of a whole orange. You can arrange the cloves in lines or patterns or just cover the entire surface of the orange. You may further scent your pomander ball by sprinkling it with a spice powder made from 2 tablespoons

The Aromas of Christmas

of cinnamon, a pinch of mace, and 1 teaspoon of orris root (Fronty 2002, 16). The intense aroma of these clove-studded orange pomanders comes from the unique combination of essential oils of clove and orange peel—a classic Christmas scent. The evocative aroma results from the perfect chemistry that exists between the phallic clove and the orange peel it penetrates.

Cloves are an especially important carrier of Christmas scent. The typical Christmas aroma of wine punch is due mostly to the presence of cloves. They are also a primary ingredient of Christmas potpourris and scented pouches, incense and scented candles, smoking tobaccos, baccy mixtures and snuffs, foods (roasts and baked goods), drinks (tea, cocoa, Christmas beer, hot drinks, punch, mead, herbal liquors), tinctures, and elixirs.

Today it is easy to find aromatic beverage mixtures of exotic spices with black or green tea under names such as Christmas Tea, Advent Tea, or Winter Magic in tea shops and natural food stores. Perfumers and scent shops proffer a plethora of essential oil blends specially formulated for Christmas. For example, according to its label, one Christmas blend contains sweet orange peel, clove, and cinnamon essential oils. Another, called Happiness in Winter, is composed of essential oils of frankincense, fir, tuberose, orris, and lime.

MAKING A CHRISTMAS ESSENTIAL OIL BLEND

It is simple and rewarding to make one's own special essential oil Christmas blend. Especially appropriate for the season are essential oils of clove *(Syzygium aromaticum)*, frankincense or olibanum *(Boswellia sacra)*, benzoin *(Styrax benzoin*, believed to make one feel very merry), myrrh *(Commiphora molmol* or *C. myrrha)*, cinnamon *(Cinnamomum verum)*, citrus *(Citrus* spp.), bergamot *(Citrus bergamia)*, lime, nutmeg and mace *(Myristica fragrans)*, cardamom *(Elettaria cardamomum)*, white sandalwood *(Santalum album)*, fir *(Abies* spp.), pine *(Pinus* spp.), spruce *(Picea* spp., especially Siberian spruce), palmarosa *(Cymbopogon martinii)*, rosewood *(Aniba rosaeodora)*, orris *(Iris germanica)*, vanilla *(Vanilla planifolia)*, and tuberose *(Polianthes tuberosa)*.

Essential oils can be purchased in scent shops, pharmacies, and natural food stores, as well as through mail-order sources. True essential oils, properly distilled from naturally grown plants, can be very expensive, especially in pharmacies. However, pharmacies and other reputable suppliers offer the advantage of being able to guarantee the natural origin and pharmaceutical quality of the essential oils they sell. In India, shops selling essential oils—often tea shops—are much less expensive, but also sell synthetic substitutes.

Blending essential oils is an art in itself. Aromatic substances react differently depending on how they are blended. But experimenting with natural essences can bring great pleasure in the long winter nights. There is one basic rule: Remember that less is more!*

*Before experimenting it would be a good idea to familiarize yourself with the properties and safety guidelines for the various essential oils. Some are toxic and can have strong effects even when inhaled.

The Aromas of Christmas

Incense for the Holy Nights

The essence of smoking is the essence of life, and the aroma of the spirit.

ARVIGO AND EPSTEIN 2001, 65

The German word for Christmas, *Weihnachten,* comes from the Middle High German *Wihenaht,* which has been documented as far back as the latter half of the twelfth century, the time of Hildegard von Bingen. The Old High German verb *wihen* comes from the adjective *weich* (holy), a usage that died out in the sixteenth century. *Weihrauch* (incense) goes back to the Middle High German *wi[h]rouch* and the Old High German *wihrouch,* which mean "holy smoke." All of this goes to prove that incense is an essential element for the Christmas ritual.

The primary meaning of the German word *weihrauch* is "smoke for invocation" or "sacred smoke." It refers in particular to the aromatic smoke that results from the burning of a smoking (or incense) substance, or a substance transformed by burning to produce a smoke that distributes itself throughout a room. In modern usage, *weihrauch* is a synonym for any substance burned to produce smoke. It is largely associated with the incense used in Catholic churches, even though this ancient "smudging" practice takes place all over the world, in numerous religions and cultures.

The use of incense is no invention of the Christian church. Smudging and incense burning are fundamentally human activities, ancient behaviors that people from all ages and regions have discovered, developed, and treasured. In the Himalayas, the shamans told us that their ancestors, the first shamans, introduced smudging around sixty thousand years ago as an essential element of shamanism. Shamans of all cultures report something along the same lines, that the incense substances they use were discovered by their first shamans or

Olibanum Eritrea, the source of resin tears ("sweat of the gods" or "tears of the gods") from the true frankincense tree *(Boswellia sacra).* Frankincense or olibanum from *B. sacra* was introduced in Greece or Rome around 500 BCE.

The Aromas of Christmas

were revealed to the shamans by messengers of the gods. Shamans all over the world also adhere to the belief that the smoke liberated by the fire that burns the incense carries the soul of the substance into the otherworld, the world of gods and goddesses. The holy smoke is transformed into a divine nectar, the most desired potion, the godly food needed to prevent aging, just like the golden apples of Idun or Freia.

The gods are as dependent on the favor of human beings as humans are on the favor of the gods. In the shamanic cosmos, there is no one god lording over his chosen people and punishing them for wrongdoing. The shamanic cosmos is holistic: Everything is part of one meaning, and in one or more different contexts everything is interdependent on all other things. Incense burning and smudging are an expression of give and take, exchange, mutuality. They represent a holistic pattern and a spiritual process, a ritual of consciousness.

Thus we see that incense burning and smudging are among the oldest ritual practices of humanity. Shamans put themselves into a trance state with the smoke that rises from certain woods, resins, and leaves. The prophet (seer) inhales the smoke of the consciousness-altering substance in order to fall into ecstasy.

The smoke or vapor emerging from the smoking chalice can contain hidden messages. The holy smoke is sometimes called "cigarettes for the gods" or "the brain of heaven."

Priestesses and priests burned resins to make contact with the gods and goddesses. With incense, one can conjure or drive out demons, sanctify and purify buildings, and introduce the sick or possessed to delicious scents or dreadful stinks. Aromatic smoke was believed to have magical and medicinal attributes; different incenses were associated with specific gods and planets. In Scandinavia, children's letters to Father Christmas were burned in the open fire, because this was the only way one could be sure the message would reach Father Christmas.

Incense for the smudging nights of Christmas fulfills most of the purposes stated here. It enables contact with the otherworld and the gods and goddesses who dwell there. It points the way to the wild chase, feeds the dead souls of the ancestors, wards off demons and evil shamans ("witches and sorcerers"), cleanses and purifies house and yard, and prevents the spread of contagious illnesses. Perhaps most important for modern people, incense gives rise to a ritualistic holy feeling. In short, it marks the time of the twelve raw nights and announces the arrival of Christmastime.

Incense Under the Christmas Tree

So it is tending the fire that makes the feast of Christmas so cozy.
APPLETON 2002, 53

Modern people still enjoy smudging and incense burning for purposes of contemplation and pleasure, not necessarily to invoke the Earth gods. But where there is smoke, there is fire! This should never be forgotten, especially when the pine needles and other evergreens are dried out because of the warmth of the home. All too quickly, a Christmas tree or wreath can catch fire.

How should one burn smoking substances in such a potentially dangerous atmosphere? The safest thing might be to forgo smudging altogether and instead set out potpourris, sprinkle essential oils in the room, or decorate with clove-studded oranges. Fortunately, human creativity has given us relatively safe ways to burn incense. We have fireproof smoking chalices, incense burners, smoking pans, and heat-resistant plates on which incense may be burned. Those who find even these methods too dangerous for the living room can turn to commercial incense coals that contain saltpeter.* After the coal is lit and begins to glow thoroughly, spoon incense onto the coal in small portions. Never leave the glowing coal unattended, and keep all burning incense out of the reach of children.

Commercial incense sticks are also relatively safe. However, they usually are of inferior quality, cheap, and saturated with synthetic aromas. Some types touted as Christmas incense do not bring up Christmas associations at all, but rather make one think of teen techno parties and music festivals. However, the little incense candles and "incense men" produced in the Erzgebirge region of Germany are different and have been developed especially for Christmas. One lights an incense candle at the pointed end, puts it in the hollow body of the incense man, and places the man on a piece of aluminum foil.

Incense candles are little pointed cones or cylinders made from different mixtures of resins (olibanum, benzoin, storax, myrrh, balsam of Peru); herbs and woods (thyme, rosemary, lavender, aloewood, rose petals, sandalwood, cedar); spices (cloves, cinnamon, cassia, nutmeg, laurel); essential oils (jasmine, rose, orange blossom); animal scents (civet musk); charcoal (*weidenkohle*, sawdust of linden); saltpeter and binding agents (dragon's blood, gum arabic, tragacanth)—in short, a wide variety of very exotic substances. Juniper, pine, and fir resin are especially popular ingredients in most regionally produced European incenses. In the GDR (East German) era, Christmas incense substances were reduced to aromatic mixtures of resins from Vietnam and Sumatra, lavender blossoms from the Balkans, pine needles from Siberia, regional pine resins and South American tonka beans—all for political reasons (Hinrichsen 1994, 59).

Incense Recipes for the Smudging Nights

For incense we used mugwort, juniper, fir and pine resin, fir and pine greens, wild rosemary, and amber; it is very likely that some crumbs of fly-agaric mushroom and hemp were in the mixture.

NAUWALD 2002, 36

Recipes for incense are like cooking recipes. Even if you follow them very closely, your results can be unexpected and unsatisfactory. This is a good reason

*You can buy "naturally pure charcoal" that is hand-pressed from herbs and wood and contains no saltpeter. These are difficult to light and burn very gradually.

to "mistrust" incense recipes, meaning they are best regarded as suggestions or loose guidelines and should not be taken too seriously.

The outcome of a recipe does not depend solely on a combination of abstract components; more often, the result is determined by the quality of individual ingredients. When working with incense and smudges, count on incorporating some artistic license. Be creative and try new things. Making incense is a method of experimenting with and experiencing nature. Thus all of your experiments will prove valuable, because through them, you will learn about nature with all of your senses.

Don't worry if you don't always end up with a beautiful aroma. Some incense smells so bad that even witches and devils flee from it! If you experience psychoactive effects with incense, you have probably inhaled too much smoke.

Juniper
Juniperus communis L., Cupressaceae (common juniper)

OTHER NAMES
Feuerbaum, juveniperus, kaddig, krammetsstrauch, kranabit, kranawitter-strauch, kranewitt ("crane wood"), *machandel, mirtesgarden, quackelbusk, queckholder, quekholder* (Middle High German, "evergreen tree"),* *rauchholter* ("smoking bush"), *rauchkraut, reckholder, wecholderbaum, wecholter* (Middle High German), *weiheicheln* ("holy berries"), *wekcholder, wehhal* (Old High German), *wodansgerte*

---

*From the Middle High German *quech* (alive, evergreen) and *ter* or *der* (tree).

The Aromas of
Christmas

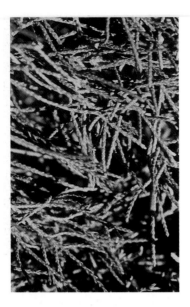

The evergreen branches of the stinking juniper *(Juniperus sabina)* are an important ingredient of smudging night incenses.

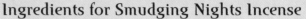

Ingredients for Smudging Nights Incense

Amber, ground
Ash wood (*Sorbus* spp.)
Benzoin *(Styrax benzoin)*
Cedar (*Thuja* spp.)
Fly agaric mushroom, dried *(Amanita muscaria)*
Fir needles (dried or fresh) and resin (*Abies* spp.)
Frankincense or olibanum *(Boswellia sacra)*
Juniper tops, berries, and resin *(Juniperus communis, J. oxycedrus, J. sabina)*
Hemp flowers (*Cannabis* spp.)
Lavender *(Lavandula angustifolia)*
Laurel *(Laurus nobilis)*
Mastic *(Pistacia lentiscus)*
Mugwort *(Artemisia vulgaris)*
Pine needles (dried or fresh) and resin (*Pinus* spp.)
Rosemary *(Rosmarinus officinalis)*
Sweetgrass *(Hierochloe odorata)*
Thyme *(Thymus vulgaris)*
Wild rosemary *(Ledum palustre)*
Wild thyme or quendel *(Thymus serpyllum)*
Yew needles *(Taxus baccata)*

INCENSE RECIPES FOR THE SMUDGING NIGHTS

Nordic Incense
Equal parts of
    Juniper berries *(Juniperus communis)*
    Mugwort herb *(Artemisia vulgaris)*
    Fir resin *(Picea abies)*
    Yew needles *(Taxus baccata)*

Grind juniper berries, chop the fir resin, and mix the two together well. Chop the mugwort herb and knead it into the mixture. Mix in chopped yew needles. If desired, you can also add ground amber, hemp blossoms *(Cannabis sativa),* and henbane *(Hyoscyamus niger).* Place by teaspoonfuls on the smoking embers. It should make little snapping noises as it burns!

Smudging Night Incense
Equal parts of
    Ground fir resin *(Picea abies)*
    Whole juniper berries *(Juniperus communis)*
    Chopped mugwort herb or stripped flowers *(Artemisia vulgaris)*
    Chopped sweetgrass *(Hierochloe odorata)**

Mix all ingredients together. Place incense by teaspoonfuls on the glowing coal.

*Fragrant sweetgrass (called *mariengras* in German) was known as Freia's grass in pagan times. Braided, it is one of the most important smudging substances of the North American Indians. In Christian Europe, the grass was called Mary's grass because of its perfume; it was used to decorate pictures of Mary.

Twelve Holy Nights*

Each ingredient stands for one of the twelve nights!

    3 parts frankincense resin
    1 part mastic resin
    2 parts herb bush mixture, consisting of:
      Mugwort
      Vervain
      Sage
      Mullein flower
      Lemon balm
      Elecampane
      St. John's wort
      Yarrow
      Mint
      Chamomile

Powder the herbs and mix them with the ground resins. Place the mixture by small spoonfuls on the glowing coal.

Incense for the Smudging Nights†

    Amber, ground
    Fir resin
    Fir needles, dried
    Juniper tops
    Fly agaric mushroom, dried
    Hemp blossoms
    Laurel leaves
    Mugwort herb

Yule Smoke‡

Equal parts of:

    Pine resin (*Pinus* spp.)
    Juniper (*Juniperus communis*)
    Cedar (*Thuja* spp.)

This incense can be used for any winter rite. You can also smudge the house with it, but only during the period from November 1 to March 21 (in other words, from the time of Samhain, the feast of All Souls, to the spring equinox).

Pagan Christmas Incense

Equal parts of:

    Juniper needles (*Juniperus communis*)
    Mugwort herb (*Artemisia vulgaris*)
    Ground pine resin (*Pinus* spp.)
    Wild rosemary (*Ledum palustre*)

Chop the herbs and mix well with the ground pine resin. Place by teaspoonfuls on the glowing coals.

---

*Recipe from Fischer-Rizzi 2001, 48.

†Recipe from Nana Nauwald, 2002. Exact quantities are not important; feel free to improvise.

‡Recipe adapted from Cunningham 1983, 120.

Wild rosemary or Labrador tea (*Ledum palustre* L., Ericaceae) is botanically related to rhododendron and heather and is among the old Nordic ritual plants. In addition to its use in smoking substances, the ancient Germans used wild rosemary as an ingredient for beer. They did not know hops; beer made with hops is an invention of Christian monks.

The smoke from juniper is part of the oldest shamanic rituals. Pictured here: *Juniperus recurva*.

The evergreen juniper is one of the most important plants in the ethnobotany of Christmas. Its branches have served as winter greens, medicinal remedies, and protective amulets. The tree's branch tops, berries, and resin have been used as incense ingredients; the berries are a cooking spice and an ingredient for beer, schnapps, and gin. Juniper wood found its way into baccy, Sunday pipes, and bonfires. Like many other plants, juniper branches also have been used as life rods: "On the Second Day of Christmas, in the Vogtland and the Saxon Erzgebirge, when the young men were beating the women and virgins with juniper rods, it could very well be while they were lying in bed" (Aigremont 1987, 52).

Juniper *(wekholder)*. (Woodcut from Brunfels 1532)

In medieval times, juniper was used as a purifying smudge against contagious illnesses. The smoke was also considered a defense against poisonous snakes. In the Engadine valley of Switzerland, farmers put milk through sieves made of juniper in order to preserve freshness. In Switzerland, up until the modern age, people smudged schoolrooms and hospitals with juniper to disinfect rooms if it was too cold outside to open the windows. Juniper was considered a symbol of the life force of Christ and his ability to overcome death in the Late Medieval period.

Juniper resin has been called "German sandaraca" and used as a substitute for frankincense. The blossom pollen of juniper was called "blossom smoke." Juniper berries were sometimes called *weiheicheln* (holy berries) in the German vernacular. Juniper berries were used in poor churches of the Slavic East as a substitute for incense.

In German-speaking countries, juniper was used as a smudge to treat a wide range of different ailments, including rheumatism, asthma, pain in the chest or side, sleepiness, depression, and lunacy. Juniper smoke was believed to protect people from evil spirits, witches, goblins, demons—even the devil himself! The plant was used in a similar way in England:

> In medieval times, the berries were used during burials in order to keep away the more intangible enemies—spirits and devils—that could be wait-

The Aromas of Christmas

ing. Green branches were burnt to smoke out the witches and drive out the dark powers; in Wales the juniper tree was considered holy, and hurting it or a dying tree was supposed to bring illness and death to the family (Drury 1989, 90).*

"Nine Herbs" Christmas Incense

The roots of the consecration of herbs reach back to the oldest mysteries of mankind. As pre-Christian thanksgiving and nature feast, the custom found a place in the Church's cult of Mary.

ABRAHAM AND THINNES 1995, 146

During holy times in old Germany—Christmas, smudging nights, New Year's Eve, and epiphany—nine consecrated herbs were burned for incense or smuding. While the combination of herbs varies, the concept behind the consecration was the same. Each herb represented one of nine mythological worlds: three worlds above, three worlds in the middle, and three underworlds. Three times three worlds, all of which are united through the world tree, is the basic shamanic cosmology.

Thus the nine herbs were dedicated to the nine worlds and their nine inhabitants. The Anglo-Saxon nine herb charm written down in the eleventh century describes nine herbs that Wotan used as medicinal magic: mugwort, "oldest of the herbs;" plantain, "mother of all herbs;" stone root, which "drives away evil" (presumably stinkweed or pennycress, *Thlaspi arvense*); wormwood (venom-loather); chamomile; *wergulu* (maybe chicory); apple; chervil; and fennel. (There is some scholarly disagreement as to exactly which herbs should be included in this verse.)

These nine might go against nine venoms.
A snake came crawling and it tore apart the human being:
So Wotan[†] took nine wonder branches
And killed the snake, so that it tore apart in nine pieces.
Thus the apple and its poison was made,
So that it would never want to come to a house again. . . .
Now the nine herbs have power against nine evil spirits
Against nine venoms and nine contagious illnesses.[‡]

In folklore, the nine herb blessing has lived on in some remote areas in the "nine herb bushes" incense mixture that is still used in certain blessings performed by the Catholic church.

Mullein *(Verbascum thapsus)*
St. John's wort *(Hypericum perforatum)*
Yarrow *(Achillea* spp.)
Valerian root *(Valeriana officinalis)*

Juniper tree *(wecholderbaum).* (Woodcut from Lonicerus 1679)

---

*"Coals of juniper wood were often found in the burial sites of ancient Germans, because it was part of the sacred wood with which the dead were burnt" (von Perger 1864, 350).

[†]"W.[otan] appears in the Old English nine herb blessing as a healing sorcerer" (Simek 1984, 466).

[‡]Taken from the Anglo-Saxon nine herb blessing as quoted in Seligmann 1996, 28f.

Nine-Herb Incense for the Smudging Nights

The old Germanic plant magic consists of the following herbs:

Elecampane *(Inula helenium)*

Hemp agrimony *(Eupatorium cannabinum)*

Mugwort *(Artemisia vulgaris)*

Southernwood *(Artemisia abrotanum)*

Wormwood *(Artemisia absinthium)*

Lady's bedstraw *(Galium verum)*

Bittersweet *(Solanum dulcamara)*

Tansy *(Tanacetum vulgare)*

Collect blossoms from these nine herbs and mix them together in equal parts. You may also add juniper berries and frankincense (von Perger 1864, 45, 347).

European centaury *(Centaurea erythraea)*

Arnica *(Arnica montana)*

Chamomile *(Chamaemelum nobile)*, thyme *(Thymus* spp.), or lady's mantle *(Alchemilla mollis)*

Wormwood *(Artemisia absinthium)*, hog's fennel *(Peucadanum palustre)*, or eyebright *(Euphrasia officinalis)*

Mint *(Mentha* spp.), basil *(Ocimum basilicum)*, or sage *(Salvia officinalis)*

The first six herbs are a vital part of the nine herb bushes mixture. The last three may vary. Some of the herbs that might be used instead include elder, wheat, hazelnut, bird berry, flax, and rosemary. The incense mixture served as a blessing and a protection charm.

The smoke of incense goes up to the sky, connecting heaven and Earth. Beyond that, incense connects the nine worlds of the world tree with the person performing the ritual.

The smudging nights of the Christmas season got their name because, when they started, the priest would go around after evening bells with a red-hot pan held in his left hand. With it, he smudged the whole house to ward off demonic influences. . . . This kept witches and devils away and protected the livestock and produce. As the custom developed, the nine herbs were used during smoke-nights; put in the troughs and wells where the horses and cows were fed, or mixed with juniper berries and incense and put on the red-hot pans—and the whole house was smudged. But this could only happen when the cows were milked and the horses fed, because after cleansing with the smoke, no one was allowed to go back into the stables. (von Perger 1864, 54).

Incense was burned to protect against evil in the German and Swiss folk custom: "The four smudging nights (consisting of the night before St. Thomas' Day and the three nights before Christmas), New Year's Eve, and epiphany are all full of terror and secrets. Ghosts are powerful and every evil has a free ride."

The witches also need nine different herbs for the making of thunderstorms: Alantroot [elecampane], lady's bedstraw, southernwood, mugwort, wormwood, valerian root, black nightshade, bittersweet (or climbing nightshade), and common tansy (von Perger 1864, 71).

The nine herbs have a very close association with old Germanic myth and ritual. Elecampane *(Inula helenium)* represented Odin's head or the head of Wotan. Lady's bedstraw *(Galium verum)* was originally the straw for Freia's bed. Southernwood was dedicated to the god Fro. Mugwort was used as a solstice girdle or belt. Like tansy, wormwood was an herb of the witch goddess.

Nine Herbs for Weather Magic Incense

Equal parts of:

Elecampane *(Inula helenium)*

Marienbettstroh, several herbs share this common name, most commonly it refers to lady's bedstraw *(Galium verum)* or wild thyme *(Thymus serpyllum)*

Southernwood *(Artemisia abrotanum)*

Mugwort *(Artemisia vulgaris)*

Wormwood *(Artemisia absinthium)*

Valerian root *(Valeriana officinalis)*

Black nightshade *(Solanum nigrum)*

Bittersweet or climbing nightshade *(Solanum dulcamara)*

Tansy *(Tanacetum vulgare)*

All of these herbs were used not only by witches, but also by farmers as Christian blessing plants—as protection, in fact, against witches, magic, sorcery, hauntings, nightmares, and thunderstorms.

Valerian root was the holy plant of Wieland, the smith, and was also called "Balder's eyebrow." "Hertha used it as a riding crop when she was riding on her noble deer (who was crowned with hops)" (Zimmerer 1896, 278). Both of the solanums (*Solanum* spp.) contain Nachtsachen, a malefic demon that brings on illnesses—but also fights them.

The following nine herbs represent a sort of "nine woods." They all come from sacred trees that are used today as Christmas trees or greens:

The carline thistle (*Carlina acaulis* L., Asteraceae), also known as "silver sun," shines like a Christmas star. The plant not only protects against lightning, but also acts as an aphrodisiac and love magic: "Nine leaves of carline thistle are supposed to give the power of nine young men" (Hiller 1989, 208). "A guy would hope for the fulfillment of all his wishes from a girl when he carried carline thistle and valerian root in red wax with him" (Hiller 1989, 24).

The Aromas of Christmas

Common juniper *(Juniperus communis)*
Larch *(Larix decidua)*
Mountain pine *(Pinus mugo)*
Scots pine *(Pinus sylvestris)*
Spruce *(Picea* spp.)
Stinking juniper *(Juniperus sabina)*
Swiss stone pine *(Pinus cembra)*
White fir *(Abies alba)*
Yew *(Taxus baccata)*

On one hand, the nine woods were believed helpful for making "magic and discovering special places to sit" (Abraham and Thinnes 1995, 212f) as well as for warding off witches and devils. On the other, they belonged to the botanical repertoire of the same witches and demonic beings that they were supposed to defend against or unmask. The wood was gathered by witches and burned as incense at Christmastime:

> In order to lure a lover, they light the wood around midnight on the winter solstice, and then they throw their dresses down in front of the door. They said: "I sit here all naked and bare. If only my beloved would come and throw my shirt back in my lap!" (Müller-Ebeling et al. 1998, 19).

In Mecklenburg, some purported witches testified that they used the nine woods for purposes of love magic: "Oak, birch, alder, hawthorn, rowan, elder, pine, whitethorn and blackthorn" (Müller-Ebeling et al. 1998, 19). The nine woods are all among the ritual plants and holy trees that were revered by pagans. With the advent of Christianity, the trees of the old pagan gods received new names that associated them either with Christ or the devil. For example, hawthorn *(Crataegus laevigata, C. monogyna)* was called Christ's thorn, just as sloe or blackthorn *(Prunus spinosa)* was called devil's thorn! "On witches' night (St. Ottilie, December 13) you put blackthorn twigs into a red-hot pan in Bavaria to smoke out witches and demons" (Weustenfeld 1996, 107).

Incense Recipes from Hildegard von Bingen

The devil flees from everything that has the power of healing,
because he himself has no such power.

HILDEGARD VON BINGEN, *PHYSICA*, III, 20

With what kind of incense was the famous herbalist Hildegard von Bingen (1098–1179) acquainted? Which of the exotic spices and resins that we count as characteristic Christmas scents did she use? A glance into her book *Physica* (which translates as "science") reveals that she was familiar with frankincense and myrrh as well as various spices, including cinnamon, nutmeg, mace, and cloves. From these substances, one can concoct a highly aromatic, seriously Christmas-scented incense. Her incense calls for a good portion of frankincense (olibanum) and the finest myrrh. Instead of the usual cinnamon sticks, use a small amount of bark from the related plant cassia *(Cinnamomum cassia)*. Mace (the seed coat of the nutmeg) and cloves round out the Christmas blend. Spoon it onto the coals and enjoy the fragrance.

From Incense to Ashes

The Yule buck and Yule log that are burned in the fireplace during the winter season are essential elements in the Nordic Yule feast. The Yule buck is braided from straw and made to resemble the mountain goat (ibex), most likely to symbolize the goats that pulled Thor's cart. The Yule log is a piece of wood—

Christmas Incense*

3 parts frankincense *(Boswellia carteri)*
2 parts myrrh *(Commiphora* spp.)
1 part cassia *(Cinnamomum cassia)*
1 part mace *(Myristica fragans)*
$1/2$ part clove buds *(Syzygium aromaticum)*

Thoroughly grind all the ingredients together in a mortar into very small parts. Place by teaspoonfuls on the smoking coals. A Christmas scent will follow very quickly!

*Adapted freely from a recipe by Hildegard von Bingen.

The *Jul* buck is braided from straw. It is burned as a sacrifice as part of the *Julfest* in Scandinavia.

often ash—burned to honor the world tree, Yggdrasil. Yule bucks and Yule logs are very often burned in combination with herbs and resins. The holy, healing ash is retained:

Especially at Christmastime, ash expresses a mystery. The phoenix, the Egyptian bird of fable, burns itself up and is resurrected to new life from its own ashes, like the infant Christ, who in the coldest dark of the snow nights (=ash) is born again every year. And, dressed in red like an Indian Sannyasin [a Brahman who dedicates his life to meditation and spiritual searching], Father Christmas emerges from the snowed-in woods with nuts and apples, like a seed of renewal. In the Lausitz, as "Klas," he comes as the rider of the white horse [=Wotan] with his sack of ashes. In the high north, the Yule log was burned on winter solstice, and its ashes were considered healing (Storl 2002, 218).

Burning the Yule buck and Yule log not only provides healing ashes, but also brings outward and inward wealth. If you make a smoking fire with ash wood at the time of the Yule feast, wealth and luck will be yours! These old Scandinavian traditions can be found in rudimentary forms in regions far from their origins. For example, in areas of the former Yugoslavia, incense and barley are burned on a log (Vossen 1985, 86).

CHRISTMAS INTOXICATIONS AND OTHER DELIGHTS

Everything that makes life worth living goes beyond boundaries,
and this is why it can be described as an intoxication.

PAPAJORGIS 1993, 12

Christmas is the time of intoxication! Moreover, these days, despite all the warnings against overconsumption, calorie counting, and dieting, we still feast and indulge in the sin of gluttony during the Christmas season. We eat and eat, filling our stomachs with goose roast, Christmas cookies, marzipan, and other high-calorie foods. We drink the tastiest beverages and consume all manner of dietary evils. We live as if still taking part in the old rites of the past. The smudging nights were celebrated with libation offerings, smoking ecstasies, orgies of smell, feast meals and baccy pipes: Smudging nights are nights of intoxication. Among the customs that have passed into our modern Christmas rituals, we still have a tradition of holy intoxication at feast time.

Yule Drinking

When the gods left the earth, beer became alcohol and the divine
intoxication became a purely mean drunkenness . . .

GRÖNBECH 1997, 180

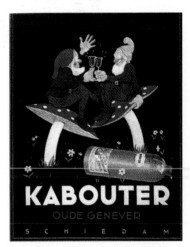

Two Christmas goblins atop fly agaric mushrooms toast each other with gin. (Poster by Jan Lavies, Amsterdam, 1960, from Lemaire 1995, xxv)

In the north, Christmas is called *Jul* or *Jule* (from the Old Nordic *jól, jol,* or Anglo-Saxon *geol*). This is the time for *Juldrinking* and *Julfeast (Joelfeast)*. In this season, one can choose among specially brewed Christmas beers, *Wodelbeers* (*Wodel*=Wotan) made from rye, and traditional Yule beers *(Julbeer)*. Old Nordic *Julbeers* were not brewed in keeping with Bavarian pureness laws, but instead included intoxicating herbs like hemp, wormwood, black henbane, fir greens, and wild rosemary.

The festive time was sometimes called "beer days" in Germany, and the tranquil atmosphere of domestic family togetherness was described by the name "beer peace."

Beer brings a festive shine with it. It does not belong to the mundane nourishment and thirst-quenching quality of everyday food, but offers a

Father Christmas loves Yule drinking. (Cartoon by Peter Gamynn, © 2001, Cartoon Concept, Hannover)

Silenus, the wild man with hair covering his whole body, was one of the followers of Dionysus. Like Father Christmas, he carries a bag of wonderful gifts over his shoulder: a wineskin. (Antique statue from Delos, Greece)

Christmas Intoxications and Other Delights

spiritual enjoyment of a higher level than milk and whey, a holy nourishment. And it is the drink that honors the high feast with its blessing, of a special power to unite gods and human beings (Grönbech 1997, 164).

The magical power of old Germanic brewing methods has been replaced largely by technology by now. Instead of intoxicating ingredients, manufacturers add the sedative plant hops to create a beer without holiness, a festive beverage made profane. However, the magic of the past still shines on modern labels, and the consciousness that accompanies the drinking can be a catalyst for a sense of Christmas holiness.

Germanic mythology, especially from the north, is full of drinking stories. According to one myth, Odin (Wotan) robbed Odhrärir of the "ecstasy drink" or the "mead of inspiration." Whoever drank this beverage would be filled with wisdom and knowledge, become inspired artistically and gifted in the art of poetry, and develop the ability to lure and seduce with words.

Thor, the thunder god, was the heaviest drinker of the gods. His thirst was unquenchable, his drinking feats legendary. One myth recounts that during a drinking competition he drank from the sea god's drinking horn, which was connected with the world sea. He gulped three times and caused high and low tides. These were some truly divine gulps! Many humans seem to want to emulate Thor, especially during Yule drinking; thus the Yule feast always ended when the people were drunk.

Love on Christmas Eve?

My head is going to find its love in intoxication . . .
BAUDELAIRE 1857, XXIII

An intoxicant may be an aphrodisiac or just the opposite, depending on the dosage. The intoxication caused by plant preparations is one of the most valuable Christmas experiences, a "border crossing" between worlds that can help celebrants understand their own position in the universe. Christmas intoxicants include special meals and drinks to put one in the right frame of mind for the feast of love and transform Christmas magic into fertility rite. There is love in the holy nights!

Plant ingredients closely associated with the aphrodisiac aspects of the Christmas feast include grain and poppy (the holy plants of the Greek mystery goddess, Demeter), flax, and hemp (the holy plants of the Germanic Freia). Such plants were essential to rites involving the Christmas love oracle and fertility magic. They were also supposed to ward off witches and sorcerers.

Poppy
Papaver somniferum L., Papaveraceae (poppy)

OTHER NAMES
Garden poppy, *magan* (Old German), opium poppy, sleep poppy

Poppy juice was the all-in-one aspirin and medicinal spirit for those times.
PIEPER 1998, 11

Why are dried poppy seedpods such a popular decoration for Christmas trees and advent wreaths? Contrary to popular belief, the opium poppy is not native

Days of Love Magic

"On some of those holy days—from times when demons were, in a sense, freer, unleashed, and had power over human beings—aphrodisiac plants became very potent. St. John's Day was the strongest of the love magic days, and Wodan, Donar, Fro, and Frigga were closer at this time to nature and to human beings. . . . After St. John's Day, the time just before and after winter solstice (December 24) is also very good for love magic. . . . It is seed time, the time when the trees inseminate one another; it is the moment of the solstice (Christ night) that is so important for the love power of the plants—when the rod of life gives health and fertility" (Aigremont 1987 II, 75f).

Left: Poppy seedpods scratched for the production of opium. (Northern Thailand, 2002)

Right: Poppy *(Papaver somniferum)* showing the Christmas colors, red and green.

to Asia, but to middle or southern Europe. This well-known cultivated plant was grown during the Neolithic period (the new Stone Age) in Northern Italy, Switzerland, and southern Germany. It has long been prized for food, but also for its intoxicating effects:

> The intoxicating and sedative attributes of the seed and the oil that can be produced from it did not escape the mound builders [of old Europe]. The frequency and quantity of poppy seeds found there and evidence of how it was used shows that it was an important cultivated plant of the mound builder (Hoops 1973, 233–234).

The cultivation of poppy in southern and northern Germanic regions must be very old. It cannot be dated accurately. The ancient Germans planted uniform fields of poppy. These fields were called "Odin's ground" *(Odainsackr)* and were seen as sacred healing sites where Odin (Wotan) manifested healing wonders (Höfler 1990, 92ff). According to folk medicine, the ingestion of poppy juice (opium) is believed to ward off demons of the night, blood-sucking vampires, nightmares, and goblins, for poppies are the servants of St. Nicholas. However, "In some valleys the belief exists that poppy seeds may be a food of witches and of the dead" (Fink 1983, 66).

Baked goods containing poppy seeds played an important and colorful role in the Christmas folk traditions of old Germany:

> At Christmastime, especially in eastern Germany, people eat baked poppy goods and cake. Even the dog gets three poppy muffins on Christmas Eve, to grow strong. The chickens get poppy seed; depending on however many they eat, they will produce that many eggs. To eat poppy on Christmas Eve brings lots of money. . . . On Christmas Eve, a girl who yearns to know where her future bridegroom will come from breaks open a poppy biscuit,

Christmas Intoxications and Other Delights

120

gives it to the dog, and drives him out of the yard. Her bridegroom will come from whichever direction the dog jumps first. Or the girl can throw poppy seeds over her head before going to bed, so that she can see her beloved in her dream. . . . Poppy seeds placed in front of the door keeps the witch from the entry because she must count them all. . . . Poppy seeds must be sown on Christmas Eve, three days before, or on a Wednesday [Day of Wotan]! And you must keep silent, or birds will eat the poppy seeds (Pieper 1998, 20).

One word of caution: "To eat poppy on Christmas Eve is supposed to bring a lot of money, but to eat too much poppy is supposed to make you stupid!" (Hiller 1989, 191).

Flax and Hemp
Linum usitatissimum L., Linaceae (flax, flaxseed)
Cannabis sativa L., Cannabaceae (hemp, marijuana)

> *The gods gave humans hemp in an act of charity, so that they could have illumination, lose fear, and maintain their sexual desire.*
> RAJA VALABHA, SANSKRIT TEXTS, SEVENTEENTH CENTURY

Flax and hemp both have a long history of association with Christmas, particularly because of their magical uses in fertility rituals and love magic. Both plants are valued as food and have also been used by farmers to ensure the fertility of the fields in the coming year. In the case of flaxseed, careful observation of nature, a lot of experience, and a little bit of mythology helped farmers with a steady hand earn a living:

Icicles tell the farmer the best time to sow flax.

In the pine tree mountains *(fichtelgebirge)*, icicles on house roofs were considered an omen that the flax would prosper. If the icicles were long and unsegmented in December, you were supposed to sow the flax in early spring. If they were at their most beautiful in January, you should sow in mid-spring; if they were longest in February, one should choose a late sowing time. If the icicles were segmented, the flax would grow the same way. Flowering flax wards off sorcery, and the flowers can enchant a whole field in such a way that, even during peaceful weather, it can seem like streaming water (von Perger 1864, 193).

Flax is the oldest cultivated plant in Europe and one of the most important sources of fabric, oil, and other products. For ages, flax has been known as a love potion. Sometimes flax played a role in love magic spells. For example, nine flax flowers woven with nine flax threads was supposed to create a binding spell of compulsive love that men could not resist. Flax has long been valued as a food, but perhaps more important, it has always carried a touch of magic, even of wonder: "On Christmas Eve, a driver saw the Holy Virgin putting flax out on the snow. He kept a handful of flax for himself, and the next morning it was changed into gold" (von Perger 1864, 177).

In old Greece, flaxseed was called *osyris* (similar to the name of the Egyptian god of vegetation, Osiris!) and used as an ingredient in aphrodisiac meals. When "mixed with honey and pepper, the cake—eaten in large portions—makes you want to make love" (Dioscorides 1610, 125). This peppered honey cake was reputed to "help the old man get back up on his horse" (Matthiolus 1626, 116b).

Hemp also has a long history of use as food, medicine, and magical plant. During the time of the old Tsarist empire in Russia, hemp mixtures were used both medicinally and ritually. Hemp seeds, called *semieniatka*, were cooked in soup and offered on Christmas night to the souls of the dead ancestors (Benet 1975, 43). The cult of the dead and the ancestors is clearly connected with hemp, especially in eastern Europe: "Even today, in Poland and Lithuania, when the dead visit their families for an hour on Christmas Eve, the people eat *semieniatka* —a soup made of hemp seed—in their honor. In the Ukraine, it is cooked for the same reason on epiphany" (Behr 1995, 42).

In numerous cultures, hemp was the sacred plant of the love goddess. The Romans called her Venus; in other regions of Europe, she was known by Freia, Freya, Frija, Holda, Frau Holle, or Frau Venus. She is the goddess of fertility, spring, and the erotic and the guardian of long life and marriage. Her sacred hemp was supposed to inspire lust, health, and fertility in human beings. In cultures that held lust and the erotic sacred, hemp was "a plant of the gods" because of this long connection with the love goddess.

The Germanic goddess of love, Freia or Freya, flew through the world in a cart pulled by two black cats. Her sacred animals were the cat and the rabbit (think of the Easter rabbit); her sacred plants were hemp and flax. Just as this

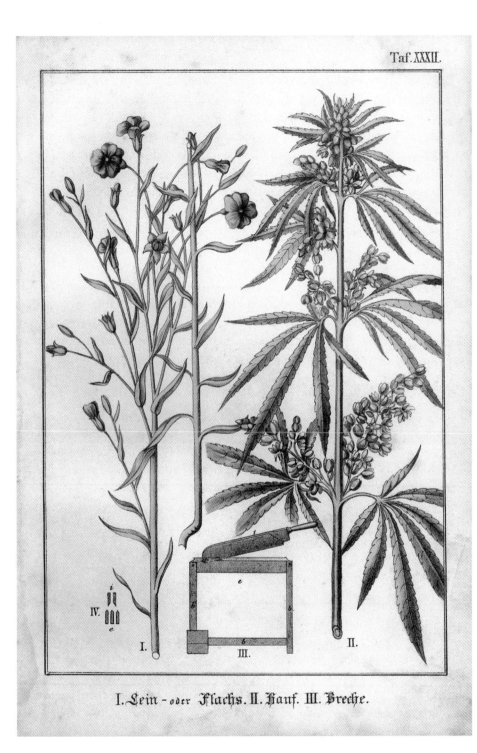

Taf. XXXII.

I. Lein - oder Flachs. II. Hanf. III. Breche.

Flax *(Linum usitatissimum)* and hemp *(Cannabis sativa)*, both sacred plants of the love goddess. Both are cultivated and used in many cultures as aphrodisiacs, love magic, oracular charms, magical protection, medicine, and food. In former times, people drove away winter with hemp stems at Christmastime. (Colored steel etching, nineteenth century Germany)

goddess was reclassified later as a witch, her holy plant hemp has become a devil's herb.*

For Germanic and Slavic peoples, hemp symbolizes human and animal fertility. It has a close association with the smudging nights and Christmas festivities:

*In the southern Tirol, hemp is called "witches' herb": "When you hang some hemp herb underneath the roof, no witch can do anything. This is a very good herb" (Behr 1995, 43).

Christmas Intoxications and Other Delights

The hemp seed seems to be a fertility symbol as well. Hemp seeds are fed to chickens so that they will lay eggs all winter long. On Christmas Eve, you eat hemp soup, poppy muffins, fish, and baked fruits (in Beuthen, Upper Silesia). The sowing of hemp is a love charm. But in Germany, it is not described as being performed by girls, as it is in England. Instead, the husband sows the hemp, and the wife brings him a meal of eggs (hemp eggs) out in the field so that the hemp will grow well. (The Slavic people also use hemp in a love charm.) For similar reasons, hemp pancakes are baked on epiphany in Transylvania. . . . The childless Hungarian woman eats Spanish flies* cooked in donkey milk and hemp blossoms every Friday [the day of the love goddess, Freia or Venus] before the sun goes down" (Lussi 1996, 133).

In old Germany, a girl who wanted to know whom she would marry was supposed to put a hemp plant on the floor while uttering certain magic words. She also had to place hemp seed in her belt. Then she was supposed to leap on the hemp plant and sing: "Andrej, Andrej, I put hemp seed on you. Will God show me with whom I am going to sleep?" (Benet, in Behr 1995, 43).

Chocolate Father Christmas: Ritual Christmas Cannibalism

With the massive enjoyment of food and drinks, massive sexual enjoyments follow at the same pace . . .

MOST 1843, 448

Theobroma cacao L., Sterculiaceae (cocoa)

OTHER NAMES

Ca-ca-huatl (Aztec, "black nut"), *cacao*, chocolate

In 1639, a book published in Europe said that the sea god Neptune had brought chocolate from the New World to Europe. Today, cocoa and the many forms of chocolate made from cocoa rank among the most popular treats enjoyed by humankind. What would Christmas be without chocolate? Are there particular reasons why we are especially keen on chocolate at Christmastime? These are questions with astonishing answers. "Chocolate is divine, a heavenly drink, sweat of the stars, seed of life, divine nectar, drink of the gods, wonderful and all-healing substance" (Geronimo Piperni, eighteenth century).

The German word for enjoyment *(genuss)* comes from *geniess*, which in turn is derived from the Middle High German *niez*, meaning "use." Thus, *genuss* indicates "communal use of something, the use of something together" (Hartwich 1911, 14). Thus, in this word for enjoyment, we find a hint about

*Spanish fly *(Lytta vesicatoria)* is not really a fly, but a beetle that contains a dangerous substance, cantharidin. It causes a strong reaction in the urinary tract and because of that is used as an aphrodisiac. However, the effective dosage is near lethal, so one should not experiment with it.

Christmas Intoxications and Other Delights

social ritual, a sense that while enjoying something in the company of others, a collective change of mood can happen.

Chocolate comes from the cocoa tree *(Theobroma cacao)*, which has long been an object of veneration in its home country, Mexico. In its native land, cocoa is considered a sacred tree and a food of the gods.* The name *chocolate* comes from the Aztec *ca-ca-huatl*, meaning "black nut." According to the report made by the Franciscan Jiménez, who was a member of the party that accompanied Conquistador Hernán Cortez to Mexico around 1520 CE, *chocolatl* means something like "foaming water." *Cacao*, the plant's species name, is a word from the Mayan language and refers to the tree, the fruit, and the drink that is made from it. The Indians made *cacao* or *chocolatl* from ground cocoa beans, corn flour, honey, vanilla, allspice, chili, cinnamon, balsam Peru, and various flowers.

The cocoa tree is one of the shamanic world trees of the Maya. The holy cocoa tree was both a wellspring of life and a portal to death. It unifies the inseparable aspects of the two poles of life and death. It is a tree of the south, the direction in which the land of the dead is located. Because of the red color of the berries, the tree is symbolically connected with blood. In the cocoa treetops sit shining red parrots, symbols of the hot tropical forests from which the cocoa comes. In their branches climb wild spider monkeys, which have a "twenty-first finger" on the end of their long tails. The Mayan hieroglyph for cocoa is a stylized monkey's head. The spider monkey is often pictured in Mayan art with a cocoa fruit in its hands and an erection, smoking a cigarette. The sexual connotation cannot be denied.

The cocoa fruit hangs from its stem like a red Christmas ball on the Christmas tree.

*Even Carl Linnaeus, the great Swedish scientist and father of modern taxonomy, seems to have taken this into consideration when he named this tropical plant *Theobroma cacao*. *Theobroma* means "divine food."

Christmas Intoxications
and Other Delights

Cocoa Recipe Anno 1528

The Spanish Conquistador Hernán Cortez is supposed to have brought the following cocoa recipe back to Spain in 1528 (Montignac 1996, 27).

    700 grams of cocoa
    750 grams of white sugar
    56 grams of cinnamon *(Cinnamomum verum)*
    14 corns of chili pepper *(Capiscum* spp.)
    14 grams of cloves or allspice *(Syzygium aromaticum* or *Pimenta dioica)*
    4 vanilla beans *(Vanilla planifolia)*
    1 handful of anise *(Pimpinella anisum)*
    1 ground hazelnut
    Musk, ambergris, and orange-flower water

Left: The holy three kings bring their true present: real Swiss chocolate! (Advertising poster for Tobler Chocolate from 1926, Kraft Foods archive postcard, © Übersee-Museum, Bremen)

Right: Here, the parrot sits on a perch, not in the world tree of the Maya, but still tells the astonished boy about the secrets of chocolate. (Old advertisement for Suchard chocolate, early twentieth century)

The evergreen cocoa tree grows up to 15 meters (about 50 feet) high and can live for 60 years. The tiny white, pink, and purple flowers, which look something like orchid blossoms, grow directly from the stem or thicker main branches. They are often present at the same time as the fruits, which also hang down the stem. A single tree produces around one hundred thousand flowers per year. The fruits are green at first, and turn yellow, red, or purple as they ripen. Cocoa beans are the seed of the delicious fruit of the cocoa tree. In old Mexico, cocoa beans were used as currency. City prostitutes were paid for their services with this aphrodisiac food of the gods.

The Ecstasy of Biedermeier

"Is the children's drink an intoxicating substance? This is not so far-fetched. On the one hand, the enjoyment of chocolate causes a release of endorphins that evoke euphoric and happy feelings, just like opium or morphine. On the other hand, the fruit of the cocoa tree itself contains stimulating substances, such as theobromine and caffeine, that raise blood pressure (a well-known effect of coffee). Recently, scientists discovered a substance called anandamide that is supposed to have the same effect as hashish. But these substances are not really present in high concentrations in chocolate. To get as 'high' as you would from smoking a joint, you would have to eat as much as 20 kg of chocolate. No reason, then, to forbid dear children their enjoyment of chocolate and all of the sweet chocolate delicacies that are everywhere plentiful in these weeks" (Feuersee 2001, 49).

Chocolate has rightfully been called "brain food" or "nerve food." Eaten regularly, it has an uplifting and comforting effect. This can be traced to the chemical compounds chocolate contains. These include the alkaloids theobromine and caffeine as well as phenylethylamine—a neurotransmitter (messenger chemical) also found in the human brain, which is believed to evoke feelings akin to those associated with falling in love. Theobromine can lead to a kind of dependency, the so-called "chocoholism"! Not long ago, researchers discovered an additional important chemical compound in cocoa, called anandamide. This is another naturally occurring neurotransmitter, that, like THC (delta-9 tetrahydrocannabinol) in *Cannabis*, produces feelings of well being.

In pre-Columbian America, cocoa was treasured as a tonic and aphrodisiac. In Europe, cocoa and chocolate were accorded the same value. In Germany, in the seventeenth and eighteenth centuries, *succolade* was made from pulverized cocoa beans, sugar, and wine and was sometimes spiced with a lot of cardamom *(Elettaria cardamomom)* and saffron *(Crocus sativus)* (Root 1996, 364). In the nineteenth century, a "spicy chocolate" was in vogue as an aphrodisiac: "It was made, like all chocolate, from roasted cocoa beans and sugar mixed with vanilla, cinnamon, and cardamom.* It is good for the weak, the emaciated, and people with cramps, but not good for anyone sick with high fever and inflammation. It is also a stimulant for men" (Most 1843, 118).

In his eighteenth-century treatise, *Diputatio Medico Diaetetica*, the Viennese doctor Johann Michael Haider reported that chocolate is an aphrodisiac, calling it *Veneris pabulum* (Venus food). It "makes the body randy" wrote Anselm von Ziegler Kliphause in a pamphlet from 1703. This is why the Catholic Church feared "excesses" due to chocolate and thought it necessary to ban cocoa and chocolate, because the last thing a celibate person needed was an aphrodisiac! Still, cocoa was permissible as a clerical fasting beverage: *Liquidum non fagit jejunum* (fluids do not break the fast) (Schwarz and Schweppe 1997, 91).

In 1655 in Rome, the Catholic cardinal Brancatio wrote an ode that sounds very pagan:

> *As long as the great heavenly light shines for me,*
> *You, tree of trees,*
> *Will be a life giver to me*
> *And a creator of my purest feelings.*
> *From you alone my spirit's power is welling*
> *O sweet gift of heaven*
> *O much praised drink of gods!*
> *Farewell to thee,*
> *You beautiful dew of the kingdom of Bacchus!*
> *In your place I honor a new well, which a god showed me.*
> *Stream on and give your relief*
> *In overabundance to the human beings!*

Sexy chocolate. Advertising and packaging for some chocolate products openly illustrates the aphrodisiac character of the food of the gods, *Theobroma*. Here, a package of prophylactics is glued to a bar of *Billy-Boy* chocolate. (2002)

*Cocoa spices in old Europe included allspice, ambergris, anise, cardamom, chili, cinnamon, cloves, ginger, jasmine blossoms, poppy seeds, musk, mace, nutmeg, orange blossoms, pepper, Peru balsam, pineapple, saffron, and vanilla. All of these typical Christmas spices are also considered aphrodisiacs or love substances (Rätsch and Müller-Ebeling, 2003). Even Spanish fly *(Lytta vesicatoria)* has been mixed into cocoa!

**Christmas Intoxications
and Other Delights**

Left: Ladybugs were sacred in pagan times and were dedicated to Freia, the love goddess. Why does this chocolate ladybug have—like the fly agaric mushroom—white instead of black dots?

Right: A tasty chocolate Father Christmas—and an invitation to a modern ritual "Christmas cannibalism." (Photo by Claudia Müller-Ebeling)

*In the Aztec "flower language," the word *xochicacahuatl* (flower chocolate) was a metaphor for good life and sensual pleasures (Coe and Coe 1997, 125).

Christmas Intoxications and Other Delights

128

Macabre Gods' Food

The Aztecs referred to chocolate or cocoa metaphorically as *yollotl, eztli*—"heart, blood."

> This is why it was said: "The heart, the blood are to be feared." It was also said that it is like jimsonweed or thorn apple (*Datura stramonium* a toxic hallucinogen); and it was said that it is like the mushroom (*Psilocybe* spp.), because it makes you drunk, it intoxicates you (Sahagun-Seler 1927).

The Aztec cocoa beverage was a vehicle for ingestion of entheogenic mushrooms, the "flowers of the earth." Even today, Mexican shamans take sacred mushrooms (*Psilocybe* spp.) along with cocoa or chocolate. In their ritual "flower language,"* the Aztec called the still-pulsating hearts taken from live human sacrifices *cacahuatl*, meaning "cocoa fruit" or "gods' food." With the bloody hearts, the priests symbolically quenched the gods' desire for chocolate. The human beings that were sacrificed were taken to the butcher. First their heads were cut off and put on a pile in the *tzompantli* (wood shelves next to the temple pyramid). Then they were butchered like animals and sold at the market. Sacrificial meat was sacred. Thus, the Aztec *xocolatl*-drinkers and *cacahuatl*-eaters were cannibals who treasured the cocoa-fruit and the living heart in equal measure as foods of the gods.

During the sacrificial rites, chocolate served as a sort of macabre healing substance that prevented the chosen human sacrificial victims from falling into depression. Instead, the beverage was used to put the victim into an ecstatic condition of intoxication.

> [The sacrificial priests] hurried to get the sacrificial knives, and washed off the blood, and made, with the dirty water, a pumpkin cup of chocolate that they gave the victim to drink. It is said that this drink had the following effect on him: he became nearly unconscious and forgot what was said to him. Then his good mood came back and he started to dance again. It is believed that, bewitched by the drink, he gave himself, full of joy and happiness before death. This drink was called *itzpacalatl,* which translates to the equivalent of "water with which obsidian blades are washed" (Diego de Durán, *Crónica, X,* as quoted in Coe and Coe, 1997, 124).*

But what does this gruesome story have to do with our tasty and beautiful Christmas chocolates? In the end we also "butcher" our Father Christmas. After we tear the wrapping paper off our chocolate Santa, we devour the *Theobroma*—the food of the gods—with pleasure. Many of us tend to first bite off the head. Even if it is only symbolic, it amounts to a sort of ritualistic cannibalism. "*Oh, divino chocolate!*" Even the Catholic Church has a symbolic connection with the Aztec sacrifice ritual. During Holy Communion, believers drink the blood of Christ in the form of red wine and eat his body as a host.

Mugwort, the Sacrificial Goose, and the Christmas Roast

The shamanic flight is not an easy enterprise. Demons and dragonlike fiends are the keepers of the entry to the otherworld. The shaman must be pure in body and soul so that he does not fall down or surrender to the demons of frenzy. One of the measures he can take is to rub on or smoke the holy herb mugwort.

STORL 1996A, 139

Artemisia vulgaris L., Asteraceae (mugwort)

OTHER NAMES
Armoise, beifuss, felon herb, *sonnwendgürtle* (Old German, "solstice girdle"), naughty man, old man, old Uncle Harry, St. John's plant, wild wormwood

In mugwort we have one of the oldest relics of the ritual life of humanity. The herb is an important incense and smudge substance for the smudging nights. It is bound up with the life rod. Mugwort was also used to spice roasts on the festive first day of Christmas and thus, in the end, is related to animal sacrifice.

Mugwort was found in huge amounts in the caves of Lascaux, France.

*The Dominican Diego de Durán (1537–1588) was born in Spain and grew up in Mexico. He wrote an extensive chronicle of ancient Mexico, especially on the Aztec culture (Coe and Coe 1997, 124).

Christmas Intoxications and Other Delights

Left: Mugwort *(Artemisia vulgaris)* in flower in Wallis, Switzerland. This wild herb is among the oldest of European ritual, magic, and healing plants. Mugwort is also one of the most important smudging substances for the smudging nights, a typical Christmas spice for sacrificial roasts, and an ingredient for beer, absinthe, and baccy.

Right: Mugwort, one of humanity's oldest shamanic plants. Mugwort is an age-old smoking substance of the shamans of old Europe, the Himalayas, modern Korea, and other parts of the world. Because of its three-toothed leaves, in Nepal it is called the trident of the old shaman Shiva. (Kalinchok, Nepal, August 1998)

---

*According to the oldest literature, mugwort was used to bring on late menstruation and abortion.

These cathedrals of the Ice Age, as they are sometimes called, were a ritual center of the Stone Age. Deposits left here by reindeer hunters at least seventeen thousand years ago show us that these reindeer hunters had as profound a connection with mugwort as the herb has with the culinary main event of our Christmas feast. This is yet more evidence that the connection between reindeer and Christmas goes all the way back to this Stone Age shamanic culture.

The German name for mugwort, *beifuss*, translates literally to "by the foot." This might be taken to imply that mugwort grows near footpaths. But the name actually comes from the medieval word *biboz*, which in German is linked with the words *beibett* (next to the bed) or *beistoss* (next to the thrusting). In this sense, the plant appears closely related to aphrodisiac attributes. And indeed, mugwort was sacred to the love goddess Freia and said to be a love magic: "Mugwort gave the power of a thunder god to the loins and opened the sacred female lap" (Storl, 1996b). When giving birth, Germanic women held a thatch of mugwort in their hands. Mugwort is holy to the Germanic birth goddess Holla (or Frau Holle) and was supposed to help the new child in the transition from the otherworld to this world.* For the same reason, the dead were provided with mugwort in the grave, and old Germanic peoples offered bunches of mugwort on bonfires to their dead.

The old German name *sonnwendgürtle* (solstice girdle) refers to the ritual role played by mugwort during both the winter and summer solstices—the longest and the shortest days and nights of the year. During solstice rituals, the people wore belts or girdles of mugwort while dancing around the fire, and later burned the mugwort belts to banish bad luck.

The association of the plant with the wild god Wotan can be clearly seen in the ancient English names old man, felon herb, naughty man, and old Uncle

Harry. The Old Nordic name Harr means "high," and was applied to Wotan (Odin).

MAGICAL AND FOLK USE

Mugwort is an old apotropaic (a substance used for protection against demons), counter spell, and amulet. It protects against lightning and was dedicated to the thunder god, Donar or Thor. The Romans put mugwort wreaths in their houses to ward off the evil eye.* As indicated by the botanical name *Artemisia*, mugwort was dedicated to Artemis, the Greek goddess of the forest and the twin sister of Apollo, the sun god. Artemis was identified with the Roman hunting goddess, Diana, who was reclassified as a witch in early modern times. Thus mugwort, like many other plants sacred in pre-Christian times, became a "witches' herb" used both for protection against witches and by the witches themselves. Mugwort was a love magic that counteracted impotence and frigidity caused by bewitchment.

The Christmas or St. Martin's Goose

> *In many myths of many cultures there is a goose that lays the golden egg from which the sun is born.*
>
> NAUWALD 2002, 34

Smudging house and stable and spicing the St. Martin's goose with mugwort goes back to old Germanic and Celtic rituals.

> St. Martin—whose day is November 11—took the place of the god of the dead, Samain, after the Christianization of the Celtic people. In the foggy, gray, sad November days, this god of the underworld defeats the sun god and takes over the country; he also captures the goddess of vegetation, the wife of the dying sun. With loud cries of despair, wild geese flying south tell of the change of the season. Now the plant goddess with her green vegetation is gone from this world, down into the dark home of her black new master. With the gathering of the gray mugwort, which may now finally be harvested, the time to pick herbs is over. All plants are now *pucca*—taboo. What is gathered and picked *now* only brings bad luck, instead of health and healing. With the last bush of mugwort, house and stable are smudged, and a goose is sacrificed for the feast of the turning of the year (Storl 1996a, 137).

Flying Balm from Goose Fat

The goose is a very obvious symbol for the flying witch, a vision of the magical flight that is known even in modern Western cultures. Frau Holle (a version of the old Nordic Hela), the goddess behind the veils of the underworld, is associated with the winter snow that is supposed to fall from the feathers of her

Anglo-Saxon Herb Blessing

"Remember, mugwort, what you said, what you said in your solemn proclamation. You, the oldest of all herbs, have all the power against three and thirty, you have the power against poison and contagious diseases, you have the power against evil that comes over the country" (quoted in Schöpf 1986, 63).

*This might be the reason for its Norwegian folk name "hut root."

Christmas Intoxications and Other Delights

131

sacred bird, the migrant goose. In English-speaking regions, we are reminded of her in the form of Mother Goose, as in the following nursery rhyme:

Old Mother Goose
When she wanted to wander
Would fly through the air
On a very fine gander.

The witch "flying" through the night often rubbed goose fat on her body as a symbolic representation of her flight. The nightly witches' flights were called grease flights, and the witches themselves grease birds or lard wings (Devereux, 2000: 131f).

In fruit and vegetable shops with a good assortment of herbs, you can find fresh mugwort at Christmastime. Mugwort is a classic spice for the roasted St. Martin's goose—"the holy goose become a Christmas goose"[*] (Storl 1996b). Mugwort is supposed to help with the digestion of heavy goose fat[†]—something for which other spices are often much more effective![‡] The real reason for this use of mugwort is much more ritualistic. The sacrificial goose is perfumed with the sacred scent of mugwort to send an olfactory signal to Wotan. The scent incites the god to pay attention to the sacrifice, so he can hear and fulfill the wishes of those making the sacrifice—if he so wishes! The smell of the sacrificial goose is, in other words, a scented wish list for Father Christmas.

What Does Sacrifice Mean?

The word sacrifice evokes complicated feelings and associations. For some, it conjures gruesome images of barbaric people sacrificing human beings and animals before the idols of their dreadful gods. Another sort of impression comes from heated debates in the German parliament over tax reforms that require citizens to "make sacrifices." However, the concept of sacrifice also has a completely different dimension: It is a way to make a connection between life and death! Animal sacrifice is a relic of the time when human beings lived purely as hunters. Hunters thanked the hunted animals for surrendering their lives to sustain the lives of human beings. The hunting and killing of animals reminded the hunters of the inevitable conclusion of life: death.

In former times, animal sacrifice was practiced in many cultures. Later, after the custom was suppressed, it was primarily expressed on a purely symbolic level. However, in some regions of the world, this religious practice has continued to the present day. In Nepal, sacrifice of various animals—such as chickens, goats, and buffalo—accompanies nearly every religious expression and is a part of daily life. Besides its social and culinary purposes, sacrifice has shamanic, magical, and consciousness-raising aspects. Animal sacrifice has not degenerated to a perfunctory act of ritual killing, but still has an important place in the thoughts and feelings of the Nepali people. Through this conscious

[*]A "man who gives everything away" is often called a "Christmas goose" (Bornemann 1974).

[†]"Goose fat is supposed to have a sexually stimulating effect" (Hiller 1989, 85).

[‡]As spices for the goose roast, the *Medieval Cookbook* suggests salt, pepper, fennel seed, cumin powder, lemon, ginger, nutmeg, cloves, and cinnamon (Ehlert 1990). Juniper berries were included in the stuffing, recalling another relationship to Wotan; in the vernacular, juniper is called Wotan's rod, Martin's rod, and life rod.

contact with death, a participant in the ritual can see his or her own place in the cosmos and can better understand life.

At Christmastime, even today, we practice customs that invoke the idea of ritual sacrifice, even if we no longer view them that way. Geese, turkeys, and carp give up their lives for us at Christmastime. We make a ritual sacrifice when we burn fir branches or incense cones. When we drink a celebratory toast to health, we make a sacrificial offering of Yule beer, punch, Christmas grog, wine, or champagne.

Rosemary and the Yule Boar

Rosemary was dedicated to Fro and Holda in the days of the gods, and the Yule buck was decorated with rosemary sprigs . . . as a plant associated with memory.

VON PERGER 1864, 143

Rosmarinus officinalis L., Lamiaceae (rosemary)

OTHER NAMES
Compass plant, *encensier, incensier* (French)

The evergreen rosemary has played a role similar to that of mugwort in the ethnobotany of Christmas. It has served not only as an incense substance, a winter green, a blossom miracle plant, and a herb for making rods, but also as a spice for seasoning another animal sacrifice that has nearly vanished from the menu: roast boar.*

A gold-bristled boar is the animal associated with Freyr, the fertility god of the pagan northern Germans. During processionals, the bristles of this boar were supposed to have shone so brightly that even the darkest night became light. The boar symbolizes sunlight in the depths of darkness. It is he who, with his enormous power, pushes the wheel of the year that has come to a standstill during the "mother nights" so that it turns again and the days grow longer (Storl 2000, 82).

The boar is the mythological animal ridden by the Wanen god Fro (also known as Frey or Freyr). Fro, sometimes considered the brother of Freia because he is the god of fertility and potency, is usually shown with a mushroom cap decoration and an erect penis. On special days, a boar might be sacrificed in his honor—at Yule time, for example, or on wedding days. The boar served a similar function in Lombardy: "Around Christmas it was killed and sold; the money went to the honor of St. Anthony" (Seligmann 1999, 51).

To this day, the Christmas boar with apple and parsley in his mouth is spiced with rosemary. The roast does not only get spicier, but also takes on the

HEYE 2002

PLEASE LIKE ME!

The future roast goose looks for protection beneath the Christmas mushroom. (Page from a pocket calendar. Munich: W. Heye Verlag, 2001)

*Rosemary is also a medieval spice for wild venison pâté.

Christmas Intoxications and Other Delights

holy smell of the incense dedicated to Fro. The Yule boar of the fertility god also lives on in Christmas representations of the wild boar, usually made from marzipan now.

There are numerous different myths about the origin of rosemary. Once, there was an Assyrian youth called Libanotis (meaning "incense"). Because he honored the gods, he was so dear to them that they changed him into a divine rosemary bush when he was driven out of his country. According to another myth, the incense bush was originally the sun's daughter, Leukothoe. It was changed into rosemary after she incestuously seduced her father. The erotic connotation has been retained in the folk custom: "In Koburg the young boys *pepper* (=engage in sexual intercourse with) or *dengel* (=expose themselves to by squeezing of testicles) the women on the first Day of Christmas. Two sprigs of rosemary were preferably used for this; this custom shows a sexual and erotic character"* (Aigremont 1987 I, 144).

The strongly aromatic rosemary herb was dedicated to the Roman house gods. Pliny wrote that "its leaves smell like incense" (Pliny the Elder XXIV, 99). This is why thatches of rosemary were burned on Roman graves. Based on this use, the plant has been known to the present day as "the incense herb"—in French, *encensier* or *incensier*. It was burned in French hospitals alone or in combination with juniper berries to purify the air: "As a smoking substance, rosemary has always been known to drive out bad spirits or germs and to help against conditions of nervous exhaustion" (Belledame 1990, 103).

Rosemary is sometimes used in smudging night or other midwinter smudgings because it was dedicated to Frau Holler, the winter Freia. "On Christmas night around twelve o'clock, all water is changed to wine and all trees are changed to rosemary" (von Perger 1864, 143). In Arabic, rosemary is called *iklil al-gabal,* "the crown of the mountain." On the winter solstice, the Berber tribes of Morocco smudge with rosemary herb *(azir)* (Venzlaff 1977, 38).

The following, a much-loved mythical story from medieval times, was altered in order to Christianize rosemary. The legend holds that Mary put up Jesus's diapers in a rosemary bush for drying. After this, the bush took on the color of heaven. Rosemary then became a symbol of faithfulness and commemoration.

*Belgian prostitutes carry boars' teeth as a lucky charm.

Christmas Intoxications and Other Delights

Merry Christmas from Mother Coca, Coca-Cola, and Santa Claus

Coca-Cola as a "Lord's supper" is a very common idea of the cultural scene.

FRITZ 1985, 88

The ethnobotanical history of human culture has more facets than our eyes can detect through the veil of Christmas romance. In every culture, certain plants have been held sacred since antiquity. These have not vanished from memory, but rather have been rededicated to new ideas, religions, and rites. Thus, plants from very diverse, faraway places conquered the snowy Christmas landscape of our own culture.

In Peru, it is said there was a special tree that gave protection to Mary; it nourished her and helped her regain her strength. It was not gorse or sticky palm, nor was it juniper or laurel. For the Peruvians, this sacred plant was the evergreen coca bush (*Erythroxylum coca*). Like other kinds of Christmas evergreens (for example, holly and spurge laurel, *Daphne mezereon*), this bush also has shining red berries.

Left: The evergreen coca bush (*Erythroxylum coca*) has shining red berries like holly and spurge laurel. No wonder coca is associated with the Christmas story in South America. (Legal coca plantation, Chulumani, Bolivia, 2000)

Right: Coca and kola (*Erythroxylum coca* and *Cola acuminata*) are the two plants whose names were taken for the internationally successful American soft drink. According to the movie *The Gods Must Be Crazy*, the Coca-Cola bottle fell from the sky into the desert of South Africa—as a Christmas present for humanity!

Even though the Spanish church has forbidden the use of coca, the folk belief gave the sacred bush a place in the syncretistic, mythical treasury of South America:

> It was said that when the Virgin Mary rested under the coca bush during her escape into Egypt, she chewed some leaves and felt refreshed and confident. According to another legend, Jesus was supposed to have blessed this bush; and from this time on, when they were used during rituals, the leaves gave power to human beings (Wiedemann 1992, 8).

Thus the coca plant made its way into Latin American Christmas folk custom, personified as the love goddess Mama Coca.

The modern beverage known as Coca-Cola got its distinctive aroma from the coca bush and, as in former times, still has the taboo energizing effect, due to a relatively high caffeine content. Coca-Cola was invented in 1886 by a pharmacist and morphine user, John Styth Pemberton (1831–1888), in Atlanta, Georgia. It was intended to be a nonalcoholic alternative to the very successful *Vin Mariani,* a coca extract that contained a good deal of alcohol and was treasured as an inspiring stimulant by the American artistic, intellectual, scientific, and political elite of the late nineteenth century.* In these times, the alcohol prohibitionists had political power and the collective folk soul was thirsting after a refreshing drink with a similar effect but no alcohol. So the inventor's concept came just in time to conquer the market, and Coca-Cola quickly became one of

*For example, Jules Verne, Robert Louis Stevenson, H. G. Wells, Thomas Edison, Jules Massenet, Charles Grounod, and the fathers of cinema, the Lumière brothers.

Christmas Intoxications and Other Delights

SOMETHING OF THE CHRISTMAS MAGIC IS GONE.

Above left: Santa Claus in front of the star-spangled sky with a sack full of surprises. (Postcard, *A Merry Christmas*, circa 1900)

Above right: Nearly a century after his introduction in advertising, Santa Claus still brings the Coca-Cola. (Cartoon by Leendert Jan Vis, © Paperclip International, 1999)

Right: *Snowballs for Santa Claus Clones.* (Postcard from G. Bauer, "Christmas 2," from around 1995)

Christmas Intoxications
and Other Delights

the most successful soft drinks (perhaps better termed a soft drug?) in history (Pendergrast 1996).

In the vernacular, Coca-Cola became "coke." Since the turn of the twentieth century, coke has also been a much-used nickname for the drug cocaine. Because what the Art Deco youth meant when they ordered coke was so ambiguous, the Coca-Cola Company secured the nickname as a company-owned brand name: Coke®. In 1903, the cocaine was removed from the drink, but an extract of good-tasting Trujillo coca *(Erythroxylum novogranatense* var. *truxillense)* from northwestern Peru remained an ingredient in the beverage. Thus, the typical taste of the sacred plant of the Incas is still important in today's Coca-Cola, even though the "soul" of the plant—the banished cocaine—has been "exorcised" (Rätsch and Ott 2003).

In 1931, the Coca-Cola Company introduced to the market a Santa Claus drawn by Haddon Sundblom (Fritz 1985, 147). The company actually secured this very public and popular mascot, the American Father Christmas, with the trademark Santa Claus®. In 1964, the American Father Christmas was simply called Coca-Cola Santa (van Renterghem 1995, 106). In 1966, the company's advertisement referred openly to Christmas: "Christmas without Coca-Cola—bah, humbug!" (Fritz 1985, 154). Even today, the Coca-Cola Company still uses Santa in Christmas advertising.

Santa Claus on a Coca-Cola can: Santa Coca!

Christmas Intoxications
and Other Delights

CHRISTMAS SPICES AND CHRISTMAS BAKING

*The smell of spices is an aroma that comes from paradise
into the human world.*

SCHIEVELBUSCH 1983, 16

In the weeks before Christmas, you can easily find spice mixtures and more unusual ingredients (for example, ammonium carbonate, also called salt of hartshorn) for Christmas baking. The smell of waffles and gingerbread, of punch and herbal sweets and teas spiced with Christmas spices caresses our noses. Hints of anise, cardamom, cinnamon, coriander, and clove oil hover over the shopping malls and Christmas markets. Advent time beguiles us with aromatic sensations from diverse worlds.

When the crusaders returned home to their castles from the Holy Land in the thirteenth and fourteenth centuries, they brought back with them the spoils of their raids and pillaging: the Christmas spices we hold so dear today. Ginger, cinnamon, cloves, pepper, and saffron quickly conquered the kitchens of central Europe. Thus it seems that, especially at Christmastime, we are truly able to take home everything the world has to offer!

Christmas spices used for baking, roasting, beverage spicing, and other facets of cooking yield an aroma that functions as a sort of incense smoke. This aroma stimulates a sense of well being and lightens the mood in dark days.

Typical Christmas baking spices come from exotic places: cardamom and ginger from Southeast Asia, star anise from China, nutmeg from the Indonesian Malaku province ("spice island"), galangal from Thailand, chili pepper from Central and South America, and cinnamon stick from Ceylon.

Many botanical ingredients used as spices and incense were also used as baccy substances, including anise, benzoin, cascarilla, cassia , cardamom, cinnamon, cloves, coriander, lemon peel, mastic, rose petals, star anise, storax, and valerian. Cardamom, cinnamon, cloves, coriander, and orrisroot had the honor of being used in mead (Wallbergen 1988, 108).

Astonishingly enough, many Christmas spices were considered aphrodisiac, including anise, cardamom, cinnamon, cloves, coriander, ginger, juniper, mugwort, nutmeg, saffron, star anise, turmeric, and vanilla.* So was the spice recipe for Nuremberg gingerbread that appears here.

CHRISTMAS SPICES

Spice name	Botanical name	Origin[†]
Allspice	*Pimenta dioica*	Caribbean
Anise	*Pimpinella anisum*	Egypt
Laurel	*Laurus nobilis*	Mediterranean
Cardamom	*Elettaria cardamomum*	India
Caraway	*Carum carvi*	Central Europe
Cassia	*Cinnamomum odoratum*	China
Chili pepper	*Capiscum annuum*	Mexico, Peru
Cinnamon	*Cinnamomum verum*	Ceylon
Cloves	*Syzygium aromaticum*	Indonesia
Coconut flakes	*Cocos nucifera*	South Pacific
Coriander	*Coriandrum sativum*	Mediterranean
Cumin	*Cuminum cyminum*	Mediterranean
Fennel	*Foeniculum vulgare*	Southeastern Europe
Galangal	*Alpinia galanga*	Southeast Asia
Ginger	*Zingiber officinale*	Southeast Asia
Hemp seed	*Cannabis sativa*	Europe
Juniper	*Juniperus communis*	Europe, Northern Hemisphere
Mace	*Myristica fragrans*	Indonesia
Mastic	*Pistacia lentiscus*	Greece
Mugwort	*Artemisia vulgaris*	Europe, worldwide
Nutmeg	*Myristica fragrans*	Indonesia
Poppy seed	*Papaver somniferum*	Central Europe
Pepper	*Piper nigrum*	India, Madagascar
Rose	*Rosa* spp.	Southern Europe
Rosemary	*Rosmarinus officinalis*	Mediterranean
Saffron	*Crocus sativus*	Eastern Mediterranean
Star anise	*Illicium verum*	China
Turmeric	*Curcuma longa*	Southeast Asia
Vanilla	*Vanilla planifolia*	Mexico

Medieval Spice Mixture for Nuremberg Gingerbread[‡]

1 part cinnamon
3 parts nutmeg
1 1/2 parts cloves
6 parts ginger
1/4 part mace

‡From Ehlert 1990, 209.

*The German word for vanilla *(Vanille)* comes from vagina (von Paczensky and Dünnebier 1999, 300).

†Most of the exotic spices of the Old World were known in ancient Europe and described by Dioscorides and Pliny. Spices were traded over long distances, as were incense substances (Schivelbusch 1983). Many of our familiar Christmas spices were already in use in the ancient Roman kitchen (Thüry and Walter 1999).

Christmas Spices and Christmas Baking

Many eastern recipes for stimulating potions and intoxicating aphrodisiacs describe very similar spice mixtures, usually combinations of cinnamon, cloves, cardamom, nutmeg, ginger, and pepper of different kinds. Most spice essential oils contain psychotropic ingredients. In order to experience the effect with the herbs themselves, however, one must take a high dose. This is why in medieval times festive meals were sprinkled "to the thickness of a finger" with spice powder, most often with pepper, nutmeg, and cloves (Schivelbusch 1983, 14f).

Anise and St. Andrew's Night

Anise should awaken sexual lust.

HILLER 1989, 15

Pimpinella anisum L., Apiaceae (anise)

OTHER NAMES
Aniseed, sweet cumin

Anise is one of today's most popular spices for Christmas baking. Use of this aromatic plant, which is believed to come from the eastern Mediterranean, is also associated with Christmas love and oracular magic in folk custom, as are so many other Christmas plants. As early as the first century CE, Dioscorides wrote that anise seeds were a love substance that stimulates sexual activity (Dioscorides III 1610, 58).

As an erotic stimulant, anise is considered especially potent with magic during St. Andrew's Night, which is why that day was called *Anishday* or simply *Anish* in old Bohemia.

> Originally occurring around the time of the winter solstice, Andrew's Night was moved to November 30 with the introduction of the Julian calendar. It was a festive time of fertility, marriage fortune, and good health—Andrew (Fro, Freyr) is the patron saint of marriage for lovers. . . . This night is connected with many practices involving love magic and love power through plants (Aigremont 1987 II, 75f).

As a love substance, people not only consumed anise seed and foods spiced with it, such as gingerbread, they also drank anise-flavored liqueurs, such as Pastis and Pernod. These beverages, which are related to absinthe, are still popular today in southern Europe. In the past, on so-called flax-swinging days (the days of the flax harvest), lovers used a mixture of gingerbread soaked in wine and anise liqueur as a love potion. This mushy drink was called a "little trough" and a girl fed it to her beloved as he knelt before her.

There is also a tinge of love magic to the other anise: star anise or spice star *(Illicium verum)*. The name *Illicium* comes from a Latin word that means "alluring," which is related to the fact that it smells like incense and has a pheromone-like effect! Star anise comes from a tree that grows up to 18 meters (about 60 feet) tall. It has white, many-petaled, star-shaped flowers that carry the typical Christmas scent and have been used for ages in Asia as an ingredient in incense powders and sticks. The smoke has a tender but hearty anise aroma that combines well with other scents. The star anise makes a natural, eight-pointed Christmas star and is used in powdered form in Christmas baking.

Finally, there is the plant commonly known as "witch anise." Black cumin *(Nigella sativa)* has been used as an ingredient for witch incense as well as in incense for the smudging nights.

Saffron: Red Gold for Christmas

Saffron was a sign of the light gods.

VON PERGER 1864, 84

Crocus sativus L., Iridaceae (saffron crocus)

OTHER NAMES
Abir (Persian), crocus (Roman), *gewürzsafran*, hay saffron, *karcom* (Hebrew), *karkom, karkum* (Persian), *kesar* (Sanskrit), *kesara* (Hindi), *kesari, krokos* (Greek), *krokus, kumkumkesari, plam phool* (Pakistani), saffron, saffron crocus, *safrankrokus, sn-wt.t* (ancient Egyptian), *z'afarân* (Arabic/Yemen), *zafran*

The saffron crocus, which comes from the eastern Mediterranean, is one of the oldest cultivated plants of all. A wild form is no longer known to exist. Saffron was cultivated in Mesopotamia and in Minoan Crete, and later across

The saffron crocus *(Crocus sativus)* is easy to recognize because of its long stigmas. It is "red gold" that has been known for ages as a spice, healing remedy, aphrodisiac, incense, and dye.

Christmas Spices and Christmas Baking

the whole Roman Empire. A very famous (and very old) area of cultivation is in Oberwallis, Switzerland. The so-called *krummenegga* (saffron fields) found there were established by returning crusaders in 1420 CE.

On the islands of Crete and Thera (now called Santorini), saffron had an important ritual significance, as can be inferred from the many pictures of saffron on frescos in the sanctuaries. The saffron crocus was obviously connected with the priests' adoration of Cybele, the Minoan goddess of nature and fertility. The wall paintings in Thera show that the saffron harvest was in fact the business of priestesses.

Saffron is often called "red gold" because it is even more expensive than gold! Around 250,000 saffron threads (stigmas) are needed to make 1 kilo (about two pounds) of the popular spice, which has been used for healing, love magic, incense, and color as well as its unique flavor. One might even imagine that the gold brought by the holy three kings was actually saffron.

Saffron is a very popular spice for Christmas baking—and in the hemp kitchen. Christmas stars made from hashish, butter, and saffron ("this one really makes the cake yellow") are a specialty. Saffron seems to enhance the oral absorption of THC and may also play its own part in the general psychoactive effect. Just as hemp was the "simple man's tobacco," turmeric *(Curcuma longa)*, the gold-colored spice from Southeast Asia, is the "poor man's saffron." However, turmeric does not produce the stimulating effect of real saffron. In old Russia, people made meals with calming, aphrodisiac, or pain-relieving effects by including hemp, saffron, nutmeg, cardamom, and honey.

> *Your stimulus is a lusty garden of pomegranate trees,*
> *With chosen fruit*
> *With cypress and roses and saffron,*
> *With spice wood and cinnamon*
> *With all kinds of frankincense*
> *With myrrh and aloe[wood]*
> *With all the noble balms.*
>
> THE SONG OF SONGS XIV

In antiquity, saffron was associated with *sol invictus,* the rebirth of the sun, and was believed to contain essences of the gods and goddesses of light and love. In old Rome, it was dedicated to Venus because it could stimulate erotic feelings. When used as an incense, it was believed to lighten human consciousness, as it was considered condensed sunlight that was set free the moment it glowed on the red-hot pan.

Christmas Baking

How deliciously it is steaming! How delicious it smells! How rich it looks! Round like a kiss, round like the horizon, round like the earth, round like the sun, moon, and stars and all the heavenly folks—this is plum pudding.

RIEMERSCHMIDT 1962, 93

In the past, pre-Christmas season started on the first day of Advent, December 1. Today, the shelves fill up with Christmas pastries and spices in September, soon after summer vacation ends, probably mainly for convenience. In earlier days, however, Advent was an important time of preparation for the coming feast. To fail to fill up your stomach on "full stomach night" (December 24) or give money to the poor was considered bad luck!

Advent time is baking time. Grandmothers lure their grandchildren into the kitchen with cookie dough and seductive spices—much like the witch of the enchanted woods in the Hänsel and Gretel story! It might be the last time in the year when grandparents, parents, and children work together in the kitchen, shaping cookie dough with little cookie-cutters and making sugar icing for gingerbread houses—all in a sticky, chaotic, wonderful-smelling paradise.

Cutting out and baking cookies in the shape of stars, fir trees, mushrooms, and crescent moons recalls the fertility rituals of days past. In remembrance of the old saying, "Sweet as a delicious gift of charity and the fullness of giving" (Riemerschmidt 1962, 106), the people used everything the kitchen and larder had to offer to make delightfully rich baked goods: English plum pudding, *hutzel* pear bread, Yule logs, cookies, and more. Today, depending on family tradition and region, popular German Christmas specialties include Nuremberg *liebkuchen* (traditional spiced cookies), Dresden *stollen* (sweet Christmas bread with dried fruit), Basle *leckerli* (gingerbread), *speculatius* (almond cookies) and *springerle* (anise cookies).

Swedish Yule pastry in symbolic shapes: fir tree (world tree), sun and moon, man (god) and woman (goddess), Yule buck, and Yule boar.

Christmas idyll in a witches' house. The witch makes the fire under the cannibal pot for cooking the kidnapped children, while her fat companion smokes a baccy pipe in happy expectation. (Wilhelm Busch, *Hänsel and Gretel*, Bilderpossen, 1864)

Christmas Spices and Christmas Baking

Grandmother's bakery.
(Christmas card with a drawing
by Elspeth Austin, England,
undated)

Marzipan

Marzipan is made from sweet and bitter almond pastes that are mixed with sugar and rosewater and formed into various shapes. In bygone days, people sometimes also added one of the gifts of the holy three kings—myrrh. The original Italian name for this popular Christmas sweet, *marci panis* (Marcus bread), harks back to the ninth century, when merchants brought the bones of St. Marcus to Venice. Marcus became the patron saint of the city of canals.

Arnalf of Villanova, a Catalan doctor who died in 1311, first documented the invention of marzipan. Since 1407, it has been among the most popular sweets of Christmas in Lübeck, Germany. The pastry chefs of Niederegger, who are among the world's best, are forbidden to take the recipe for marzipan out of the house; it has been kept secret for hundreds of years. A recipe for making marzipan appears in the handwritten cookbook started in 1533 by an Augsburg patrician's daughter, Sabina Welserin (Ehlert 1990, 13).

Gingerbread and Christmas Pepper
Piper nigrum L., Piperaceae

OTHER NAMES
Black pepper, pfeffer

Pepper *(Piper nigrum)* comes from "the country where pepper is growing"—more succinctly, from India. In England, chili pepper (*Capsicum annum* L., Solanaceae) is called Christmas pepper, perhaps simply because the fresh peppers are colored green and red.

The German word for pepper, *pfeffer,* is reflected in the German name for the gingerbread—*pfefferkuchen. Pfefferkuchen* is made with spices similar to those used in *pfeffernüsse* and *liebkuchen,* traditional German spiced cookies made from recipes handed down from medieval convent bakeries. Nuremberg *liebkuchen* contained cinnamon, nutmeg, mace, ginger, cloves, and rosewater—but strangely enough, no pepper! Whence, then, comes this German name for gingerbread?

In German, "pepper" is a folk synonym for a multitude of spices. The word also relates to the old custom of "peppering"—the ritualized beating of young girls with the life rod on December 28, the day of the innocent children. The friends attending the peppering received a pepper cake *(pfefferkuchen)* as a thank-you present from the beaten girl. The priests forbade this old fertility ritual and renamed the peppery pastry in remembrance of the martyred St. Stephen, who was killed by stoning, a kind of peppering. "The name recalled the stones with which Stephen was killed; and thus they really made believers taste the fact that, for the faithful, the hardest and the most bitter thing can yet become sweet" (quoted in Vossen 1985, 103).

A mix of peppercorns in all the Christmas colors.

Today, these old customs drive some feminists crazy. On December 28, 2002, the newspaper *Harburger Wochenblatt* published an account of a ruling against Father Christmas under the title "Grievous Bodily Harm and Provocation." The announcement stated, "Father Christmas is guilty of grievous bodily harm by means of the husband (provocation), according to criminal code §223. Thank God." This amusing anecdote shows how the old peppering custom handed down through the centuries has commanded attention right up to the present day—now more out of misunderstanding, ignorance, and lack of sense of humor than anything else.

Finally, here's something uplifting and healing on the subject:

> Gingerbread was used medicinally against fever, when it was written on and eaten in a special way; against backaches, when one carried it in one's pocket and ate from it during the time from Christmas to Candlemas (February 2); and against worms, when cooked as a mash with yeast liquor and used as a compress on the stomach. In the convents, gingerbread was baked with healing herbs (Hiller 1989, 174).

Cinnamon Stars
Cinnamomum verum J. Presl., Lauraceae (cinnamon)

Unlike pepper cake (gingerbread), which contains no pepper, cinnamon stars actually contain cinnamon *(Cinnamomum verum)*. This spice too may have some unwanted side effects. In the area of the Lüneburger heath in Germany, it was said that cinnamon stars sometimes were made so well that Father Christmas, magically attracted, would come for the farmer's wife. Given the

Christmas Spices and Christmas Baking

right dosage and the proper preparation, cinnamon may very well contribute to erotic seduction.

In antiquity, cinnamon was among the best known and most widely used spices and aromatic substances. Even though the Greeks were not acquainted with the cinnamon tree, there were some legends there about its origin. The people believed that the cinnamon tree grew in Arabia. In the Bible, cinnamon is mentioned several times as *kinnamon* and described as a perfume and incense (Rätsch and Müller-Ebeling 2003, 731).

In combination with dried orange slices and walnuts, cinnamon sticks are also a very popular Christmas decoration.

Nutmeg and the Lucky Cookies of Hildegard von Bingen
Myristica fragrans Houtt., Myristicaceae (nutmeg and mace)

OTHER NAMES
Almendra de la semilla, balla (Banda), Banda nutmeg, *bazbaz* (Persian), *bisbâsa al-hindî* (Arabic/Yemen), *buah pala* (Malayalam), *bush-apal, chan-thet* (Laotian), *hindî, jaephal* (Hindi), *jan-thet* (Tahi), *jauz-i-bûyâ* (Arabic, "fragrant nut"), *ju-tou-k'ou, juz, mada shaunda, massa, miskad, moscada, moscata miristica* (Italian), *moschocaria, moschocarydia, muscade, muscadier, muscadier cultivé, muscatennußbaum, muschatennuß, muskach'u* (Callawaya), *muskatnußbaum, musque, myristica moschata, noix muscade, nootmuskaat* (Dutch), *noz moscada, nuce muscata, nuez moscada,* nutmeg, nutmeg tree, *pala banda, roudoukou* (Chinese)

> *There are scents that sing the way of the senses, others of the spirit.*
>
> BAUDELAIRE 1857

Nutmegs are the seed of the *Myristica fragrans* fruit, which is coated with a golden-yellow seed coat, the "nutmeg flower" or mace. Nutmeg is the psychoactive ingredient of Hildegard von Bingen's "happy cookies."

Christmas Spices and Christmas Baking

Nutmeg and mace (the seed coat of the nutmeg) are most appropriate spices for the Christmas feast of love. The two are well known in India, the Middle East, and Europe, where they have been used as aphrodisiac substances and love magic as well as spices. In medieval times, nutmeg was considered helpful for encouraging "Venus trading."*

The nutmeg tree is from the Southeast Asian "spice island" known as the Island of Banda and is among the oldest cultivated trees of humanity. Botanically speaking, the nut is the seed of the plant's fruit. Mace, the so-called "nutmeg flower" is the dried seed coat (arillus). Both not only are good tasting and aromatic, they may also have a consciousness-altering effect at higher doses. Nutmeg has a musk-like smell and a pheromone-like effect.

The medieval herbalist and abbess Hildegard von Bingen was well acquainted with the uplifting effect of nutmeg:

> The nutmeg has a great warmth and a good mixture in its powers. When a human being eats nutmeg it opens his heart, and his sense is pure, and it puts him a good state of mind. Take nutmeg and (in the same amount) cinnamon and some cloves and grind them up. And then, from this powder and some water, make flour—and roll out some little tarts. Eat these often and it will lower the bitterness of your heart and your mind and open your heart and your numbed senses. It will make your spirit happy, purify and cleanse your mind, lower all bad fluids in you, give your blood a good tonic, and make you strong (Hildegard von Bingen, *Physica*, I, 21).

Cookies for Preventing Sadness

Based on a recipe by Hildegard von Bingen

- 22 g ground nutmeg
- 22 g ground cinnamon
- 5 g cloves
- 500 g spelt flour
- 150 g cane sugar
- 250 g butter
- 2 eggs
- A pinch of salt
- 100 g almond pieces

Bake cookies at 350° (180° Celsius) for 5 to 10 minutes. Beware! They have a strong effect.

* *Venushandel*, or "Venus trading," is an old German vernacular term for sexual intercourse.

Christmas Spices and
Christmas Baking

THE REBIRTH
OF THE SUN

Hail to you, sun!
Hail to you, light!
Hail to you, shining day!
Long was my sleep;
I woke up.

BRÜNHILDE IN WAGNER, *SIEGFRIED*, 3RD ACT

For our pre-Christian ancestors, the winter solstice—the day of the year with the shortest daytime and the longest nighttime—nourished hope for the return of the sun. Pliny the Elder tells us that the sun

. . . brings the light to things and takes away darkness; it lightens and covers the other stars. Following the laws of nature, it leads the change of season and the ever-changing year. It breaks up the cloudy skies; and lightens up the cloudy darkness of the human mind. It yields her light to the other stars—shining, exceptional, seeing and hearing everything . . . (Pliny the Elder, *Naturkunde* II, 13).

Spices and smudgings can bring out the sun in human beings because sunlight brings out the green power of plants. Today, we call this power chlorophyll. Rosemary was dedicated to the Germanic sun god, Freyr (Old Nordic for "lord"), brother of the love goddess, Freya (Freia). In Old Germany, Freyr was known as Fro (Old High German for "lord") and in Greece, Helios (Greek, "sun god"). "Freyr is the noblest of the gods. He reigns over rain and sunshine, and thus, in so far as this, over the growing things of the earth. It is good to ask him for a good harvest and peace; he oversees the bounty of human beings" (Snorri-Edda, *Glyf* 23 F).

Typical sun spices include lesser galangal *(Alpinia officinarum)*, turmeric *(Curcuma longa)*, ginger *(Zingiber officinale)*, nutmeg *(Myristica fragrans)*, saffron *(Crocus sativus)*, and cinnamon *(Cinnamomum verum)* (Madejsky and Rippe 1997, 56).

The sun comes from the smoke of the cinnamon rind in much the same way the legendary phoenix rises from its ashes. In ancient times, cinnamon was among the most popular spices and aromatic substances with pheromone-like effects. It was believed that the cinnamon tree grew in Arabia—not, however, on the ground, but instead in the nests of phoenix birds built high up on steep rocks. According to the story, in order to get to the cinnamon, the people had

> ### Sun Incense
>
> Based on a recipe from Sédir*
>
> **Ingredients**
> 3 parts frankincense (olibanum, *Boswellia sacra*)
> 1 part cinnamon bark *(Cinnamomum verum)* or cassia *(Cinnamomum aromaticum)*
> 1 part cardamom seed *(Elettaria cardamomum)*
>
> Grind ingredients together with a mortar and pestle. Place by small spoonfuls on the coals.
>
> ―――――――
>
> *Sédir is the pseudonym of Yvon de Loup (1871–1926), a French occultist and member of the Martinist Order. The recipe comes from his studies of occult botany (Belledame 1990, 117).

to trick the birds. Thus they put out parts of dead or sacrificed animals near the nests. When the birds left their nests to get the meat, the cinnamon collectors had just enough time to obtain some cinnamon from the nest.

Sun Gods: Apollo, Mithras, and Jesus

Listen to me, blissful! Reigning
The all-seeing, eternal eyes
Far up strolling, heavenly light,
Sparkling gold Titan,
Never tired, self-made
Fair sight of the living!

ORPHIC HYMN TO HELIOS

Without the sun there would be no life. Without the sun there would be no plants, and without plants, there would be no oxygen. Without oxygen, there would be no animals or human beings!

Like many pre-Christian customs and beliefs, the old feast commemorating the yearly return of the sun was rededicated to the birth of Christ. In the year 274 CE, the Roman emperor Aurelianus established the cult of *Deus sol invictus*—"God of the invincible sun"—which was celebrated on December 25, even though the actual day of the winter solstice is the twenty-first or twenty-second day of the month. Why? Perhaps this was the first day on which the people could actually discern the elevated position of the sun and see that it truly was coming back from the depths of darkness. The feast associated with the event was called the "rebirth of the sun." At the same time the Romans rededicated the rebirth of the sun to the birth of Christ, they also took over the cult of the Persian sun god Mithras, whose birthday was also celebrated on December 25. "The [Mithraic] mystery started with his initiation into a heavenly soul voyage" (Giebel 1990, 200).

Many of the gods of the past were associated with the sun: Ra and Osiris, the Egyptian sun and vegetation gods; Helios and Apollo, Greek gods of the sun and light; and the Germanic Wotan, who searches for the sun in the time of darkness with his wild army, to name just a few. The power of each of these important gods was attributed to the reigning emperor or king of the day. The sun was the giver of life for plants and thus also for human beings.* Therefore, the first day of the week—Sunday—was named after the day once dedicated to Helios, the sun god.

In the context of this cosmological and mythological background, the idea that Jesus was a descendent of the former sun gods was only logical, and it is easy to see why his followers associated the rebirth of the sun with his birth. But there remains a significant difference. According to Christian belief, the sun itself is not divine, but is "a mere creation that God has given special duties. . . . The pagan belief remained centered on the divine beauty of His work, and worshipped *it*, in their adoration of God, instead of only comprehending the Creator" (Forstner 1986, 96).

This is why the Church was so keen to point out that the pagan admiration of the sun really amounted to adoration of the "glowing light from the heights."[†]

Mystery Cults

Soon, oh soon, the light
Ours to shape for all time, ours the right
The sun will lead us
Our reason to be here

YES, *The Gates of Delirium*, 1974[‡]

In order to see into the mystery of life and death, human beings have devised techniques and rituals available only to those initiated into the ways of particular mystery cults. In 375 CE, Epiphanius, Bishop of Constantia,[§] described the pagan winter solstice feasts and mystery cults:

> This feast was celebrated by the Greeks (I mean the pagans) on December 25—the day called Saturnalia by the Romans, Kronia in Egypt, and Kykellia by the Alexandrians. On December 25, then, a *cut* happens that is also a *turn*; and it begins to grow. This is the day when the light becomes *more* (Vossen 1985, 72).

In Egypt, Kykellia is called "the rite of Isis." Like the smudging nights, this

---

*In the cold, dark north, the sun barely clears the horizon on the winter solstice. This has a big impact on the people living there, and is one of the reasons many struggle with winter depression.

†Luke 1:78, quoted in Forstner 1986, 97.

‡Translator's note: Original lyrics in English.

§Today a Cypriot city, Salamis.

The Rebirth of
the Sun

is a twelve-day feast. It begins with a torch procession in honor of the birth of Horus, the son of Isis: "The birth of the new sun is the intended meaning, and that was connected with the announcement of the sowing [of wheat] in the earth, freshly fertilized (with dung) and flooded by the Nile" (Vossen 1985, 72f). The sowing was done on December 27, during the feast celebrating the ascension of Horus to the throne. The meaning of the name Isis is equivalent to "Earth."

Who is not familiar with the image of the Mary holding the baby Jesus? This classic tableau has found expression in countless examples of European art. This depiction of mother and child is not merely a sentimental evocation of motherhood, nor did it originate with the birth of Christ. It actually began with Egyptian pictures of Isis and the Horus child, giving us yet another example of the mysteriously subtle interweaving of religious iconography and meaning in art from diverse cultures.

The rebirth of the sun is the mystery of the winter solstice, symbolized by the rejuvenation of the wheat crop. Wheat is sacred because it delivers sustenance, healing, and intoxicating substances (like Yule beer). The earthly wheat also provides straw for Christmas stars, which are the signs of Helios, the sun god, hung on the evergreen world tree. Thus on Christmas night, in the candle-lit darkness, wheat reminds us of the mythical rebirth of the sun that shines at midnight.

For centuries, wheat has served as a botanical symbol of the Great Goddess, Demeter or Ceres, also known as the wheat or poppy goddess. Wheat is found in many Christmas arrangements. It is dedicated to St. Barbara and finds expression in St. Barbara's wheat rituals. (Late Antique relief from Eleusis, Greece)

Kyphi: Incense for the Smudging Nights

Every day the scents carry me into the magic worlds of otherwise unreachable paths of beauty, of the spirit of love. And without them I feel alone and left out.

CHIN CHIA, HAN DYNASTY, 200 CE

Our Christmas feast has roots in every ancient celebration of the rebirth of the sun. The most important source of information on sun rites from antiquity is the book *About Isis and Osiris* by the Greek philosopher Plutarch (circa 46–119 CE). Plutarch, a priest of Delphi, was intimately acquainted with the holy rites of Apollo and Helios and initiated into the mysteries of Isis and Osiris. He also had a sharp mind and literary sensibility. Here, he writes about the original Egyptian ritual:

Around the time of the winter solstice, they carry a cow seven times around the sun temple, and this walk is called the visit of Osiris. . . . One had to walk seven times around the temple, because the sun finishes its walk from the winter to summer solstice in the seventh month. Horus, the son of Isis, is supposed to have made a sacrifice to Helios on the fourth day of the month, as in the book called *Birthday of Horus*. To make an incense offering for Helios three times a day, offer resin at dusk, myrrh at midday, and so-called kyphi at dawn. . . . These are believed to show favor to Helios and to serve him (Plutarch 1850, 93f).

INGREDIENTS FOR KYPHI-INCENSE, FROM PLUTARCH*

Substance/Egyptian Name	Source
Honey *(meli)*	
Wine *(oinos)*	
Raisin *(staphides)*	
Cyperus, papyrus *(kyperos)*	*Cyperus* spp.
Resin *(setion)*	General term for resins and frankincense (olibanum)
Myrrh *(smyrna)*	*Commiphora* spp.
Broom *(aspalathos)*	*Cytisus* spp.
Hartwort *(seseleos)*	*Bupleurum* spp.
Mastic resin *(schinos)*	*Pistacia lentiscus*
Bitumen *(asphaltos)*	Asphalt[†]
Gum juniper *(thryon)*	possibly *Tetraclinis articulata*
Curly dock *(lapathos)*	*Rumex crispus*
Prickly juniper *(arkeuthis)*	*Juniperus oxycedrus*
Big juniper cardamom *(kardamom)*	*Juniperus* spp.
Cardamom *(kardamom)*	*Elettaria cardamomum*
Calamus, sweet flag *(kalamos)*	*Acorus calamus*
Citronella	*Cymbopogon nardus*

* Adapted from Plutarch, *About Isis and Osiris,* Chapter 81.

† It is believed that this asphalt is resined petroleum.

Kyphi: Egyptian Incense

The Hellenized word *kyphi* means "incense substance." It is, like the word incense, a general term for a variety of substances. Incense was considered "the divine maker" in Egypt because it was supposed to sanctify the environment when burned.

Many authors have speculated about recipes for the legendary Egyptian kyphi incenses, which were considered magical. Kyphi was the "favorite dish" of the sun god. Whoever worshipped him needed kyphi—*good* kyphi. Some recipes handed down from antiquity contain ingredient lists that are an indecipherable riddle today, perhaps because of spelling errors or sloppy recording.

Probably the most useful recipe is the sixteen-ingredient kyphi from Plutarch (Plutarch 1850 [Orig. pub. 2nd century CE]).

Plutarch writes:

It is not simply a matter of blending ingredients together, just like that! While the balm-makers are mixing the incense, people read them holy scriptures. . . . Kyphi is used as a drink and a medicine. As a drink, it purifies the inner organs because it seems to soften the lower part of the belly. Resin and myrrh are made by the sun; the plants sweat it out, as it were, in the midday heat. Some of the ingredients of kyphi—those that nourish themselves with cool air, shadow, dew, and humidity—grow better at night. This is because the daylight is a unified entity, and thus simpler, while the night air is a more complex mixture of many happenings, of lights and powers that come like seeds from the stars. Thus the approach to blending the incense must create a balance between simple things made by the sun during the day and the more elaborate things (things with many attributes) formed in the beginning of the night (Plutarch 1850 [Orig. pub. 2nd century CE]).

An Egyptian priest (recognizable because of his bald head) sacrificing incense balls. (After a wall painting in a nineteenth dynasty tomb in Memphis, Egypt)

The Egyptian *Papyrus Ebers,* the oldest existing medical text (written around 1553–1550 BCE), states:

Kyphi is used to make the house or clothes smell more pleasant: Dried myrrh, juniper berries, incense, spruce, aloewood, sebet-resin, calmus from Thailand (in Asia), inekkun-corns, mastic, and juice from the niiuben tree [styrax] are ground, combined, and put on the fire (*Papyrus Ebers,* XCVIII).

This recipe is difficult to reconstruct, as the botanical identifications cannot be verified. But we can say with confidence that basic incense combinations of

Mastic resin from Greece is an ancient incense substance used in the Egyptian kyphi recipe. In European occultism, mastic was associated with the sun, the waking of the "second face," and the conjuring of spirits. When burned, mastic vaporizes with a white smoke and gives off an aroma that is resiny but not sweet, reminiscent of frankincense.

The Rebirth of the Sun

153

frankincense and myrrh (or even frankincense and juniper) were used as offerings to the sun gods as far back as the time of the pharaohs.

Saturn, the God of Incense

The return of Saturn
Who was once in the Golden Age
The spring of humanity
Reigning as king
Was promised these days in oracles.

SIMON 1990, 196

During the Roman Saturnalia, people made offerings of presents to one another, especially candles and clay dolls symbolizing "life lights" and human beings. These were the predecessors of Christmas tree lights and gifts. In the pagan tradition, the Saturnalia often included a good deal of feasting and intoxication in addition to rest, relaxation, and general merry-making.

Saturn, or, more precisely, Saturnus, was the Roman god of agriculture. Even in antiquity, he was associated with the Greek god Kronos, symbolizing time itself. Saturnus was the husband of Ops (=Cybele), the Roman goddess of sowing and the harvest, and the father of Jupiter (=Zeus), who robbed him of his reign and drove him away. Under the reign of Saturn, humanity experienced the Golden Age *(Saturnia regna)*, a time of happiness without sorrow. One of Saturn's attributes is the sickle or wine grower's knife, which is also an attribute of Sylvanus, the god of the forest. The sickle was symbolic of the idea that, in the Golden Age, it was not necessary to sow, only to harvest.

In recollection of the Golden Age and as homage to the old, kind god,* the Saturnalia was celebrated in ancient Rome from December 17 to December 19. (Later on, during the time of the Roman emperors, the celebration was extended to the seven days following December 17.) It was a feast that did away with limits and relaxed normal social boundaries. This was especially true on December 19, the day on which master and slave switched roles and clothing. Thus, at least once in the year, social differences were eliminated, although it seems that the temporary switch would have made the differences even more obvious.

The most important source of information about the Saturnalia is the work of a Roman state official and Latin scribe, Macrobius (circa 400 CE). His writings present Saturnalia from the perspective of late antiquity and therefore provide us with a synthesis of many interpretations.

Saturnus and Janus were seen as guardians of the doors of the state treasuries. A candelabra that has survived from this time period illustrates their multifaceted symbolism. On one side of Augustine's marble candelabra was the image of Saturn riding on a peaceful donkey—a representation of the zodiac sign of Sagittarius, a centaur. On his divine thighs is an eagle, the eagle of

*As a merciless judge of time who reigned over those with melancholy temperaments, the old representation of Saturn had some negative characteristics as well.

The Rebirth of
the Sun

Jupiter. On the other side of the same candelabra, Sol (the sun god, Apollo) represents the zodiacal sign of Cancer. "The planet Saturnus rides on the zodiac sign of December, because its feast occurs in that month, while Apollo, as lord of the *Ludi Apollinares* [an Apollonian feast that took place July 6–13] rides on the star sign of July" (Simon 1990, 198f). Thus the two solstices, winter and summer, are depicted on the two sides of the candelabra.

The planet Saturn was also connected with the Greek god Phaeton, the "shining one." Because Phaeton was the son of the sun god Helios, he was sometimes called "little sun," or "son of the sun."

God of the Incense Altars

> *Magic Carthage of the sea! Even if you are no more, your*
> *aroma climbs up from these bare rocks and speaks: from*
> *incense, from the balm tree and from roses.*
>
> PIERRE FOUQUET, QUOTED IN ROVESTI 1995, 217

Saturn was the god of incense. Accounts of Phoenician worship show this clearly. In the ancient city–state of Carthage in North Africa, Saturnus was identified with the locally reigning Phoenician god Baal Hammon, whom the Phoenicians had worshipped as a fertility god since the ninth century BCE. At the same time, the main god of Carthage was Hammanim, "lord of the smoking altars" (Simon 1990, 194), because Phoenician merchants ruled the incense trade. This trade was not only lucrative, but was also politically important, because the monopoly led to conflict, war, and, in the end, the destruction of the city.

Through this Phoenician trade, the cult of the god of incense altars came early to Malta, Sicily, and Sardinia, and from there extended all over the world. Thus the lord of the incense altars became the predecessor of the Erzgebirge smoking men! A god under whose all-knowing eye smoking substances as important as myrrh and incense became very important at Christmastime.

Saturn's Plants

> *Astrologically speaking, the herbs of Saturn are all the plants that*
> *come under the reign of the planet Saturn. These are the following:*
> *hemlock, hellebore, mandrake, savin tree, nightshade and so*
> *on—and henbane is the most important of all.*
>
> SCHIERING 1927

In antiquity, many plants were dedicated to gods and goddesses. By association with particular gods, these plants also were connected with their planets and stars.

Occult botany defines the plants of Saturn according to their astrological signature:

The plants that carry Saturn's signature grow very slowly. They are heavy, sticky, and draw together. They have a bitter, sharp, or acid taste. These plants produce fruits without blossoms; they often carry black berries. Their smell is strong, even penetrating, and they often look gloomy and spooky. They contain a lot of resin, have a numbing effect, and are connected with death and the ceremonies of mourning (Belledame 1990, 25f).

During the Roman Saturnalia, the people hung holly as the ritual evergreen. According to the famous English doctor and astrologer Nicolas Culpeper (1616–1645), holly is a Saturnian tree; Saturn influences its evergreen power. Other plants associated with Saturn included the olive tree, bindweed (Father Christmas beards), European wild ginger, mistletoe, rye *(Secale cornutum)*, and horsetail (little Christmas tree).

Many incense plants in contemporary Christmas ethnobotany have been associated with Saturn since antiquity: fir, spruce, pine, yew, cypress, cedar, costus, storax (or styrax), male fern, common fumitory, European wild ginger, henbane, rue, asafetida, valerian root, hemp, hellebore, mandrake, opium, sage, nightshade, aconite, belladonna, hemlock, and ivy. Because the planet and the god Saturn (the guardian of the threshold) are associated with all psychoactive plants (for example, mandrake, henbane, hemp, and aconite), one can presume that his alchemical elixirs can also have spirit-moving effects.

Many Saturn plants have reputations as aphrodisiacs: "Saturn and Venus together make a big tree come out" (Belledame 1990, 31). Thus, the use of Saturn plants seems to result in the same kind of wild goings-on that happened during the Saturnalia.

The Erotic Bean Feast

In the seventeenth century, bean soup had a reputation so erotic that it was forbidden in the convent of San Jeronimo in order to prevent conditions that might result in indecent arousal. But that order no longer stands, since the nuns gave up their habit.

ALLENDE 1998, 197

Phaesolus vulgaris L., Fabaceae (garden bean)

Beans, also influenced by Saturn, played an important role in the Saturnalia and other ecstatic mystery cults and celebrations in old Rome. Beans are ancient cultured plants from legume family (Fabaceae). An ancient form of bean known in old Rome was called "the erotic chick pea" (*Cicer* spp.): "The religious cult uses it after festivals" (Pliny the Elder XVIII, 32). Most types of beans eaten today are from the New World, especially tropical Mexico—home of many other plants important in the ethnobotany of Christmas.

The Bean Feast by Jakob Jordaens. During the bean feast, the people elected a ritual master called the bean king: "On the last smudging night (December 6) a cake was baked in which a single bean was hidden. Whoever got the bean became the bean king. He directed a big drinking feast and led the singing of obscene songs" (Aigremont 1987 I, 123).

In German mythology, there is a suspicion about the pea (similar to the bean) in regard to the cultic meal of the elben [fairies connected to the Elbe River], which they eat in the twelve smudging nights. You were not supposed to eat it; if you did, you got skin spots, or you were spellbound by the elben. This is why you must catch the wild women with beautiful long hair who entrance young boys in the pea field. Peas are used in German love magic; if placed behind a door, a pod containing nine (!) peas will make the next person that enters the room say one's bridegroom's name aloud. . . . The pea belonged to Donar, the god of marriage. It makes things fertile and brings blessings. . . . Peas were also thrown to the animals in the stalls on Christmas night to make them fertile (Aigremont 1987 I, 125f).

In old Germany, the January feast grew out of the concept of the Roman Saturnalia. It was a time to celebrate the awakening of the Earth from its winter sleep. Because the bean was the center of ritual attention as a fertility symbol, the German folk vernacular called this feast—with its sexually excessive orgies and Saturnalian drinking and eating—the "bean feast."* The bean clearly had a sexual connotation: "On *Walpurgisnacht*, at Blocksberg, the lover presented his beloved with a bean blessed by incantations of the helper spirits. In later Christian traditions, these spirits were demonized as devilish sexual partners for the lover and the beloved. Because of its testicular shape, the bean holds the

*The Roman *Fabriae* (bean feasts) took place in June. In celebration of the summer solstice, the people offered fresh beans to the gods.

The Bean Feast: January 6

"The symbolic meaning of the reawakening of nature was expressed in the medieval January feast that developed from the Roman Saturnalia. Just as in Rome, in Germany, the Netherlands, and France, this led not only to big drinking and eating feasts, but also to sexual orgies. This was called the bean feast in the vernacular, because the bean was considered a sexual symbol in all of the Germanic tribes" (Bornemann 1974, I).

power of life. In the folk language, 'bean soup' is a description of male semen" (Hirschfeld and Linsert 1930, 192).

What made beans so important in this context? The fact that they were considered a fertility symbol during the Saturnalia, or that they have served as a symbol of the testicles and of the power of life since antiquity? Or perhaps it is simply that throughout the world, beans are considered one of the most important sources of protein in the plant kingdom. In the mythology of Christmas, beans were considered a divine food and sacrificial offering, as they were the favorite meal of the demons of the smudging nights: "In German belief, it was forbidden to eat beans or peas during the twelve smudging nights because, at this time, the souls that have joined the wild army over the earth have first claim on any food that comes along" (Seligmann 1996, 77).

To this day in Germany, during children's birthday parties, a bean king is crowned. A hard, dried bean or pea is baked in the birthday cake. Whoever bites into it is celebrated as the bean king. Little does the child know that he or she represents the sun god Apollo's chosen one!

NEW YEAR'S EVE: THE WILD FEAST OF SYLVESTER

Profound and magical charm that gets us drunk
In the present on the restored past!
Like the lover from an adored body
Culls the exquisite flower of memory.

BAUDELAIRE 1857, *THE FLOWERS OF EVIL*

When talking about Sylvester or New Year's Eve, who doesn't think of wild parties, drinking feats, and a big headache afterwards?

According to the etymological dictionary, the name Sylvester goes back to Pope Sylvester I (314–335), who became a Catholic saint whose day fell on December 31. The word sylvan comes from the Latin and means "wooded, wood, or wilderness." The etymological dictionary is no more specific than this. But we know that Sylvester is also a god of the forest, who later became "the strange old man of the woods"—the *waldschrat*. After the long road to Catholic sainthood, the word came back to its origins. Sylvester is a wild feast day that falls on the furthest border of the year's cycle.

Protection and Fertility Rites

The smudging and incense rituals of the smudging nights marked the completion of the cycle of the year. On Sylvester the juniper twigs that had been collected at the beginning of the year were burned to protect the house and the court. The people cut fresh elder (*Sambucus* spp.), braided it into the shape of a wheel, and put it in the house as a traditional protection against fire. To protect the animals on Christmas and on the night of Sylvester, they smudged the stalls with wormwood *(Artemisia absinthium)*. "In Frankonia, on Christmas and Sylvester night, you take a handful of different varieties of corn and mix it in a baking bowl with clover. And then you give it to the animals, in order to ward off witches" (Seligmann 1996, 152). Horses were fed stolen cabbage *(Brassica oleraceae)* to keep them in good health during the coming year. In order to make fruit trees fertile, the people beat them with little sacks of peas on Sylvester.

People also believed that wild pears could protect against death (*Pyrus pyraster*, called dragontree in the Lausitz region): "Right at midnight, if you put a broth made of the fruit on the threshold, then death would not enter the house that year" (Seligmann 1996, 75). Common speedwell *(Veronica officinalis)* served a special protection and healing function. Vernacular names for

Like a *Hagedize* (hedge rider=witch) among the rose hips, the baby Jesus is perched between Christmas worlds.

Red rose hips *(Rosa canina)* were dedicated to Freia or Holda. They also played a role in a practical joke for Sylvester, in which children put rose hip seeds inside people's shirts as a sort of itching powder.

this plant include Sylvester flower, *maennertreu* (faithfulness of men), and *allerweltshei* (world healer). These names illustrate the folk belief that on Sylvester, love magic makes men become faithful, and this brings about a healing of the whole world.

Rose hips are a good remedy against accidents and maladies of the coming year if you eat three (while sober!) on Christmas Eve, Boxing Day (St. Stephen's Day), and New Year's Eve—and especially on New Year's Day. The people were supposed to pass the three rose hips through a window without saying a word. These three rose hips had a reputation for providing protection, especially against sore throats, pains in the side and stomach, gout, and erysipelas. A decoction of pulverized rose hips collected on Christmas Eve was supposed to help with kidney stones and other such problems in the kidneys, the gall bladder, and other organs (Hiller 1989, 113).

The meals prepared on this special day were not only for purposes of nourishment, but also for future happiness and good fortune. To be blessed with luck and money, one had to eat millet gruel. Other lucky foods included fish, carrots, and lentils:

Whoever eats a scaly fish during Sylvester will make enough money the following year. And this was also the case if you had carrots, or a lentil meal on the table. . . . A hemp cord should not be left dangling during the Sylvester night, because sorrow could come through it into the New Year (Hiller 1989, 265).

One could learn just how much and what kind of sorrow would cross over into the New Year from plant oracles: "During Sylvester night, you put an evergreen leaf of *Vinca minor* on a plate filled with water. If it remained green the following night, health could be expected the following year. But stains prophesied illnesses—and blackness, death itself" (Hiller 1989, 140).

Lucky Plants

In the last days of December, the plants that show up in the flower shops and supermarkets remind us of old rituals that, for the inhabitants of the house, serve to keep good luck going for the coming year. These include little pots or miniature beds of hyacinth, anemones, four-leaf clover, winter aconite, and

Sylvester Punch

This northern German recipe consists of five ingredients. (Vossen 1985, 141) (The word punch has roots in the Hindi *panc,* meaning "five.")

Arrak (rice brandy or corn schnapps)

Sugar

Lemon juice

Water or tea

Spices (cloves, cinnamon, cardamom, nutmeg, saffron)

"Punch made from hot water, sugar, lemon juice, and arrak, or made from wine, water, sugar, lemon juice, and good Jamaica rum, served hot, and drunk in two or four glass rations, is a great way to warm up, and feel alive again, and even to produce sweat" (Most 1843, 513f).

similar fast-growing and symbolic plants. These little plantings grown for Sylvester go all the way back to the ritual gardens of Adonis.

Adonis, a beautiful young god of oriental and Phoenician descent, was a lover of Aphrodite. During ancient feasts of Adonis, the people grew anemones and Adonis roses in the famous Adonis gardens to commemorate Aphrodite's famous lover. These gardens were, in fact, clay pots filled with earth. Without being conscious of it today, we are worshipping the sacred plants of Adonis every time we carry home a Sylvester pot and water it thoroughly. The fast-growing, fast-flowering, and fast-withering plants show us how life renews itself, but also demonstrate the vanity of life—just as our Sylvester pots and beds do today.

Anemones *(Anemone* spp.) and the Adonis rose *(Adonis vernalis)* were often confused with one another in the past and have been used in the same fashion. Both are members of the buttercup family (Ranunculaceae) and are associated with Aphrodite and the youthful Adonis, "the one who nourishes flowers." The Adonis rose is also generally associated with fast-withering youth.* The genus name *Anemone* comes from the Greek *anemos,* meaning "wind." In antiquity, it was believed that the wind had a love affair with this plant; in truth, the blowing wind fertilizes the plant. Thus the plant goes by the folk name windflower.

The wild anemone *(Anemone coronaria)* has blood red petal leaves and reminds us in appearance of a red-blooming opium poppy *(Papaver somniferum)* or field poppy *(Papaver rhoeas).* It was believed to have grown from the blood of Adonis, the youthful lover of Aphrodite. While the love goddess was flying through the air in her swan wagon, Adonis was hurt by a boar in a dangerous chase. When the goddess came back to Cyprus, she could talk only to her dying lover:

*The Adonis rose *(Adonis vernalis)* is also called by the folk names Bohemian hellebore (Schoen 1963, 51), spring Adonis, pheasant's eye (Ahrends 1935, 55), and devil's eye.

New Year's Eve

Luck times three: A Sylvester pot in the form of a fly agaric mushroom, containing four-leaf clover and guarded by a chimney sweep. (Germany, 1999)

"The memory of my mourning will go on forever, Adonis, and a festive commemoration of your death will be an annual part of my mourning of you. Your blood will become a flower. . . ." After these words, she put scented nectar on the blood; touched by it, it rose, and from the brown mud air was coming up. It did not take longer than an hour before the blood was a flower, red like a pomegranate that hides its seeds under the hard peel. But you can only enjoy the flower for a short instance, because it is very tender and it falls down when the wind touches it, and the winds that gave her the name (animus) carry it away (Ovid, *Metamorphoses* X, 724ff).*

In ancient mythology, the hyacinth *(Hyacinthus orientalis)* grew from the dead body of a king's son who was beloved by the sun god Apollo. The god gave life to his ashes, but in the form of the beautiful hyacinth, with its alluring, aphrodisiac scent.

Winter aconite *(Eranthis hyemalis)* is a typical Christmas decoration in North America, even though it contains very poisonous chemicals known as cardiac glycosides. From December to March, it puts forth yellow blossoms, like little suns, that sit between bright green leaves. With its miraculous flowers, this floral New Year's gift brings new light and new life to the house.

*Even though the anemone seems to have been established as the flower described here, it is also possible that it is the poppy.

New Year's Eve

162

HAPPY NEW YEAR

Every year returns to the origins of time in its beginning;
it is a repetition of cosmogony.

ELIADE 1966, 49

At twelve o'clock midnight on December 31, the witching hour arrives and the new year begins. There is something magical about the moment in which one year passes and the next begins. Traditionally, we make a toast to the New Year with sparkling wine or champagne; we toast and wish one another good luck and good health.* We embrace and kiss our beloved, and we toast and hope for future luck in love. Then follow the resolutions—made mostly in vain—for the new year.

Thunder and Witch Flour

With the explosions and the beating of the whip, bad spirits that could
disturb the New Year were driven away. And the air was heated up over
the cornfields and the fruit trees in order to awaken their fertility . . .

HILLER 1989, 205F

There seems to be something of the homeopathic concept "like cures like" in the way magic works: One can defeat or protect against illness or evil by using something similar in defense. Thus, the best way to be safe from lightning is to create artificial lightning, and fireworks make this possible in multiple colors. In the old days, people called upon plants for this purpose. To be more precise, they used plants to make a powder variously called witch, thunder, or lightning powder or flour. This produced dramatic natural fireworks that could be used for a number of purposes.

Called "thunder and witch lightning" in earlier times, the Sylvester (New Year's Eve) fireworks explode with bright lights on the winter sky, driving out the demons of the old year and clearing the way for the new. In early times, the lights and noise of the fireworks was considered protection and a way to drive bad weather away from house and court. Today, we feel safe against thunder and lightning because we have lightning rods on the roof; only animals hide when they hear the unexpected noise.

The use of fireworks to welcome the new year goes back to Stone Age shamanism. As they tended the fire, Paleolithic shamans must have noticed that certain nonflowering plants exploded on the flames with bright lights and a sudden noise, producing a dramatic, theatrical effect and a natural magic.[†] To this day, lightning powder or witch flour is the folk name for the thick, yellow, fluid

*The German toast, *prosit*, is Latin (the third person singular, present tense, conjunctive, active form of *prodesse*) and means: "to be good for something, to be handy." This toast has been in use since the beginning of the eighteenth century. The Germanized Latin came from university student vernacular.

†"The Stone Age magician used this dramatic effect as much as the theatre directors of past centuries" (Müller-Ebeling et al. 1998, 20).

163

spore powder produced by the running clubmoss (*Lycopodium clavatum*):

> . . . A part of the powder is blown into the open flame, and there it burns quickly in the form of a very bright sparkling without any trace of smoke. This intense explosion of the burning lightning, like rapid combustion, is so astonishing that you find you can't keep from burning little doses of the powder. In such peacefulness and such a heat, it feels so easy to just slip away into the fire—into such a bright light! (Schenk 1960, 67).

Stag horn clubmoss *(Lycopodium clavatum),* a shamanic "bear plant," is also an old magic substance of the Celtic druids. It is known in the vernacular as black henbane, devil's claw, *Erdschwefel,* selago, witches' herb, and wolf's claw. Names used for the clubmoss spores in folk medicine include *Alpenmoss,* devil's snuff, druid's moss, *Neunheilpulver, Waldstaub,* and witches' moss. The druids used this "flour" to create lightning on their altars, to the astonishment of their awestruck fellow humans. "The druids of the Gauls have said that this plant [the magic plant selago] should be carried around to ward off every evil, and that its smoke helps with eye injuries"* (Pliny the Elder XXVI, 103).

We now know that *Lycopodium* causes fireworks because it contains aluminum, which the plant absorbs from the soil. But until modern times, this aluminum-containing "witch flour" was considered a magical substance: "It brings luck, drives witches away, makes you attractive to the ladies, makes you invisible and, all in all, gives the carrier superhuman attributes" (Schenk 1960, 68). What more could you want?

Teacher Laempel is the victim of Max and Moritz's joke. They put not baccy or tobacco in his pipe, but a mixture of exploding powder made from coal, sulfur, and saltpeter. (Wilhelm Busch, *Max und Moritz,* 1865)

*"In Irish folk medicine, the yellow golden spore powder was heated and the smoke was wafted into inflamed eyes" (Storl 2000b, 243).

From Incense to Fireworks

The Sylvester explosions woke up the seeds of the plants. Bad spirits were driven out by shooting over the wells.

FRUEH 2000, 49

It is possible that the use of noise-making substances on Sylvester's Eve originated with ingredients used to burn incense. Even in the past, people knew that incense-smoking coals burned better and glittered more when enriched with saltpeter. To ward off devils and witches, one was supposed to light the coal (using wood from the buckthorn, alder, linden, beech, or poplar) and then add sulfur. In the combination of saltpeter and sulfur, we have the basic ingredients for what was known as black powder.

Black powder was invented in 1200 CE in China. The Chinese used the substance to drive off demons, vultures, and devils. Black powder was rediscovered in fourteenth century Europe by the legendary monk and alchemist Berthold Schwarz.* Today, black powder is part of the ethnobotany of our Sylvester and New Year's Eve celebrations.

When fireworks go off, flames rise and sparks fly. This can easily result in a fire. Today, as in the past, special precautions are needed to prevent disaster. In earlier times, the father of the house made four piles of dirt (one for each direction the wind might blow) for use in putting out potential fires.

Lucky Mushrooms and Chimney Sweeps

Whoever is acquainted with the effects of fly agaric mushroom will understand how one might see ghosts during the winter solstice, or hear animals talk. Even today, the fly agaric mushroom, which can be smoked when dried, is considered a good luck charm for the coming year.

MADJESKY AND RIPPE 1997, 166

What makes the fly agaric mushroom *(Amanita muscaria)* the archetypical lucky mushroom? It is one of the most secret symbols of our modern world, omnipresent but still not understood. In German, a lottery winner is called "a lucky mushroom." Yet at the same time, the fly agaric mushroom is feared because of a belief that it contains a lethal poison. How did these contradictory connotations develop?

The German word *Glück* ("luck") leads us to the first clue. In the old Germanic language, Glück means "hail" and "to be blessed."

Luck can particularly be described as a very special condition of human consciousness. Luck belongs to the *form* of being. It is nothing of substance itself; it is not something you can physically own. A quest for luck

*In Freiburg im Breisgau, a town that goes back to the founding of the Alemannic dukes from Zaehringen, there is a monument that memorializes "black Berthold."

Happy New Year

165

is a search for the thing you hope will *make* you lucky, not luck itself. The search for luck is indeed always a search for the origin of luck (Hofmann 1997, 108).

Contrary to popular belief, the fly agaric mushroom is not a lethal poison. Strangely enough, it is the third most popular edible mushroom in the whole world. Eaten with knowledge and in small enough doses, it alters the sense of orientation, perception, and dreams. The fly agaric mushroom opens the door to other worlds—shamanic worlds—because it is an age-old shamanic substance. Since ancient times, it has given human beings hidden knowledge and happy insights into the mysteries of life.

And so, in Central Europe, the beautiful, white-spotted fly agaric mushroom is not only a lucky symbol, but also a doorway to the world of fairies, nymphs, dwarfs, and goblins.

Chimney Sweeps

After the fly agaric mushroom, the chimney sweep is the most important lucky charm for the new year. Popular since human beings invented chimneys, chimney sweep figures intended to ensure a happy new year are still frequently found in modern Sylvester pots. Other lucky symbols that may appear along with the chimney sweep include horseshoes, fly agaric mushrooms, and ladders (a representation of the shamanic ladder to heaven). Often, the chimney sweeps carry brooms, an attribute of St. Nicholas as well as witches.

Chimneys and open fires in the house are doors to the other world. These

Chimney-Sweep Plants

In German folk botany, the following plants are all called by the name *Schornsteinfeger* (chimney sweep). These chimney-sweep plants became symbols for the cleansing chimney broom because of their appearance.

Carex spp., Cyperaceae (sedge)

Equisetum arvense, Equisetaceae (horsetail)

Hemerocallis spp., Liliaceae (daylily hybrids)

Ilex aquifolium, Aquifoliaceae (holly)

Luzula campestris, Junacaceae (woodrush)

Plantago lanceolata, Plantaginaceae (plantain)

Polygonum bistorta, Polygonaceae (bistort)

Sanguisorba officinalis, Rosaceae (salad burnet)

Tragopogon pratensis, Asteraceae (salsify)

Typha latifolia, Typhaceae (cattail)

Plants with chimney-sweep-related names also include:

Iris germanica, Iridaceae, iris or orris (chimney-sweep flower)

Luzula campestris (chimney-sweep grass)

Typha latifolia (chimney-sweep cleaner)

Mushroom miracle in the winter forest. A chimney sweep harvests the lucky mushroom for Sylvester and the New Year. (Postcard, 1900)

"pipes of the house" are an alchemical distilling flask, a huge smoking pot. Thus the chimney sweep, a member of the "ritual cleaning staff," clears the way to the other world. He climbs into chimneys and, by cleaning them, takes away the darkness and makes a clear passage for the smoke. "Chimney sweeps are considered messengers of good luck, especially when you meet them first thing in the morning" (Hiller 1989, 148).

Chimney sweeps climb through the chimney just like ancestor spirits, witches, sorcerers, shamans, Befana (the Christmas witch), St. Nicholas, and Santa Claus. They are all considered a connection between heaven and Earth. The chimney sweep, with a fly agaric mushroom in his hands, may be another of the many forms of Father Christmas.

Happy New Year

Left: Many people wrongly fear the fly agaric mushroom, believing it is poisonous. At the same time, it is widely treasured as a lucky mushroom. In Europe, huge fly agaric mushroom fireworks (*tischfeuerwerk*, or "table bomb" fireworks) are burned as a lucky symbol for Sylvester and the new year.

Right: New Year's day is the day of the lucky mushroom. (Illustration by Martina Schoenenberger, *Lucky Collector*, postcard, 2001)

---

*"Laurel will protect everything born of the earth from being struck by lightening" (Pliny the Elder II, 146).

Happy New Year

New Year's Day

Whoever is last to finish his meal on New Year's Day will be too late to get into heaven.

OLD SAYING

New Year's Day calls for a great deal of attention to detail. There are rules for meals, incense-burning, gift-giving, and treating hangovers, all to ensure that the new year is cleansed of whatever may be left over from the old year, like a chimney swept clean of last year's cinders.

To protect the house at this important time, people decorated with evergreen wreaths and aromatic herbs. The Romans put laurel branches on their doors at dawn to ward off evil spirits.* For the same reason, Germanic peoples put mugwort on the roof on New Year's Day. "Sown on New Year's Day along the whole courtyard and mixed with flax and salt, dill was supposed to be a protection for the whole year against evil spirits and haunting" (Abraham and Thinnes 1995, 50). Hangovers and heartburn could be cured with gingerbread leftover from Christmas, which was put into brandy and lit on fire before being consumed. It was important to eat this on an empty stomach.

Who were the evil spirits from whom the people needed protection? The *Encyclopedia of Antiquity and Christianity* gives the following explanation:

The totally negative connotation of demons (and, to a lesser degree, of spirits) as destroyers and enemies of humanity started when Christianity damned and downgraded the pagan gods and beings that may have been called spirits or demons in a neutral, good, or ambivalent way (Stuttgart 1976, 546).

"On the first of January, the Romans sent New Year gifts to each other, which were supposed to bring good luck throughout the year. Baked goods were among these presents" (Seligmann 1996, 45). Numerous recommendations and warnings were made about the brewing of drinks and preparation of food for New Year's Day. The consumption of nettle cake, beer, and carrots was supposed to bring money and good health. Apples, on the other hand, were not to be eaten because they caused tumors (von Perger 1864, 202; Hiller 1989, 206f). It was also believed that one could prevent illnesses of the skin by eating a dish of peas on New Year's Day. In yet another custom, you were protected from fever when you ate pea soup on New Year's, but if you did not, you had reason to fear worse illness (Hiller 1989, 63).

In the Catholic Church, January 1 is the day of the circumcision of Jesus, eight days after his birth.

Magical, Shamanic Clover

Four-leaf clover is believed to bring luck and was considered a love magic: It was even supposed to make anyone who possessed it clairvoyant. Whoever found a four-leaf clover at midnight could expect a big inheritance. A four-leaf clover in the house was supposed to ward off lightning.

HILLER 1989, 156

Trifolium pratense L., Fabaceae (red clover)
T. repens L., Fabaceae (white clover)
Oxalis spp. L., Oxalidaceae (wood sorrel, lucky clover)

Lucky four-leaf clover leaves are a famous motif on good luck postcards for the New Year. But the only clover that offers protection against witchcraft is the four-leaf clover that occasionally can be found among white clover or red clover *(Trifolium repens* or *T. pratense)*, which normally have only three leaves.

The druids were supposed to have worshipped the clover *(Trifolium pratense)* because of its three leaves. In the early period of Christianity, it was the symbol of the holy trinity, and in Ireland it was considered the national symbol—St. Patrick gave it this meaning. It wards off magic spells and devil's tricks and strengthens weapons. A four-leaf clover is considered a lucky sign and this is why it is stuck on the traveler's clothes without their knowledge (von Perger 1864, 195f).

Around 1440 CE, Johannes Hartlieb wrote about clover *(Trifolium* spp.), especially the four-leaf form, in his *Herb Book:* "The masters of necromancy use the same. Other sorcerers make a great art with it that is not a decent thing to write about for this book." In this writing, he alludes to but does not tell

Happy New Year

The magic clover *(Trifolium)* in Johannes Hartlieb's *Herb Book* (circa 1440, 99v).

* "We may not seek the principle of such great (magical) operations outside of us; there is a spirit living in us that can well do whatever unbelievable and wonderful things mathematics, magicians, alchemists, and necromancers are capable of doing," writes Agrippa von Nettesheim (von Nettesheim, XXIX, 14th century).

† "Magic taught for the purposes of making poison," according to Johannes Praetorius (1630–1680) (Praetorius 1688, 50).

Happy New Year

us the most important information, which is subsequently pointed out by the editors of the *Herb Book:* "A residual belief in old pagan gods can clearly be seen here and is in contradiction to the Christian view" (Werneck and Speta, 1980).

The "masters of necromancy" (black magic) were sorcerers, magicians, and conjurers of the dead—in short, black magicians. The legendary Dr. Johannes Faust, who died in 1539, was called a "strange *Nigromanta*" (black magician).* *Nigrumencia* is one of the many spellings of necromancy and means "black fortune telling" or "sorcery."† *Nigromantie*, a new word of the Middle Ages, was coined by Isidor, Archbishop of Seville (circa 560–636 CE); *Nekromantie* implied fortune-telling by means of conjuring the dead. According to Hartlieb, sorcerers used a magic ointment called *Unguentum pharelis* for "exiting" or "driving out" (Hartlieb, Chapter 32). This is the legendary witch flying ointment, the medium of shamanic travel.

> Especially *because* he described these remedies of the "ridiculed arts, magic and unbelief" in such detail—even if he does not encourage their use—he became the one who handed down the old folk customs; which in their original meaning, free of all the later additions, is the Celtic and Germanic knowledge in the pre-Christian belief of both peoples (Werneck and Septa 1980, 61f).

Associations of the magic clover with sorcery, traveling, and flying recall numerous myths that commemorate shamanic initiation, from both the Old and the New Worlds: myths of the shamanic consecration of the wanderer, the world wanderer, the bestowal of magic abilities by immortal deities, and the visionary bird flight. Here too are the stories of Wotan who seeks knowledge, the love-hungry Tannhäuser, and the somnambulant dreamer.

Oxalis, commonly known as wood sorrel or sour grass, is another plant that is sometimes called "lucky clover." Like many other plants that have come to fame as part of the ethnobotany of Christmas, the ornamental lucky clover *Oxalis tetraphylla* is originally from Mexico. In Aztec, it is called *xocoyoli*, "sour nut." The root is edible; all other parts contain oxalic acid. It was first described in the fifteenth century by Bernardino de Sahagun, a Spanish missionary, who wrote that it was a cure for inflammation.

Happy New Year

THE NIGHT OF BEFANA, THE CHRISTMAS WITCH

Lieve Baeten

Die kleine Hexe feiert Weihnachten

Oetinger

The Little Witch Celebrates Christmas. Children's book. (Baeten 1996)

See, there she comes, Befana
Over rocks, mountains and valleys
Rain, snow and hail
Make her voyage painful
But she still comes.

See, there she comes, Befana,
Poor thing, with her arms crossed before her breast
Covered with a coat of snow
Frost protects her like a shield
Her voice is the wind
When she comes around the corners.

Befana feels and sees
When human beings suffer:
Is a house without bread?
Is a child ill and near to death?
Is a family suffering?
She helps without anyone seeing it.

Italian folk song (from Kleinau 2002, 222)

Christmas witches are familiar to European children. Operas such as *Hänsel and Gretel** by the German composer Englebert Humperdinck (1854–1921) serve as Christmas season entertainment, and books like *The Little Witch Celebrates Christmas* (Baeten 1996) are given as gifts under the Christmas tree. Witch houses made from gingerbread are an important part of Christmas baking. Why are witches so popular around Christmastime? The tradition likely comes from the Italian folk custom of Befana, the Christmas witch.

The name Befana (or Befania) comes from *Epiphanias* (epiphany), the feast commemorating the baptism of Christ, also known as Three Kings Day in some regions. In Italian folk custom, this became "the day the friendly witch goes from house to house," distributing presents the same way St. Nicholas does in Germany (Kleinau 2002, 233). In Italy, the long-nosed Befana—the three king witch or fairy—comes in through the chimney and fills the boots of good children with sweets, chestnuts, and other treats on the night of January 4. For bad children, Befana brings ashes, coal, and garlic. The night of Befana

*First staged under the direction of Richard Strauss on December 23, 1893.

A witch under the Christmas tree, wearing a fly agaric-patterned scarf and distributing her gift of golden apples. (Illustration by Wilhelm Petersen, *Mecki and the Seven Dwarfs* [Köln: Lingen Verlag, undated])

is Three Kings Night, which falls on the last of the smudging nights or twelve days of Christmas.

The Befana custom combines the tradition of helper Ruprecht with the ghost army of the smudging nights and the typical motifs of the European witch belief. Before the Christian church gave the three magi from the east a steady place in our calendar, in Germany the night of the sixth of January was the holy night of Berchta, North German goddess of winter and witchcraft. Berchta—also known as or associated with *Eisenberta* (Iron Berta), Frau Bert, Frau Holle, Mother Goose, and Perchta—belongs to the ghost army of the wild hunt that races through the clouds at the darkest time of the year.* During Berchta's journey through the clouds with her followers, she descends to Earth, where humans lay a table full of good food and drinks for her in the open air. In return, Berchta bestows her favors. Berchta, "the shining," brought so much light into the darkness that people were not only enlightened, they could also even be blinded. Thus it was important to protect oneself from direct eye contact with any supernatural power, as well as from the unwise use of fireworks.

Thus Befana is one of the spirits who haunt people in the smudging nights.

On the day of the three magi in the Colle Santa Lucia, all old brooms are collected and burned in a snow hole, and the people scream out: "Bread and wine, bread and soup and the hat of the witch on the chimney!" (Fink 1983, 151).

In Switzerland, *sträggele* (from the Italian *strega*, "witch") are among the winter demons. Folk custom includes the very gruesome belief that the *sträggele*

*Until the reform of the calendar in 1582, this time was counted as December 13 through December 25. December 13 was dedicated to the goddess of light, identified with the Christian St. Lucia. Today in Sweden, where there is no sunlight at this time of the year, Lucia brides wearing crowns of candles still play an important role during the Christmas season (December 12 through the night of January 6) (Vossen 1985, 59).

The Night of Befana, the Christmas Witch

"rob all bad children, and tear them to pieces in the air" (Lussi 1996, 60). Similarly, the Germanic Frau Faste "tears out [the] bowels" of lazybones to teach them a lesson (Riemerschmidt 1962, 118). It is easy to see the similarities between these witches and helper Ruprecht.

The wild celebration called the Perchten run,* still practiced in German-speaking regions, is associated with the protection and fertility rituals practiced during the smudging nights of old. During the Christmas season, people don dreadful masks and take to the streets with a great deal of noise and screaming in order to drive out infertile winter spirits.

To drive out the powers of darkness, the people lit massive straw wheels and rolled them down to the valley where, in the darkest days, they fertilize the icy ground with the light that plants need in order to grow.

Holy Bushes that Protect Against Witches

A hat or a scarf that has been smudged on Three
Kings Night helps prevent headaches.

FRÜH 2000, 62

*An exotic (but also purely erotic) interpretation: When Perchta is the birth lock, which is the hymen, the Perchten key is the penis. The Perchten run, then, is a symbolic intercourse.

Christmas Eve, New Year's Eve (Sylvester), and the eve of Epiphany (Berchten night, Befana night, or Twelfth Night)—the three most important eves of Christmastime—are all part of the smudging nights. In order to protect house and stables from the much-feared "butter-and-stable witch," the people performed smudgings with holy smoke. In southern Tirol, the following custom was still alive in 1983:

The Night of Befana,
the Christmas Witch

174

In Pfunders, even today, on all three smudging nights all rooms in the fire and food houses are smudged out by the farmers. On Christmas Eve, hats and scarves are held chest-high over the smoke; on New Year's Eve, head-high; and on Three Kings Eve, as high up as arms can reach—as high up as the wheat shall be on the fields in summer, this is the wish (Fink 1983, 35).

For this reason the house is smudged with holy herbs known as *Frauendreißiger* (literally "women-thirties")—a bunch of herbs collected between the time of Mary's ascension (August 15) and Mary's birth (September 8). These holy herb bunches are made up of seven, nine, thirty-three, or seventy-three herbs—the old pagan god and these so-called thirty flowers.

The following herbs are associated with the "women thirties":* hazelnut twigs (*Corylus* spp.), mullein (*Verbascum* spp.), witches' herb or enchanter's nightshade *(Circaea lutetiana)*, raspberry leaf *(Rubus* spp.), yarrow *(Achillea* spp.), wormwood *(Artemisia absinthium)*, St. John's wort *(Hypericum perforatum)*, European bird cherry *(Prunus padus)*, *mutterkraut* or feverfew *(Tanacetum parthenium)*, common corn cockle *(Agrostemma githago)*, valerian *(Valeriana officinalis)*, parsley *(Petroselinum crispum)*, plantain *(Plantago* spp.), primrose *(Primula* spp.), *Bettelabbiss (Clematis* spp. [?]), white sweet clover *(Melilotus alba)*, rue *(Ruta graveolens)*, *Vermeinkraut (?)*, *Toningkeaut (?)*, common toadflax *(Linaria vulgaris)*, *Schussmalte (?)*, horehound *(Marrubium vulgare)*, red clover *(Trifolium pratense)*, *Holzkraut* (Wolfsmilch [?]), vervain *(Verbena* spp.), paradise plant *(Daphne* spp.), chamomile *(Matricaria recutita* or *Chamaemelum nobile)*, and fumitory *(Fumaria officinalis)*. The most important rule in making the herb bunch was to take what you could get at this time of year.

Plantain *(Plantago major)* is an important plant among the thirty herbs, because it was also used in witches' incense. The plantain root had to be dug up with a tool made from a material other than iron. The root was incorporated in amulet necklaces according to magic numbers. People were supposed to put three, seven, nine, or ninety-nine roots in amulets around the neck in order to ward off worms, fevers, and evil spirits; to protect against love charms; or to win a lawsuit (Storl 1996b, 104).

Valerian (also called witches' herb, witch-smoking root, or cat herb) belonged in every thirty-herb bunch. In addition, it was used to make a "thirty powder" that served as an amulet to guard against lightning and contagious diseases.

A little sprig on the hat protects the wanderer during a night of evil and evil spirits. Valerian tea prolongs life and helps the visual power of the eyes. . . . In Villanders, valerian flowers are cut before the blessing and put in a scarf on the altar. On Three Kings Eve, the dried flowers were ground up and put on the glowing pan for smoking (Fink 1983, 73, 75).

Witch Smudge†

Make a mixture of:
  Garden rue *(Ruta graveolens)*
  Stonecrop *(Sedum acre)*
  Belladonna *(Atropa belladonna)*
  Chamomile *(Matricaria recutita* or *Chamaemelum nobile)*
  Plantain *(Plantago major)*
  Asafetida *(Ferula assafoetida)*
  Stinking juniper *(Juniperus sabina)*

---

†From Höfler 1994, 117.

---

*The plants with a question mark in parenthesis—(?)—are at this time not fully understood.

The Night of Befana, the Christmas Witch

With its green leaves and red fruit, the paradise plant *(Daphne mezereum)* is part of our Christmas ethnobotany. (Detail, plate XV from Dr. von Ahles, *Our Most Important Poisonous Plants,* 4th edition [Esslingen and Munich: F. Schreiber, circa 1875])

Paradise Plant

The paradise plant is said to be so strong that you can bind the devil's legs with it, and whoever decorates his horse with this herb is protected from a witches' curse.

FINK 1983, 80

Daphne mezereum L., Thymelaeaceae (daphne)

OTHER NAMES
Buschweide, daphne, *elendsbluem, gemeiner kellerhals, seidelbas,* spurge laurel

Of all the thirty herbs, paradise plant or daphne has perhaps the most complex relationship with Christmas and the smudging nights:

According to legend, the plant was once, long ago, a mighty tree. But when the cross of Christ was made from its wood, it degenerated more and more and became a lowly shrub (Prahn 1922, 157).

The poisonous paradise plant was very popular with witches: "With the rind, the mark, the seed of the paradise plant, and toads, a very strong poison was made for the Sabbath," explained the inquisitor Pierre de Lancre in the year 1612 (Fillipetti and Trotereau 1979, 41). Presumably, this is why paradise plant was called "deadly nightshade" in old Bohemia!

The botanical name of the plant goes back to the Greek *dáphne,* which originally meant laurel. Because the paradise plant (also sometimes known as wood laurel) looks a little like laurel and the name *Laurus* had already been given to the bay laurel, the poisonous plant was called *Daphne.* In earlier times, girls used the red fruit of the paradise plant as a beauty trick to make their cheeks red—instant Christmas cheeks! (Schenk 1943b, 106).

Devil's Dirt and Witches' Smoke

On the twelfth night or eve of epiphany, in Catholic areas of Germany, houses and stables were smudged with frankincense as a protection against witches and bad women.

SELIGMANN 1996, 285

Smudging with smoke is a magic practiced to protect against witches—but also to help witches or to summon them. Witches themselves smudge as part of their magic art. From the roof of the world to the Alps, from the Far East to the Baltic Sea, many recipes for witch smudges have been handed down to us. Witch smoke is an inheritance from shamanic culture that is still in practice, according to current ethnobotanical lore. "Witch smoke" is supposed to be an offering made in return for well being and magical protection. Often, the smudging incense is made from the very same substances that witches use for their witchcraft. So just as nine-herb bunches were an old Germanic magic and smoking substance for the smudging nights, it is the same substance the witches used to create their lightning magic. In this manner, the "nine herbs" are akin to the folk Christian "holy bush."

Asafetida is the resin of *Ferula assa-foetida,* a plant in the parsley family that is called food of the gods in English, *merde du diable* (devil's dung) in French, and *teufelsdreck* (devil's dirt) in German. "Just imagine that you are standing at the entrance to hell, and you will know how the devil's dung smells" (Wieshammer 1995, 97).

The smoke of pure asafetida is supposed to help cleanse and drive out impurities. This foul-smelling "devil's dirt" has been used as an aphrodisiac and is also used, in very small amounts, as a kitchen spice. "That we, on the continent, just as much as the English, take devil's dirt in spicy sauces, on mutton, etc., is known to every gourmet" (Most 1843, 580). Today asafetida is valued especially in the Indian kitchen and gives crispy *papadam* its characteristic aroma.

The combination of asafetida and black cumin seed *(Nigella sativa)* as a witch smudge or a basis for other smudge mixtures was very popular in Germany. The belief in the protective power of black cumin seed is ages old: "Black cumin seeds are in medicine for all illnesses but death," says an Arabic proverb. In earlier times, black cumin seed was often mixed with seeds of thorn apple *(Datura stramonium)* (von Chamisso 1987, 190).

[In Old Germany] A mixture of asafetida and stinking juniper *(Juniperus sabina)* combined with "blackstone oil" (Ol. Animale foet.) was used to "drive out witches" (Höfler 1994, 108). In Transylvania, on epiphany, people baked hemp pancakes to ward menacing witches away from the fire. Common juniper *(Juniperus communis)* was also popular for this purpose:

Witches' Smoke*

The following three smudging substances are called "witches' smoke" in the German vernacular:

Frankincense or olibanum *(Boswellia carteri)*

Asafetida *(Ferula assa-foetida)* and black seed *(Nigella sativa)*

Valerian root *(Valeriana officinalis)*

---

*From Arends 1935, 122.

The Night of Befana, the Christmas Witch

"Witch smoke." Devil's dirt or asafetida ground together with fenugreek and black cumin seed is used as a smudge against witches and the devil.

Smudge to Protect Against Witches*

Ingredients
4 parts devil's bit scabious *(Succisa pratensis)*
1 part asafetida *(Ferula assa-foetida)*
4 parts alpine leek *(Allium victorialis)*
½ part black cumin seed *(Nigella sativa)*

Thoroughly grind and mix the ingredients. Place the powder on the burning embers in small portions. Three knife points of the powder should be swallowed (Söhns 1920, 45).

---

*From Mecklenburg, Germany

. . . the smoke of juniper "drives out snakes and any other poisonous things . . . and purifies the air of evil foul pests." . . . When the farmer from the Alps goes through the house and stables with his smoking pan on the eve of epiphany to ward off evil spirits, the smoke has a purely magical meaning—and then, for the same reason, he writes the initials of the three magi on the doors (Nemec 1976, 90).

THREE KINGS DAY: THE END OF THE CHRISTMAS SEASON

Because the New Year repeats the cosmogonic act, even today, the twelve days that separate Christmas from epiphany can be considered a prefiguration of the twelve months of the year.

ELIADE 1966, 57

The smudging nights end with Three Kings Day, which signals the end of the Christmas season. The children may now plunder the Christmas tree. Now is also the time of epiphany, the holy day with which the Befana custom is associated. "The Almighty wakes bodies and souls on the day of epiphany" (Ephraim the Syrian, *Hymn*, I, 1).

Depending on one's cultural background, January 6 is a Christian holiday celebrating the three kings, a pagan one honoring Befana or Frau Holle, or the birthday of the Greek god Dionysus. Dionysus is, above all, the god of vegetation, of all fruit trees, and especially of grapes. This is why he appears with a face covered with leaves on the capitals of Roman basilicas. His cult and his other names reflect the floral nature of his being: *Bakchos* (shoot), *Anthios* (blossom god; literally, holy flower), *Dendrites* (tree god), and *Kissos* (ivy god; literally, ivy). Many trees were holy to him, including the spruce, the oak, and the laurel. Of all the flowers, roses and lilies were most dear to him. In a sense, he is the godfather of the evergreen Christmas botany. "Dionysus is the god of a wonderful and enchanted world" (Merkelbach 1988, 109). "On the island of Andros . . . the people believe that in the temple of Dionysus a source of liquid with the taste of wine flows every *nonen* of January [January 5]: This day is called 'God's gift'" (Pliny the Elder II, 231).

In his work *Protreptikos*, the Church father Clement of Alexandria (140–215 CE) wrote that Dionysus's birthday was on January 6 and associated it with the birth of Jesus: "The birth of God

On epiphany (January 6), Dionysus, the ancient Greek god of ecstasy and the "age-old ram," was born. Here, the baby Dionysus, crowned with ivy and riding a ram, jumps over the threshold into reality and toasts the world. (Advertisement for Berlin Schultheiss brewery; tin plaque from twentieth-century Germany)

Schultheiss' Bock

happened with a lot of Dionysian wonders, such as the changing of water into wine" (Giani 1994, 123). It is no surprise then that "On Three Kings Day, as many stars as you can see through the chimney is the number of glasses of wine may you drink that night" (Früh 2000, 61). On the same day, the Christian feast of epiphany celebrates the event in which Jesus changed water into wine at a wedding.

The Pagan Magi from the East

Age-old magic! Practiced for thousands of years by priests and kings all over the world, you raise the human being up to a higher consciousness, and you make him live up to your age-old picture, and teach him to see the hidden things in his life!

ROVESTI 1995, 80

In our calendar, January 6 has a solid place as the holiday of the three magi, commonly known as Three Kings Day. Even today, priests go from house to house in the Black Forest on January 6, smudging them for protection from evil influences. With chalk sanctified with blessed salt, they write the letters C., M., and B., plus the year, over house and stable doors. This magic formula is supposed to keep away witches and devils and ward off evil in order to protect the animals and the stored bounty brought in from the fields. The letters are the initials of the three magi: Caspar, Melchior, and Balthazar. Yet the original, often-forgotten meaning of the three letters is the Latin blessing *Christus mansionem benedicat* (may Christ bless this house) (Schilli 1968, 36).

Similarly forgotten is the cult of the three kings, who are celebrated as saints under the supervision of the Church only in Cologne. Apart from this city—with one exception—the cult has been acknowledged nowhere else. The exception is Milan, Italy, where the relics of the three kings were kept in the Basilica of the Three Kings between the ninth and twelfth centuries. Later, Rainald von Dassel, Barbarossa's chancellor in the twelfth century, presented

It's a girl! A subtle parody of the three magi. (Christmas card, Germany, from around 1998)

Three Kings Day

180

the relics as a gift to Cologne. Ever since, the three kings have been worshipped there too.

The Christian worship of the holy three kings comes from the worship of the newborn king of the Jews. The three magi from the "land of the morning" not only followed the light of the star shining above the stable at Bethlehem, but the passage that describes the star in the Bible was inspired by the words of the Roman poet Pliny the Elder (23–79 CE): "There is also a white comet with a silver tail. And from such a glittering brightness that you can hardly bear to look at it, within is revealed the picture of a God in human form" (Pliny the Elder II, 90). The only part of the New Testament that mentions worship of the three magi is the book of Matthew, which was written about the same time as Pliny's work:*

> Now when Jesus was born in Bethlehem of Judea in the days of Herod the king, behold there came wise men from the east to Jerusalem, saying "Where is He that is born King of the Jews? For we have seen His star in the east, and are come to worship Him" (Matt. 2: 1–12).

Thus, the three magi played a role in the ethnobotany of the Christmas season in old Germany:

> In old folklore, wishing rods for the detection of gold, silver, and water are associated with the three magi. At the same time, one should remember to cut down branches of a white hazelnut with three cuts, in the name of the three magi. The cut must be made with an unused knife. The three branches are baptized with the names of the three magi, so success will come (Fink 1983, 317).

WHO WERE THE THREE KINGS?

Who were these far-traveled ones who brought presents for the newborn babe from the morning land of the east? Depending on the source and Bible translation, the three are variously called "kings," "wise men," or heathen "magi." The Greek word *magoi* means "astrologers." According to Greek sources from antiquity, the Persian priests under the ancient prophet Zoroaster (sixth century BCE), who came from the east, were called *magoi*.

"These wise ones from the east are priest-kings, noble Chaldeans; their knowledge of occult things includes astrology and can be defined as the 'wisdom of Solomon'"(Luck 1990, 387). Sicardus, Bishop of Cremona (circa 1215 CE), called them "mathematicians from the royal family of the Zoroaster." In the *Legenda Aurea*,[†] they were described as star-interpreters, philosophers, and magicians. From the perspective of his pagan contemporaries, Jesus himself was among those considered *magoi* (Graf 1996, 99).

The Persian priests of the sun god Mithras were called *magoi* as well. The

*Its time of creation was dated by biblical scholars from the eighth decade of the first century CE.

†*The Golden Legend*, a medieval book about the lives of the saints written by Jacobus de Voragine around 1260 CE.

Three Kings Day

181

The holy three kings bring Christmas beer to the manger of the baby Jesus. (Beer bottle)

meaning of this amounts to "those who are initiated in the rites of the worship service." Mithras said about himself, "I am a star that goes with you on its path and lights up the depth" (Giebel 1990, 210). Did the three magi see Mithras in the star of Bethlehem? Is the baby Jesus Mithras reborn?

The Church father Tertullian (circa 160–225 CE) was the first to call the three magi "kings." In his verdict, astrology was invented by fallen angels and should not be practiced by any Christian. Yet he also believed that the three wise men from the east were astrologers (Luck 1990, 390). From the severe perspective of the Church, this carried a touch of heathenism and explains the restraint of the Church with regard to worshipping the three magi.

Since the twelfth century, artistic renderings have associated the three kings with the three stages of life: Caspar represented childhood and youth, Melchior age, and Balthazar adulthood. In the thirteenth century, the three magi were connected with the three known continents of the world: Africa, Asia, and Europe, respectively. Caspar became a dark-skinned Moorish king. Thus, the three collectively embodied old and young and all races of humanity, legitimizing the worldwide worship of the newborn founder of a new religion.

The Gifts of the Three Magi

> Of myrrh [Hebrew mor] and aloe[wood] of cassia, your dress smells.
>
> PSALMS 45: 9

Boswellia sacra Flueckiger, Burseraceae (frankincense, olibanum)
Commiphora molmol Engl., Burseraceae (myrrh)
Commiphora myrrha (Nees) Engl., Burseraceae (myrrh)
Commiphora opobalsamum (L.) Engl., Burseraceae (Mecca myrrh)

The wise men from the east brought the "King of the Jews" three presents: frankincense, myrrh, and gold.* Caspar brought the myrrh; Melchior embodied "the light" of the orient (Asia) and bestowed frankincense; and Balthazar, "the lord of the treasure," gave the gold. Frankincense is for religion, myrrh for the art of healing, and gold for earthly power. We do not know which gift the baby Jesus grabbed for first, as the written sources and paintings are silent on this matter.

Frankincense and myrrh were among the most precious treasures of antiquity. Myrrh, the resin of the myrrh tree *(Commiphora molmol, C. myrrha)* was considered a miraculous substance and was used medicinally in many ways by ancient peoples. Its perfume and its healing effect were believed to prolong life beyond death, which is why the ancient Egyptians used it for embalming. Even today, it remains an ingredient in herbal medicines.

Frankincense or olibanum (Hebrew *levonah*, Arabic *luban*) is the name of the resin of the true frankincense tree, *Boswellia sacra*, a member of the plant family Burseraceae. The tree comes from Somalia and southern Arabia. The

*It is possible that the "gold" brought by the three magi was not the shining metal, but Mecca balm from *Commiphora opobalsamum*, a plant for which the Arabic word is written much like the Arabic word for gold, *dhb* (Sellar and Watt 1997, 32). "The balm is of royal nature" (Hildegard von Bingen, *Physica* I, 177).

Three Kings Day

resin, the most important incense substance of the Old World, is collected from cuts made in the bark of the tree.

All three of the royal presents are used as incense substances. To the present day, the incenses used in Catholic and Greek Orthodox churches are liturgical mixtures of frankincense, myrrh, and gold leaf. In honor of epiphany, the English King Edward I sacrificed gold, myrrh, and frankincense in his church—a gift from one king to another, so to speak. "Just like gold, frankincense and myrrh seem to have been symbolic of our inner need to communicate with the gods or with our higher self" (Sellar and Watt 1997, 142).

Gold,* myrrh, and frankincense (olibanum) have also been used as aphrodisiacs and love magic!

"When a person had the 'heavy need' for the first time" it helped to carry an amulet, a piece of paper on which the following Latin phrases were written:

Caspar sert myrrham, thus Melchior,
  Balthasar aurum
Haec tria qui secum portabit nomina
  regum
Solvitur a morbo Christi pietate caduco.[†]

Postcard for Three Kings Day. (Köpenicker Cartoon Gesellschaft, from around 2001)

We don't really know what "heavy need" refers to: melancholy or moral scruples, perhaps. However, whoever had been overcome by this need was supposed to carry around the amulet for protection.

SYMBOLIC ATTRIBUTES OF THE THREE KINGS

Name	Age	Origin	Gift	Interpretation
Caspar	Childhood and youth	Africa	Myrrh	Healer
Melchior	Old age	Asia	Frankincense	Priest
Balthazar	Midlife	Europe	Gold	Lord, king

*"Because the gold is made by the help of the sun and is related to it, it was also considered to have life-prolonging powers" (Hiller 1989, 102).

†"Caspar brought myrrh, Melchior frankincense, and Balthazar gold/ in the name of their royal reign/ they save the fallen through Christ's mercy."

Three Kings Day

Benzoin is a resin that has been used in many mixtures for the smudging nights, especially at the end, on Three Kings Day. This sweet resin, which smells a little like vanilla, is one of the most important shamanic and magic smoking substances of Southeast Asia. It comes from the benzoin tree *(Styrax benzoin).* "Benzoin is often used in erotic incense" (Rovesti 1995, 100).

Three Magi Smoking Substance

This mixture is known throughout Arabic and Islamic culture and serves as a basis for many holy and protective incense and smudging rituals.

> 2 parts frankincense *(Boswellia sacra)*
>
> 1 part myrrh *(Commiphora* spp.)
>
> 1 part Syrian rue seed *(Peganum harmala)*

Grind frankincense and myrrh and mix with the Syrian rue seed.* Place small amounts of the mixture on the burning embers. The perfume is very relaxing and has a warm, spicy, resinous quality.

Kings' Incense Recipes

Three Kings Incense

> 3 parts frankincense (olibanum)
>
> 2 parts myrrh
>
> 1 part storax
>
> 1 part cinnamon rind
>
> 1 part star anise

Grind frankincense, myrrh, cinnamon, and star anise in the mortar. Mix the powdered blend with the sticky storax and knead. Place in small amounts on the embers. The perfume spreads out slowly: sweet, warm, and spicy.

Three Kings Frankincense[†]

> 3 parts frankincense
>
> 2 parts myrrh
>
> 1 part benzoin
>
> 1 part mastic
>
> $\frac{1}{2}$ part cinnamon rind

Grind and mix all ingredients. Place by teaspoonfuls on the glowing coals. The smoke has a lovely aroma, composed of solemn frankincense, festive myrrh, warm benzoin, fresh mastic, and spicy cinnamon.

---

*In Afghanistan on New Year's Day, for a little money, children will do a smudge for you with Syrian rue seeds.

†From Fischer-Rizzi 2001, 144.

Frankincense, the Secret of Old Arabia

The smoke that comes from those frankincense containers [censers] that the celibate churchmen swing around not only helps with worship, but also helps arouse sexual feelings, because frankincense is an aphrodisiac. Is this why so many old ladies go to church?

Caravans of dreams once wandered through the desert sands, bringing precious goods and gifts. Punt, the legendary land of frankincense, may have been present-day Yemen, part of the penisula known as Arabia. Many hints carved into stone refer to the ancient frankincense trade. The "illustrated wall paper" of Bir Hima, in the southernmost part of Arabia, is among the oldest petroglyphs of humanity. There are pictures of shamanic hunting rituals, camels, and other fertility symbols, such as rams: "For around nine thousand years, the nomads, warlords, and caravan leaders left thousands and thousands of carvings: scenes from their lives, from their time, a huge encyclopedia of the natural and cultural history of Arabia" (George 2002, 39).

In antiquity, the most commonly used name for the southernmost part of the Arabian Peninsula was Arabia Felix. From this region

. . . come the treasures of Arabia . . . of this land with the name of "the lucky," and "the blessed." Its most important products were frankincense and myrrh;* and the latter comes also from the land of the troglodytes [cave people]. Frankincense comes only from Arabia, and even there it cannot be found everywhere. In the middle of Arabia live the Atramites [an

---

Incense from Sheba

3 parts frankincense, *Boswellia sacra*

2 parts myrrh, *Commiphora* spp.

2 parts aloewood (eagle wood), *Aquillaria agallocha*

1 part cassia, *Cinnamomum cassia*

1 part storax, *Styrax officinalis*

1 part cardamom, *Elettaria cardamomum*

Grind, mix, and pulverize the ingredients. Place small portions on the burning embers. It is important to grind the aloewood very finely. Otherwise, its special scent will not be apparent in this mixture.

This incense is also intended to perfume the body and the clothes. To do this, put the smoking pan on the floor and stand with legs wide apart above it. And just like that, you can be Queen of Sheba!

*Muslims consider myrrh sacred and believe that it comes from Mecca.

Three Kings Day

A nugget of olibanum (frankincense).

Arabic ethnic group], in a district of the Sabaeans, with the capital of their region, Sabota [=Sabbatha], high up on a mountain. From there it takes an eight-day journey to get to the place of frankincense, which is called Sariba, which means—in the interpretation of the Greeks—"secret" (Pliny the Elder II, 51f).

The Minoans, the Arabian neighbors of the Atramitans, claimed that they were descended from the Cretan king, Minos:

These people were the first of all to have traded in frankincense, and today they are still very important in the trade—which is why frankincense is also called "Mineaic." Apart from them, no Arab recognizes the frankincense tree on sight; only three thousand families are supposed to know it. They have, one might say, the right formula for success in this area, but also an understanding of the special nature of their right to it. For they are considered holy, and are not supposed to dirty themselves (with women or funerals) during the time they are cutting down the trees or harvesting them. This insures that the "holiness" of the goods is even greater. Some say that the frankincense in the forests belongs to all the people; others say that they share it only once every year (Pliny the Elder II, 54).

Thus it seems that the *holy ones* were Minoans; they kept the secret of the lucky and blessed land. Maybe the three kings—or at least the one that brought the frankincense—were Minoans, also.

Frankincense for All!

. . . frankincense contains—like hashish—the substance tetrahydrocannabiol (THC).

HADERER 2002, 40

Many modern people assume that frankincense is just an old element of the Christian Church. But the use of frankincense began in late antiquity, with the Roman Emperor Flavius Valerius Constantinus I (Constantine the Great, 272–337 CE). This is same Constantinus who made Christianity the Roman state religion in the year 324–325 CE. No one should be surprised to learn that the most important incense substances of the Christian Church are identical to those used by the pagans. Indeed, frankincense and myrrh were very important pagan smoking substances. By state decree, they were Christianized—meaning that they were profaned for the pagans and sanctified for the Christians.

Church Incense

Adapted from Frerichs et al. 1938 II, 307

Ingredients
2 parts frankincense, *Olibani* (200 g)
3 parts storax, *Styracis calamit* (300 g)*
3 parts benzoin, *Benzoes* (300 g)
1 part amber, *Succini* (100 g)
2½ parts myrrh, *Myrrhae* (250 g)
1 part lavender blossoms, *Florum lavendulae* (100 g)†

Grind all ingredients finely and mix together well. Aromatic essences can be blended into the powder. Some churches use frankincense blended with essential oils of lavender, bergamot, cloves, and cinnamon.

---

*The storax (also sometimes called styrax) to which this recipe refers is a pressed byproduct of the winnowing process, which is used as an incense substance. The plant source of this storax is the oriental amber tree *(Liquidambar orientalis)* from Syria. Its resin contains 30 percent cinnamon oil, some cinnamon esters, 2 percent vanillin, sterols, and resin.

†"In the Alps, the lavender herb is very holy. It works against the devil, and can even save witches being pursued by the devil—they only need to sit on it! This is all an echo of pagan times" (Söhns 1920, 62).

The smoke of frankincense can cause pharmacological effects. Approximately two-thirds of its constituents are expressed unchanged in the smoke, and thus can be taken in directly through the mucous membranes when inhaled. From there, they circulate into the blood. The aroma of frankincense also may have a strong psychological impact. For some people, the scent may call up bad memories of childhood, images of dark and cold churches, or priests who prey upon the acolytes. Some may even draw an association with Christian morality and experience feelings of inhibition. For other people, however, this aroma can evoke passionate, fiery love; erotic feelings; and sensual joy. Thus for some, frankincense is an aphrodisiac, while for others, it has just the opposite effect. Everyone must follow his or her own nose!

Here ends our journey through the ethnobotany of Christmas. It has led us along twisting pathways to many unexpected and amazing discoveries. We have found that the ritual use of plants associated worldwide with the celebration of Christmas and the birth of Jesus Christ, actually has its roots in much older pagan traditions that celebrate the cycle of nature's fertility and the resurrection of the sun. Despite individual interpretations and belief systems, the message of these plants is clear: Let us trust in the never-ending cycle of life!

Three Kings Day

BIBLIOGRAPHY

Abraham, Hartwig, and Inge Thinnes. 1995. *Hexenkraut und Zaubertrank*. Greifenberg: Urs Freund.

Aigremont, Dr. (pseudonym). 1987. *Volkserotik und Pflanzenwelt*. Berlin: Express Edition. (Reprint of the volumes from 1907/1910 in one volume).

Alcorn, Janis B. 1984. *Hustaec Mayan Ethnobotany*. Austin: University of Texas Press.

Allegro, John M. 1971. *Der Geheimkult des heiligen Pilzes: Rauschgift als Ursprung unserer Religion*. Vienna: Molden.

———. 1977. *Lost Gods*. London: Michael Joseph.

———. 2000. Der heilige Pilz und das Christentum. In: *Der Fliegenpilz: Traumkult, Märchenzauber, Mythenrausch*. eds. Wolfgang Bauer et al. 31–45. Aarau: AT Verlag.

Allende, Isabel. 1998. *Aphrodite: Eine Feier der Sinne*. Reinbek: Rowohlt.

Andersen, Hans Christian. 1991. *Der Tannenbaum* [The Fir Tree]. Berlin: Der KinderBuchVerlag. (Orig. pub. 1845.)

Anderson, William. 1990. *Green Man: The Archetype of Our Oneness with the Earth*. London and San Francisco: Harper Collins.

Anisimov, A. F. 1991. *Kosmologische Vorstellungen der Völker Nordasiens*. Hamburg: Schletzer.

Anon., ed. 1989. *Der Fliegenpilz: Herkunft, Bedeutung und Anwendung*. Amsterdam: Gods Press. (Bootleg printing; a compilation of different offprints.)

Appleton, Tom. 2002. Der Schamane im Rentierschlitten. *Universum* 12: 52–56.

Arends, G. 1935. *Volkstümliche Namen der Arzneimittel, Drogen, Heilkräuter und Chemikalien*. 12th ed. Berlin: Julius Springer.

Arvigo, Rosita, and Nadine Epstein. 2001. *Die Maya Hausmedizin*. Munich: Integral.

Baeten, Lieve. 1996. *Die kleine Hexe feiert Weihnachten*. Hamburg: Verlag Friedrich Oetinger.

Balabanova, Svetlana. 1997. *Die Geschichte der Tabakpflanze vor Columbus außerhalb Amerikas sowie das Rauchen im Spiegel der Zeiten*. Seeheim-Jungenheim: Innovations-Verlags-Gesellschaft.

Baudelaire, Charles. 1993. *The Flowers of Evil*. James McGowen, trans. Oxford: Oxford University Press. (Orig. pub. 1857.)

Bauer, Wolfgang, Edzard Klapp, and Alexandra Rosenbohm. 2000. *Der Fliegenpilz: Traumkult, Märchenzauber, Mythenrausch*. Aarau: AT Verlag.

Becker, Hans, and Helga Schmoll. 1986. *Mistel: Arzneipflanze, Brauchtum, Kunstmotiv im Jugendstil* [Mistletoe: Medicinal Plant, Customs, and Art Motifs in Art Deco.] Stuttgart: Wissenschaftliche Verlagsgesellschaft.

Beckmann, Dieter, and Barbara Beckmann. 1990. *Alraune, Beifuß und andere. Hexenkräuter: Alltagswissen vergangener Zeiten*. Frankfurt/M. and New York: Campus.

Behr, Hans-Georg. 1995. *Von Hanf ist die Rede: Kultur und Politik einer Pflanze*. Rev. ed. Frankfurt/M.: Zweitausendeins.

Belledame, ed. 1990. *Die persönliche Magie der Pflanzen: Traditionelle Grundlagen der Aromatherapie*. Bad Münstereifel: Edition Tramontane.

Benet, Sula. 1975. Early diffusion and folk uses of hemp. In: *Cannabis and Culture*, ed. V. Rubin. 39–49. The Hague: Mouton.

Berendes, Julius. 1891. *Die Pharmacie bei den alten Culturvölkern*. Halle: Tausch & Grosse.

Berger, Markus. 2002a. Psychoaktive Gewürze. *Entheogene Blätter* 6: 4–13.

_____. 2002b. *Psychoaktive Kakteen: Mehr als 293 entheogene Kakteen-Arten aus 72 Gattungen*. Löhrbach: Edition Rauschkunde.

Bock, Hieronymus. 1577. *Kreütterbuch*. Strasbourg: Rihel.

Bornemann, Ernest. 1974. *Sex im Volksmund: Der obszöne Wortschatz der Deutsche*. 2 vols. Reinbek: Rowohlt.

_____. 1984. *Lexikon der Sexualität*. Herrsching: Pawlak.

Bourke, John Gregory. 1996. *Der Unrat in Sitte, Brauch, Glauben und Gewohnheitrecht der Völker*. Frankfurt/M.: Eichborn (Orig. pub. 1913.)

Braem, Harald. 1995. *Magische Riten und Kulte: das dunkle Europa*. Stuttgart and Vienna: Weitbrecht.

Brandon, Reiko Mochinaga, and Barbara B. Stephan. 1994. *Spirit and Symbol: The Japanese New Year*. Honolulu: Academy of Arts and University of Hawaii Press.

Bremness, Lesley. 1994. *Kräuter, Gewürze und Heilpflanzen*. Ravensburg: Ravensburger Buchverlag. (Orig. pub. in 1994 as an Eyewitness Handbook. *Herbs*. London: Dorland Kindersly.)

Bröckers, Mathias. 2002. *Cannabis*. Aarau: AT Verlag/Solothurn: Nachtschatten Verlag.

Brosse, Jacques. 1990. *Mythologie der Bäume*. Olten and Freiburg: Walter-Verlag.

Bruhn, Jan G. 1971. Carnegiea gigantea: The saguaro and its uses. *Economic Botany* 25(3): 320–329.

Brunken, Ulrike, et al. 2000. *Wo der Pfeffer wächst: Ein Festival der Kräuter und Gewürze*, Frankfurt/M.: Palmengarten (Sonderheft 32).

Brunfels, Otto. 1532. *Kreüterbuch*. Strasbourg: Schotten.

Caldecott, Moyra. 1993. *Myths of the Sacred Tree*. Rochester, Vt.: Destiny Books.

Callejo Cabo, Jesús. 2000. *Gnomos y otros espíritus masculinos de la naturaleza*. 6th ed. Madrid, México, and Buenos Aires: EDAF (Guía d los Seres mágicos de España).

Coe, Sophie, and Michael D. Coe. 1997. *Die wahre Geschichte der Schokolade*. Frankfurt/M.: S. Fischer.

Conte Corti, Egon. 1986. *Geschichte des Rauchens: "Die trockene Trunkenheit."* Frankfurt/M.: Insel. (Orig. pub. 1930.)

Cook, Roger. 1988. *The Tree of Life: Images of the Cosmos.* London: Thames and Hudson.

Cosack, Ralph. 1995. Die anspruchsvolle Droge: Erfahrungen mit dem Fliegenpilz. *Jahrbuch für Ethnomedizin und Bewusstseinsforschung* 3: 207–41.

Crumlin-Pedersen, Ole, and Birgitte Munch Thye. 1995. *The Ship as a Symbol— in Prehistoric and Medieval Scandinavia.* Copenhagen: National Museum. PNM Vol. 1.

Cunningham, Scott. 1983. *Magical Herbalism.* St. Paul, Minn.: Llewellyn Publications.

_____. 1989. *Cunningham's Encyclopedia of Magical Herbs.* St. Paul, Minn.: Llewellyn Publications.

Davis, Courtney. 2000. *A Treasury of Viking Design.* London: Constable.

Daxelmüller, Christoph. 1996. *Aberglaube, Hexenzauber, Höllenängste.* Munich: DTV.

de La Cruz, Martín. 1996. *Libellus de Medicinalibus Indorum Herbis*: *Manuscrito Aztec de 1552.* Fondo de Cultura Economica USA. (Orig. pub. 1552.)

de Milleville, René. 2002. *The Rhododendrons of Nepal.* Lalitpur: Himal Books.

Detienne, Marcel. 1994. *The Gardens of Adonis: Spices in Greek Mythology.* Princeton, N.J.: Princeton University Press.

Devereux, Paul. 2000. Schamanische Landschaften. In *Rituale des Heilens: Ethnomedizin, Naturerkenntnis und Heilkraft,* eds. Franz-Theo Gottwald and Christian Rätsch. 121–37. Aarau: AT Verlag.

de Vries, Herman. 1984. *Natural relations I—die marokkanische sammlung.* Nürnberg: Institut für moderne Kunst/Stuttgart: Galerie d+c mueller-roth.

Dieck, Alfred. 1993. Eine bronzezeitliche Schamanendarstellung aus Schweden. *Curare* 3/4: 189–90.

Dierbach, Johann Heinrich. 1833. Flora Mythologica oder Pflanzenkunde in Bezug auf Mythologie und Symbolik der Griechen und Römer, Schaan/ Liechtenstein: Sändig. (Reprinted in 1981.)

Dioscorides, Pedanios. 1610. *Kreutterbuch.* Frankfurt/M.: Conrad Corthons.

_____. 1902. *Arzneimittellehre.* Stuttgart: Enke.

Drury, Nevill. 1988. *Lexikon esoterischen Wissens.* Munich: Knaur.

_____. 1989. *Der Schamane und der Magier: Reisen zwischen den Welten.* Basel: Sphinx.

Dutchman, E. 1983. Weihnachtsbräuche aus alter und neuer Zeit. *Unicorn* 7: 188–91.

Ehlert, Trude. 1990. *Das Kochbuch des Mittelalters.* Zurich and Munich: Artemis.

Eliade, Mircea. 1957. *Das Heilige und das Profane: Vom Wesen des Religiösen.* Hamburg: Rowohlt.

_____. 1966. *Kosmos und Geschichte: Der Mythos der ewigen Wiederkehr.* Reinbek: Rowohlt.

Emboden, William A. 1974. *Bizarre Plants: Magical, Monstrous, Mythical.* New York: Macmillan.

Engel, Fritz-Martin. 1978. *Zauberpflanzen—Pflanzenzauber*. Hannover: Landbuch-Verlag.

Fabich, Fred. 1991. *Bauernmedizin*. Rosenheim: Rosenheimer Verlagshaus.

Fankhauser, Manfred. 2002. *Haschisch als Medikament: Zur Bedeutung von Cannabis sativa in der westlichen Medizin*. Liebefeld: SGGP/SSHP/Schweiz. Apothekerverein.

Faure, Paul. 1990. *Magie der Düfte: Eine Kulturgeschichte der Wohlgerüche von den Pharaonen zu den Römern*. Munich and Zurich: Artemis.

Feuersee, Hermann. 2001. *Der kulinarische Adventsbegleiter* [The Culinary Advent Companion]. 3rd ed. Munich: Piper.

Fillipetti, Hervé, und Janine Trotereau. 1979. *Zauber, Riten und Symbole: Magisches Brauchtum im Volksglauben*. Freiburg: Bauer.

Fink, Hans. 1980. *Südtiroler Küche, Tisch und Keller*. Bozen: Athesia.

_____. 1983. *Verzaubertes Land: Volkskult und Ahnenbrauch in Südtirol*. Innsbruck, Vienna: Tyrolia.

Fischer, L. 1917. Ein "Hexenrauch": Eine volkskundlich-liturgiegeschichtliche Studie. *Bayerische Hefte für Volkskunde* 4: 193–212.

Fischer-Rizzi, Susanne. 2000. *Gold in der Küche: Das Safrankochbuch*. Aarau: AT Verlag.

_____. 2001. *Botschaft an den Himmel: Anwendung, Wirkung und Geschichten von duftendem Räucherwerk*. Aarau: AT Verlag. (Orig. pub. Munich: Hugendubel, 1996.)

_____. 2002. *Himmlische Düfte: Aromatherapie*. Aarau: AT Verlag. (Orig. pub. Munich: Hugendubel, 1989.)

Flüeler, Niklas, and Sebastian Speich, eds. 1975. *Gold*. Luzern: Bucher.

Forstner, Dorothea. 1986. *Die Welt der christlichen Symbole*. 5th ed. Innsbruck, Vienna: Tyrolia-Verlag.

Frerichs, G., G. Arends, and H. Zörnig, eds. 1938. *Hagers Handbuch der pharmazeutischen Praxis*. Berlin: J. Springer. [Note: *Hagers Handbuch* receives annual updates.]

Fritz, Helmut. 1985. *Das Evangelium der Erfrischung: Coca-Colas Weltmission*. Reinbek: Rowohlt.

Frond, Brian, and Alan Lee. 1979. *Das große Buch der Geister*. Oldenburg and Munich: Stalling.

Fronty, Laura. 2002. *Paradies der Düfte*. Weil der Stadt: Hädecke.

Früh, Sigrid. 2000. Rauhnächte: Märchen, Brauchtum, Aberglaube (6th ed.). Waiblingen: Verlag Stendel. (Orig. pub. 1998.)

Fuchs, Eduard. 1909. *Illustrierte Sittengeschichte vom Mittelalter bis zur Gegenwart: Renaissance*. Munich: Albert Langen Verlag für Literatur und Kunst.

Fuchs, Leonhart. 1543. *New Kreüterbuch*. Basel: Michel Isingrin.

_____. 1545. *Laebliche abbildung und contrafaytung aller kreüter*. Basel: Michel Isingrin.

George, Uwe. 2002. Rub Al-Khali, Teil 2: Expedition durch Jahrtausende. *Geo* 12: 26–54.

Georgiades, Christos Ch. 1987. *Flowers of Cyprus. Plants of Medicine.* 2 vols. Nicosia: Cosmos Press.

Germer, Renate. 1985. *Flora des pharaonischen Ägypten.* Mainz: Philipp von Zabern.

_____. 1986. *Die Pflanzen des Alten Ägypten.* Berlin: Verlag Botanisches Museum.

Geschwinde, Thomas. 1996. *Rauschdrogen: Marktformen und Wirkungsweisen.* Berlin: Springer-Verlag.

Gessmann, Gustav W. 1922. *Die Pflanze im Zauberglauben und in der spagyrischen (okkulten) Heilkunst. Katechismus der Zauberbotanik mit einem Anhang über Pflanzensymbolik* (2., ergänzte und erweiterte Auflage). Berlin: Siegismund. O. J. Die Pflanze im Zauberglauben, The Hague: J. J. Couvreur (reprint).

Giani, Leo Maria. 1994. *In heiliger Leidenschaft: Mythen, Kulte und Mysterien.* Munich: Kösel.

Giebel, Marion. 1990. *Das Geheimnis der Mysterien: Antike Kulte in Griechenland, Rom und Ägypten.* Zurich, Munich: Artemis.

Gieschen, Jens Peter, and Klaus Meier. 1993. *Der Fall "Christkind": Juristisches Gutachten über die denkwürdigen Umstände von Zeugung und Geburt eines Glaubensstifters.* Frankfurt/M.: Eichborn.

Ginzburg, Carlo. 1980. *Die Benandanti: Feldkulte und Hexenwesen im 16. und 17. Jahrhundert.* Frankfurt/M.: Syndikat.

_____. 1990. *Hexensabbat: Entzifferung einer nächtlichen Geschichte.* Berlin: Wagenbach.

Glauser, Friedrich. 1989. *Wachtmeister Studer.* Zurich: Diogenes.

Golowin, Sergius. 1985. *Die Magie der verbotenen Märchen: Von Hexendrogen und Feenkräutern.* 5th ed. Gifkendorf: Merlin. (Orig. pub. Merlin Verlag, Hamburg, 1973.)

Golowin, Sergius, ed. 1982. *Kult und Brauch der Kräuterpfeife in Europa.* Allmendingen: Verlag der Melusine.

_____. 2003. *Von Elfenpfeifen und Hexenbier: Magie um unsere Genussmittel.* Solothurn: Nachtschatten Verlag.

Graf, Fritz. 1996. *Gottesnähe und Schadenzauber: Die Magie in der griechisch-römischen Antike.* Munich: Beck.

Grigson, Geoffrey. 1978. *Aphrodite: Göttin der Liebe.* Bergisch-Gladbach: Gustav Lübbe Verlag.

Grimm, Jakob. 1968. *Deutsche Mythologie* (Reprint of 4th ed., Berlin 1875–1878). [Graz: Akademische Druck- und Verlagsanstalt] Wiesbaden: Drei Lilien Edition (3 vols.).

Grönbech, Wilhelm. 1997. *Kultur und Religion der Germanen.* 12th ed. Darmstadt: Primus/WBG.

Guter, Josef, ed. 1978. *Märchen aus Sibirien.* Frankfurt/M.: Fischer.

Haderer, Gerhard. 2002. *Das Leben des Jesus.* Vienna: Ueberreuter.

Haid, Hans. 1992. *Mythos und Kult in den Alpen.* 2nd ed. Rosenheim: Rosenheimer.

Hartel, Klaus D. 1977. *Das Taschenbuch vom Schnupftabak*. Munich: Heyne.

Hartlieb, Johannes. 1973. *Kräuterbuch* [Herb Book]. Graz: ADEVA. (Orig. pub. 1440.)

Hartwich, Carl. 1911. *Die menschlichen Genussmittel*. Leipzig: Tauchnitz.

Haseneier, Martin. 1992. Der Kahlkopf und das kollektive Unbewusste. *Integration* 2/3: 5–38.

Hecker, Ulrich. 1995. *Bäume und Sträucher*. Munich: BLV.

Heinrich, Clark. 2002. *Magic Mushrooms in Religion and Alchemy*. Rochester, Vt.: Park Street Press.

Hepper, F. Nigel. 1969. Arabian and African frankincense trees. *Journal of Egyptian Archaeology* 55: 66–72.

_____. 1992 *Pflanzenwelt der Bibel*. Stuttgart: Deutsche Bibelgesellschaft.

Hiller, Helmut. 1989. *Lexikon des Aberglaubens: Alte Volksweisheiten und Bräuche*. Bergisch-Gladbach: Bastei-Lübbe.

Hinrichsen, Torkild. 1994. *Erzgebirge: Der Duft des Himmels*. Hamburg: Altonaer Museum.

Hirschfeld, Magnus, and Richard Linsert. 1930. *Liebesmittel: Eine Darstellung der geschlechtlichen Reizmittel (Aphrodisiaca)*. Berlin: Man Verlag.

Hodge, Carle. 1991. *All about saguaros*. Phoenix: Arizona Highways Books.

Höfler, Max. 1892. *Wald- und Baumkult in Beziehung zur Volksmedicin Oberbayerns*. Munich: Stahl.

_____. 1911. Volksmedizinische Botanik der Kelten. *Archiv für Geschichte der Medizin* 5(1/2): 1–35; 5(4/5): 241–279.

_____. 1990. *Volksmedizinische Botanik der Germanen*. Berlin: VWB. (Orig. pub. 1908.)

_____. 1994. *Volksmedizin und Aberglaube in Oberbayern Gegenwart und Vergangenheit*. Vaduz/Liechtenstein: Sändig. (Orig. pub. 1888.)

Hofmann, Albert. 1997. Die Suche nach Glück und Sinn. In: *Die Suche nach Glück und Sinn: Beiträge zu den Basler Psychotherapietagen*, ed. Lothar Riedel, 103–112. Rheinfelden: Mandala Media.

Hoops, Johannes. 1973. Mohn. In: *Reallexikon der germanischen Altertumskunde*. Vol. 3, 233–234. Berlin and New York: Walter de Gruyter. (Orig. pub. in 4 vols. 1911–1919.)

Hyslop, Jon, and Paul Ratcliffe. 1989. *A Folk Herbal*. Oxford: Radiation Publications.

Italiaander, Rolf. 1982. *Xocolatl: Ein süßes Kapitel unserer Kulturgeschichte*. 2nd ed. Düsseldorf: Droste Verlag.

Jordans, Wilhelm. 1933. *Der germanische Volksglaube von den Toten und Dämonen im Berg und ihrer Beschwichtigung*. Bonn: Hanstein (Bonner Studien zur englischen Philologie, Heft XVII).

Kaplan, Reid W. 1975. The sacred mushroom in Scandinavia. *Man N.S.* 10: 72–79.

Karageorghis, Vasso. 1976. A twelfth-century BC opium pipe from Kition. *Antiquity* 50: 125–129.

Kaster, Heinrich L. 1986. *Die Weihrauchstraße: Handelswege im alten Orient.* Frankfurt/M.: Umschau.

Keewaydinoquay. 1979. The Legend of Miskwedo. *Journal of Psychedelic Drugs* 11(1–2): 29–31.

Kemper, Wolf-R. 2003. Die "Cocaine Blues" Story, Einführung von Christian Rätsch, Nachwort von Konstantin Wecker. Löhrbach: WeltBeat in der Edition Rauschkunde.

Kerényi, Karl. 1966. *Die Mythologie der Griechen.* Munich: DTV.

_____. 1983. *Apollo.* Dallas, Texas: Spring Publications.

Klapp, Edzard. 1985. Rabenbrot. *Curare Sonderband* 3: 67–72.

Klapper, Joseph. 1936. *Der schlesische Berggeist Rübezahl.* Reihe: Schlesienbändchen, hrsg. v. Landesstelle für Heimatpflege in Niederschlesien. Breslau: Flemmings Verlag.

Klauser, Theodor, ed. 1976. *Reallexikon für Antike und Christentum* [Encyclopedia of Antiquity and Christianity], vol. IX. Stuttgart: Anton Hiersemann.

Kleinau, Tilmann, ed. 2002. *Die Weihnachtshexe: Weihnachtliche Geschichten aus Italien.* 2nd ed. Munich: DTV.

Klessmann, Eckart. 1995. *Das Hamburger Weihnachtsbuch.* Hamburg: Kabel.

Kluge, Heidelore. 1988. *Zaubertränke und Hexenküche: Die geheimen Rezepte und Tinkturen der weisen Frauen.* Munich: Heyne.

Kluge, Heidelore, R. Charles Fernando, and Edzard F. Keibel. 1999. *Weihrauch, Gold und Myrrhe: Nutzen Sie die Heilschätze der Natur.* Heidelberg: Haug.

Knuf, Joachim. 1985. Traditioneller Blitzschutz als Kommunikationsproblem. *Volkskunst* 8(4): 18–22.

Kölbl, Konrad. 1983. Kölbl's Kräuterfibel. 20th ed. Grünwald: Reprint-Verlag Konrad Kölbl.

Kräutermann, Valentino. 1725. *Der Curieuse und vernünfftige Zauber-Arzt.* Frankfurt and Leipzig: E. L. Riedt.

Krause, Wolfgang. 1970. *Runen.* Berlin: De Gruyter.

Kronfeld, E. M. 1906. *Der Weihnachtsbaum: Botanik und Geschichte des Weihnachtsgrüns.* Oldenburg und Leipzig: Schulzesche Hof-Buch-Handlung.

Krützfeld, Kerstin. 2002. Muskat, die psychoaktive Nuss: Vom aphrodisischen Moschusduft zum synthetischen Entaktogen. *Deutsche Apotheker Zeitung* 142(46): 58–67.

Küster, Hansjörg. 2001. Die Suche nach Yggdrasil. *Der Palmengarten* 65(1): 7–12.

Kutsch, Angelika, ed. 1996. *Weihnachten, als ich klein war.* Hamburg: Friedrich Oetinger.

Labouvie, Eva. 1991. *Zauberei und Hexenwerk: Ländlicher Hexenglaube in der frühen Neuzeit.* Frankfurt/M.: Fischer.

Landy, Eugene E. 1971. *The Underground Dictionary.* New York: Simon & Schuster.

Lemaire, Tom. 1995. *Godenspijs of duivelsbrood: Op het spoor van de vliegen-zwam.* Baarn: Ambo. ["Ambrosia or Devil's Bread? On the Search for Fly Agaric"]

Lewin, Louis. 1998. *Phantastica*. Rochester, Vt.: Park Street Press. (Orig. pub. 1924.)

Liebs, Elke. 1988. *Das Köstlichste von allem: Von der Lust am Essen und dem Hunger nach Liebe*. Zurich: Kreuz Verlag.

Lommel, Herman. 1949. Mithra und das Stieropfer. *Paideuma* 3(6/7): 207–18.

Lonicerus, Adamus. 1679. *Kreuterbuch*. Frankfurt: Matthius Wagner.

Lucretius Carus, Titus. *On the Nature of Things*. Martin Ferguson Smith, trans. Hackett Classics Series, rev. ed. Indianapolis, Ind.: Hackett Publishing Company, 2001. (Orig. pub. 50 BC.)

Luck, Georg. 1990. *Magie und andere Geheimlehren in der Antike*. Stuttgart: Kröner.

Ludlow, Fitz Hugh. 2001. *Der Haschisch-Esser (Klassiker der berauschten Literatur)*. Solothurn: Nachtschatten Verlag.

Lurker, Manfred. 1987. *Lexikon der Götter und Symbole der alten Ägypter*, Bern usw.: Scherz.

Lussi, Kurt. 1996. Verbotene Lust: Nächtliche Tänze und blühende Hanffelder im Luzerner. Hexenwesen. *Jahrbuch für Ethnomedizin und Bewusstseinsforschung* 4: 115–42.

_____. 2002. *Im Reich der Geister und tanzenden Hexen: Jenseitsvorstellungen, Dämonen und Zauberglaube*. Aarau: AT Verlag.

Madejsky, Margret, and Olaf Rippe. 1997. *Heilmittel der Sonne*. Munich: Verlag Peter Erd.

Majupuria, Trilok Chandra, and D. P. Joshi. 1988. *Religious and Useful Plants of Nepal and India*. Lalitpur: M. Gupta.

Manandhar, N. P. 2002. *Plants and People of Nepal*. Portland, Ore.: Timber Press.

Martinetz, Dieter, Karlheinz Lohs, and Jörg Janzen. 1989. *Weihrauch und Myrrhe*. Stuttgart: WVG.

Martinetz, Dieter. 1994. *Rauschdrogen und Stimulatien: Geschichte—Fakten—Trends*. Leipzig, Jena, Berlin: Urania.

Marzell, Heinrich. 1926. *Alte Heilkräuter*. Jena: Eugen Diederichs.

_____. 1935. *Volksbotanik: Die Pflanze im Deutschen Brauchtum*. Berlin: Verlag Enckehaus.

_____. 1964. *Zauberpflanzen—Hexentränke*. Stuttgart: Kosmos.

Matthiolus, Pierandrea. 1626. *Kreuttterbuch*. Frankfurt/M.: J. Fischers Erben.

Mautner, Uli, and Bernd Küllenberg. 1989. *Arzneigewürze*. Wiesbaden: Jopp.

Mehling, Marianne, ed. 1981. *Frohe Weihnacht: Geschichten, Lieder und Gedichte zur Advents- und Weihnachtszeit*. Würzburg: Edition Mehling.

Mercatante, Anthony. 1980. *Der magische Garten*. Zurich: Schweizer Verlagshaus.

Merkelbach, Reinhold. 1984. *Mithras*. Königstein/Ts.: Hain.

_____. 1988. *Die Hirten des Dionysos*. Stuttgart: Teubner.

Messner, Reinhold. 1998. *Yeti—Legende und Wirklichkeit*. Frankfurt/M.: S. Fischer.

Metzner, Ralph. 1988. The mystical symbolic psychology of Hildegard von Bingen. *ReVISION* 11(2): 3–12. (See also Metzner 2000: 73–87.)

_____. 1993. Die schwarze Göttin, der grüne Gott und der wilde Mensch. In: *Naturverehrung und Heilkunst.* C. Rätsch, ed. 37–63. Südergellersen: Bruno Martin.

_____. 1994. *Der Brunnen der Erinnerung.* Braunschweig: Aurum.

_____. 2000. *Das Mystische Grün: Die Wiedervereinigung des Heiligen mit dem Natürlichen.* Engerda: Arun-Verlag.

Moerman, Daniel E. 1998. *Native American Ethnobotany.* Portland, Ore.: Timber Press.

Modick, Klaus. 2002. *Vierundzwanzig Türen.* Munich: DTV.

Möllmann, Klaus, ed. 1998. *Weihnacht bei den Trollen: Weihnachtliche Geschichten aus Skandinavien.* Munich: DTV.

Montignac, Michel. 1996. *Gesund mit Schokolade.* Offenburg: Artulen-Verlag.

Mookerjee, Ajit. 1988. *Kali—The Feminine Force.* London: Thames and Hudson.

Most, Georg Friedrich. 1843. *Encyclopädie der gesammten Volksmedicin.* Leipzig: F. A. Brockhaus. (Repr. Graz: Akademische Druck und Verlagsanstalt, 1984.)

Müller, Irmgard. 1982. Die *pflanzlichen Heilmittel bei Hildegard von Bingen.* Salzburg: Otto Müller.

Müller-Ebeling, Claudia. 1991. Wolf und Bilsenkraut, Himmel und Hölle: Ein Beitrag zur Dämonisierung der Natur. In *Gaia—Das Erwachen der Göttin.* Susanne G. Seiler, ed. 163–82. Braunschweig: Aurum.

_____. 1993. Die Dämonisierung der Natur. In: *Naturverehrung und Heilkunst.* C. Rätsch, ed. 23–35. Südergellersen: Bruno Martin.

Müller-Ebeling, Claudia, Christian Rätsch, and Wolf-Dieter Storl. 2003. *Witchcraft Medicine: Healing Arts, Shamanic Practices, and Forbidden Plants.* Annabel Lee, trans. Rochester, Vt.: Inner Traditions.

Müller-Ebeling, Claudia, Christian Rätsch, and Surendra Bahadur Shahi. 2002. *Shamanism and Tantra in the Himalayas.* Annabel Lee, trans. Rochester, Vt.: Inner Traditions.

Muthmann, Friedrich. 1982. *Der Granatapfel: Symbol des Lebens in der Alten Welt.* Bern: Verlag Office du Livre (Schriften der Abegg-Stiftung).

Nauwald, Nana. 2002. *Bärenkraft und Jaguarmedizin: Die bewusstseinsöffnenden Techniken der Schamanen.* Aarau: AT Verlag.

Navarro, Fray Juan. 1992. *Historia natural o Jardín Americano (manuscrito de 1801).* México City: UNAM.

Nemec, Helmut. 1976. *Zauberzeichen: Magie im volkstümlichen Bereich.* Vienna and Munich: Verlag Anton Schroll.

Nietzsche, Freidrich. 1886. *Jenseits von Gut und Böse* [Beyond Good and Evil], Sprüche und Zwischenspiele, 152.

Norman, Jill. 1991. *Das grosse Buch der Gewürze.* Aarau: AT Verlag.

Ovid. 1998. *Metamorphoses.* A. D. Melville, Trans. Oxford World Classics pbk. reissue. New York: Oxford University Press. (Orig. pub. 1st century BC.)

Pahlow, Mannfried. 1993. *Das große Buch der Heilpflanzen*. Munich: Gräfe und Unzer.

Papajorgis, Kostis. 1993. *Der Rausch: Ein philosophischer Aperitif*. Stuttgart: Klett-Cotta.

Papyrus Ebers. Das älteste Buch über Heilkunde. 1890. From the Egyptian translated for the first time in its entirety, by Dr. med. H. Joachim. Berlin: Print and Publisher's House Georg Reimer (Reprint: Walter de Gruyter, Berlin, New York, 1973). See Hermann, Grapow, Von den medizinischen Texten: Art, Inhalt, Sprache und Stil der medizinischen Einzeltexte sowie Überlieferung, Bestand und Analyse der medizinischen Papyri, Berlin: Akademie-Verlag (Grundriss der Medizin der Alten Ägypter II), 1959, 77ff.

Pendergrast, Mark. 1993. *For God, Country and Coca-Cola: The Definitive History of the Great American Soft Drink and the Company that Makes It*. New York: C. Scribner's Sons. (2nd ed. 2000, Basic Books, New York).

Peuckert, Will-Erich. 1951. *Geheimkulte*. Heidelberg: Carl Pfeffer Verlag (Reprinted by Hildesheim, Olms Verlag, 1988).

———. 1978. *Deutscher Volksglaube im Spätmittelalter*. Hildesheim und New York: Georg Olms Verlag (Reprint of 1942 ed.).

Pausanius. *Description of Greece* (5 vols.). W. H. S. Jones, trans. Loeb Classical Library. Cambridge, Mass.: Harvard University Press.

Pfyl, Paul, and Heinz Knieriemen. 1998. *Vogelbeere, Schlehe, Hagebutte: Die besten Rezepte*. Aarau: AT Verlag.

Philpot, J. H. 1994. *The Sacred Tree or the Tree in Religion and Myth*. Felinfach: Llanerch Publishers. (Orig. pub. 1897.)

Pieper, Werner. 1998. *Die Geschichte des O.: Opiumfreuden—Opiumkriege*. Löhrbach: Edition Rauschkunde.

Plinius, C. Secundus d. Ä. [Pliny the Elder]. 1973ff. *Nature Study*. (37-book series), Edited and translated by Roderich König in collaboration with Gerhard Winkler. Munich: Heimeran.

Plowman, Timothy. 1977. Brunfelsia in ethnomedicine. *Botanical Museum Leaflets* 25(10): 289–320.

Plutarch. "The Roman Questions" in *Moralia* vol. IV. Frank Cole Babbit, trans. Loeb Classical Library. Cambridge, Mass.: Harvard University Press.

Pogue, Robert Wälder. 1992. *Ursprung und Spiegel der Kultur*. Munich: Carl Hanser.

Pohlhausen, Henn. 1953. Zum Motiv der Rentierversenkung der Hamburger und Ahrensburger Stufe. *Anthropos* 48: 987–90.

Prahn, Hermann. 1922. *Pflanzennamen*. 3rd ed. Berlin: Schnetter & Dr. Lindemeyer.

Praetorius, Johannes. 1669. *Blocks Berg Verrichtung*. Leipzig/Frankfurt: Johann Scheiben/Friedrich Amsten.

Pursey, Helen L. 1977. *The Strange World of the Mushrooms*. Zollikon: Albatros.

Rahner, Hugo. 1957. *Griechische Mythen in christlicher Deutung*. Zurich: Rhein–Verlag.

Rätsch, Christian. 1987. Der Rauch von Delphi: Eine ethnopharmakologische Annäherung. *Curare* 10(4): 215–28.

_____. 1992. Die heiligen Pflanzen unserer Ahnen. In: *Das Tor zu inneren Räumen.* C. Rätsch, ed. 95–103. Südergellersen: Verlag Bruno Martin.

_____. 1994a. Der Met der Begeisterung und die Zauberpflanzen der Germanen. In: *Der Brunnen der Erinnerung.* Ralph Metzner, ed. 231–49. Braunschweig: Aurum.

_____. 1994b. Die Alraune in der Antike. *Annali dei Musei Civici dei Rovereto* 10: 249–96.

_____. 1995. *Heilpflanzen der Antike in Ägypten, Griechenland und Rom.* Munich: Diederichs.

_____. 1996a. *Räucherstoffe—Der Atem des Drachen: Ethnobotanik, Rituale und praktische Anwendungen.* Aarau and Stuttgart: AT Verlag.

_____. 1996b. *Urbock: Bier jenseits von Hopfen und Malz.* Aarau: AT Verlag.

_____. 1998a. *Hanf als Heilmittel: Ethnomedizin, Anwendungen und Rezepte.* (New revised ed.). Aarau: AT Verlag.

_____. 2000. Tengu—Der Geist des Fliegenpilzes. In: *Der Fliegenpilz: Traumkult, Märchenzauber, Mythenrausch.* Wolfgang Bauer, et al. eds. 66–71. Aarau: AT Verlag.

_____. 2002a. *Aztekenkakao, Echter Kakao und Jaguarbaum.* In: Schokolade. Hartmut Roder, ed. 91–99. Bremen: Edition Temmen/Übersee-Museum.

_____. 2002b. *Schamanenpflanze Tabak. Band 1: Kultur und Geschichte des Tabaks in der Neuen Welt.* Solothurn: Nachtschatten Verlag.

_____. 2002c. *War der Weihnachtsman ein Schamane? Glückspilze unterm Tannenbaum. KGS* 12: 14–15.

———. 2005. *The Encyclopedia of Psychoactive Plants: Ethnopharmacology and Its Applications.* John R. Baker, trans. with Annabel Lee and Cornelia Ballent. Rochester, Vt.: Park Street Press.

Rätsch, Christian, and Claudia Müller-Ebeling. 2003. *Lexikon der Liebesmittel: Pflanzliche, mineralische, tierische und synthetische Aphrodisiaka.* Aarau: AT Verlag.

Rätsch, Christian, and Jonathan Ott. 2003. *Coca und Kokain: Ethnobotanik, Kunst und Chemie.* Aarau: AT Verlag.

Rätsch, Christian, and Heinz Probst. 1985. *Namaste Yeti: Geschichten vom wilden Mann.* Munich: Knaur.

Reko, Victor A. 1938. *Magische Gifte: Rausch- und Betäubungsmittel der neuen Welt* (2nd revised ed.). Stuttgart: Enke.

Rias-Bucher, Barbara. 2001. *Das Weihnachts–ABC.* Munich: DTV.

Rippe, Olaf, Margret Madejsky, Max Amann, Patricia Ochsner, and Christian Rätsch. 2001. *Paracelsusmedizin: Altes Wissen in der Heilkunst von heute.* Aarau: AT Verlag.

Riemerschmidt, Ulrich. 1962. *Weihnachten: Kult und Brauch—einst und jetzt.* Hamburg: Marion von Schröder Verlag.

Root, Waverley. 1996. *Wachtel, Trüffel, Schokolade: Die Enzyklopädie der kulinarischen Köstlichkeiten.* Munich: Goldmann.

Rosenbohm, Alexandra. 1991. *Halluzinogene Drogen im Schamanismus*. Berlin: Reimer.

_____. 1995. Zwischen Mythologie und Mykologie: Der Fliegenpilz als Heilmittel. *Curare* 18(1): 15–23.

Roth, Lutz, Max Daunderer, and Kurt Kormann. 1994. *Giftpflanzen— Pflanzengifte*. 4th ed. Munich: Ecomed.

Rovesti, Paolo, hrsg. von Susanne Fischer-Rizzi. 1995. *Auf der Suche nach den verlorenen Düften: Eine aromatische*. Kulturgeschichte, Munich: Hugendubel (Irisiana).

Rüttner-Cova, Sonja. 1988. *Frau Holle: Die gestürzte Göttin*. Basel: Sphinx.

Rust, Jürgen. 1983. *Aberglaube und Hexenwahn in Schleswig-Holstein*. Garding: Cobra-Verlag.

Sahagun, Fray Bernardino de. 1978. Florentine Codex. J. O. Anderson and C. E. Dibble, trans. 12 vols. Santa Fe, N.M.: The School of American Research and the University of Utah. (Written in the 16th century.)

Sahagun-Seler, Eduard. 1927. *Einige ausgewählte Kapitel aus dem Geschichtswerke des Fray Bernardino de Sahagun*. Stuttgart: Strecker und Schröder.

Samorini, Giorgio. 2002. *Liebestolle Katzen und berauschte Kühe: Vom Drogenkonsum der Tiere*. Aarau: AT Verlag.

Schadewaldt, Wolfgang. 1980. *Sternsagen*. Frankfurt/M.: Insel.

_____. 1990. *Der Gott von Delphi*. Frankfurt/M.: Insel.

Schenk, Gustav. 1943a. *Das wunderbare Leben—Roman*. Berlin: Verlag Die Heimbücherei John Jahr.

_____. 1943b. *Traum und Tat—Aufzeichnungen aus zwei Jahrzehnten*. Hannover: Adolf Sponholtz Verlag.

_____. 1948. *Schatten der Nacht*. Hannover: Adolf Sponholtz Verlag.

_____. 1954. *Das Buch der Gifte*. Berlin: Safari-Verlag.

_____. 1959. *Vor der Schwelle der letzten Dinge: Über die neuesten Forschungen und Erkenntnisse der Chemie und Physik*. Berlin: Safari-Verlag (New ed.).

_____. 1960. Die Bärlapp-Dynastie: *Eine Pflanze erobert die Erde*. West Berlin: Herrenalb/Schw., Frankfurt/M.: Verlag für Internationalen Kulturaustausch.

Schiering, Walther. 1927. Bilsenkraut: Eine okkultistisch-kulturgeschichtliche Betrachtung. In: *Zentralblatt für Okkultismus*. 23–31, Leipzig.

Schilli, Hermann. 1968. *Guide to the Black Forest Open-air Museum*. Freiburg: Department of the Ortenaukreis, Offenburg.

Schipperges, Heinrich. 1990. *Der Garten der Gesundheit: Medizin im Mittelalter*. Munich: DTV.

Schivelbusch, Wolfgang. 1983. *Das Paradies, der Geschmack und die Vernunft: Eine Geschichte der Genussmittel*. Frankfurt/M.: Ullstein.

Schlechta, Karl. 1967. *Nietzsche index zu den Werken in drei Banden*. Darmstadt: Wissenschaftliche Buchgesellschaft.

Schmidt, Brian B. 1995. The "witch" of Endor, 1 Samuel 28, and ancient Near Eastern necromancy. In: *Ancient Magic and Ritual Power*. Marvin Meyer and Paul Mireckim, eds. 111–29. Leiden: E. J. Brill.

Schoen, Ernest. 1963. *Nomina popularia plantarum medicinalium*. [Schweiz]: Galenica.

Schöpf, Hans. 1986. *Zauberkräuter*. Graz: Adeva.

———. 2001. *Volksmagie: Vom Beschwören, Heilen und Liebe zaubern*. Graz, Vienna, and Cologne: Styria.

Schopen, Armin. 1983. *Traditionelle Heilmittel in Jemen*. Wiesbaden: Franz Steiner Verlag.

Schwarz, Aljoscha, and Ronald Schweppe. 1997. *Von der Heilkraft der Schokolade: Geniessen ist gesund*. Munich: Verlag Peter Erd.

Seligmann, Siegfried. 1996. *Die magischen Heil- und Schutzmittel aus der belebten Natur: Das Pflanzenreich*. Berlin: Reimer. (Prepared from notes and fragments found in Seligmann's estate by Jürgen Zwernemann.)

———. 1999. *Die magischen Heil- und Schutzmittel aus der belebten Natur: Das Tierreich*. (Prepared from notes and fragments found in Seligmann's estate by Jürgen Zwernemann.)

Sellar, Wanda, and Martin Watt. 1997. *Weihrauch und Myrrhe: Anwendung in Geschichte und Gegenwart*. Munich: Knaur.

Seyfried, Gerhard. 2003. *Cannabis Collection—Kiff-cartoons 1973–2003*. Solothurn: Nachtschatten Verlag.

Siegel, Ronald K. 1995. *Rauschdrogen: Sehnsucht nach dem Künstlichen Paradies*. Frankfurt/M.: Eichborn.

Simek, Rudolf. 1984. *Lexikon der germanischen Mythologie*. Stuttgart: Kröner.

Simon, Erika. 1990. *Die Götter der Römer*. Munich: Hirmer.

Smith, Kile. 2000. William Henry Fry (1813–1864), in the leaflet accompanying the CD American Classics: William Henry Fry—Santa Claus Symphony, Royal Scottish National Orchestra conducted by Tony Rowe (Naxos, HNH International Ltd., 8.559057).

Söhns, Franz. 1920. *Unsere Pflanzen. Ihre Namenserklärung und ihre Stellung in der Mythologie und im Volksglauben*. 6th ed. Leipzig: Teubner.

Spamer, Adolf. 1937. *Weihnachten in alter und neuer Zeit*. Jena: Eugen Diederichs Verlag.

Starks, Michael. 1981. *The Fabulous Illustrated History of Psychoactive Plants or Great Grandma's Pleasures*. Mason, Mich.: Loompanics Unlimited.

Stewart, F. E. 1885. Coca-leaf cigars and cigarettes. *Philadelphia Medical Times and Register* 15: 933–35.

Stoffler, Hans-Dieter. 1978. *Der Hortulus des Walahfried Strabo: Aus dem Kräutergärten des Klosters Reichenau*. Sigmaringen: Jan Thorbecke Verlag.

Storl, Wolf-Dieter. 1988. *Feuer und Asche, Dunkel und Licht: Shiva—Urbild des Menschen*. Freiburg i. B.: Bauer.

———. 1993. *Von Heilkräutern und Pflanzengottheiten*. Braunschweig: Aurum.

———. 1996a. *Kräuterkunde*. Braunschweig: Aurum.

_____. 1996b. *Heilkräuter und Zauberpflanzen zwischen Haustür und Gartentor.* Aarau: AT Verlag.

_____. 1997. *Pflanzendevas—Die Göttin und ihre Pflanzenengel.* Aarau: AT Verlag.

_____. 2000a. *Götterpflanze Bilsenkraut.* Solothurn: Nachtschatten Verlag.

_____. 2000b. *Pflanzen der Kelten.* Aarau: AT Verlag.

_____. 2000c. Die Werkzeuge der Wurzelgräber: Elemente archaischer Pflanzensammelrituale. In: *Rituale des Heilens: Ethnomedizin, Naturerkenntnis und Heilkraft.* Franz-Theo Gottwald und Christian Rätsch, eds. 91–100 Aarau: AT Verlag.

_____. 2004. *Shiva: The Wild God of Power and Ecstasy.* Rochester, Vt.: Inner Traditions.

Strassmann, René A. 1994. *Baumheilkunde.* Aarau: AT Verlag.

Ströter-Bender, Jutta. 1994. *Liebesgöttinnen: Von der Großen Mutter zum Hollywoodstar.* Köln: DuMont.

Stutley, Margaret. 1985. *The Illustrated Dictionary of Hindu Iconography.* London: Routledge & Kegan Paul.

Tabernæmontanus, Jacobus Theodorus. 1731. *Neu Vollkommen Kräuter-Buch.* Supplemented by Casparum und Hieronymum Bauhinium. Basel: Verlag Johann Ludwig König.

Tacitus. 1988. *Germania—Bericht über Germanien.* Josef Lindauer, trans. Munich: DTV. (Orig. pub. in Roman antiquity.)

Thüry, Günther E., and Johannes Walter. 1999. *Condimenta: Gewürzpflanzen in Koch- und Backrezepten aus der römischen Antike.* 3rd ed. Herrsching: Rudolf Spann Verlag.

Usteri, A. 1926. *Pflanzenmärchen und -sagen.* Basel: Rudolf Seering.

van Renterghem, Tony. 1995. *When Santa Was a Shaman: The Ancient Origins of Santa Claus and the Christmas Tree.* St. Paul, Minn.: Llewellyn.

Vaupel, Elisabeth. 2002. *Gewürze—Acht kulturhistorische Porträts.* Munich: Katalog des Deutschen Museums.

Venzlaff, Helga. 1977. *Der marokkanische Drogenhändler und seine Ware.* Wiesbaden: Franz Steiner.

Vinci, Leo. 1980. *Incense: Its Ritual Significance, Use and Preparation.* New York: Samuel Weiser.

Vlček, Emanuel. 1959. Old literary evidence for the existence of the "snow man" in Tibet and Mongolia. *Man* 203/204: 133–134, plate H.

Vlček, Emanuel, Josef Kolmas, and Pavel Poucha. 1960. Diagnosis of the "wild man" according to Buddhist literary sources from Tibet, Mongolia, and China. *Man* 193/194: 153–155.

Vonarburg, Bruno. 1993. Wie die Innerrhoder "räuchelen." *Natürlich* 13(12): 13.

_____. 2002a. Sonne tanken bei der Christrose. *Natürlich* 22(1): 66–68.

_____. 2002b. Weihnächtliche Pflanzensymbole. *Natürlich* 22(12): 20–22.

von Bibra, Baron Ernst. 1995. Plant Intoxicants: A Classic Text on the Use of Mind-Altering Plants. Hedwig Schleiffer, trans. Rochester, Vt.: Healing

Arts Press. (Orig. pub. in German in 1855 under the title *Die narkotischen Genussmittel und der Mensch*.)

von Bingen, Hildegard. 1985. *Ursachen und Behandlung der Krankheiten.* Heidelberg: Haug. (Orig. pub. in 12th century.)

_____. 1991. *Heilkraft der Natur: "Physica."* Augsburg: Pattloch (erste textkritische Übersetzung). (Orig. pub. in 12th century.)

_____. 1997. *Scivias—Wisse die Wege.* Augsburg: Pattloch (Weltbild Verlag). (Orig. pub. in 12th century.)

von Chamisso, Adelbert. 1987. *Illustriertes Heil-, Gift- und Nutzpflanzenbuch.* Berlin: Dietrich Reimer.

von Hovorka, O., and A. Kronfeld. 1908. Vergleichende Volksmedizin. Stuttgart: von Nettesheim, Agrippa, and Heinrich Cornelius. 1982. *Die magischen Werke.* Wiesbaden: Fourier.

von Paczensky, Gert, and Anna Dünnebier. 1999. *Kulturgeschichte des Essens und Trinkens.* Munich: Orbis Verlag.

von Perger, K. Ritter. 1864. *Deutsche Pflanzensagen.* Stuttgart und Oehringen: Schaber.

von Weltzien, Diane. 1994. Ritual des Todes—Tod des Rituals. *Connection* 10(1): 8–12.

Vossen, Rüdiger. 1985. *Weihnachtsbräuche in aller.* Welt: Weihnachtszeit–Wende.

_____. 1985a. Hermel, harmel, harmal, Peganum harmala, die steppenraute, ihr gebrauch in marokko als heilpflanze und psychotherapeutikum. *Salix* 1(1): 36–40.

_____. 1989. *Natural relations.* Nürnberg: Verlag für moderne Kunst.

_____. 1993. Heilige bäume, bilsenkraut und bildzeitunge. In: *Naturverehrung und Heilkunst,* ed. C. Rätsch. 65–83. Südergellersen: Verlag Bruno Martin.

Wallbergen, Johann. 1988. [*Johann Wallbergens Sammlung*] *Natürlicher Zauberkünste* (1769), hrsg. und mit einem Essay versehen von Christopf Hein, Leipzig und Weimar: Gustav Kiepenheuer Verlag (Bibliothek des 18. Jahrhunderts).

Wasson, R. Gordon. 1968. *Soma: Divine Mushroom of Immortality.* New York: Harcourt Brace Jovanovich.

_____. 1986. Lightningbolt and Mushrooms. In *Persephone's Quest: Entheogens and the Origins of Religion,* eds. R.G. Wasson et al. 83–94. New Haven and London: Yale University Press.

Weber-Kellerman, Ingeborg. 1987. *Das Weihnachtsfest: Eine Kultur—und Sozialgeschichte der Weinachtszeit.* Munich, Luzern: Bucher.

Werfel, Franz. 1981. *Stern der Ungeborenen—Ein Reiseroman,* Frankfurt/M.: Fischer TB.

Werneck, Heinrich L., and Franz Speta. 1980. *Das Kräuterbuch des Johannes Hartlieb.* Graz: Akademische Druck- und Verlagsanstalt (Adeva).

Weustenfeld, Wilfried. 1995. *Zauberkräuter von A bis Z: Heilende und mystische Wirkung.* Munich: Verlag Peter Erd.

_____. 1996. *Heilkraft, Kult und Mythos von Bäumen und Sträuchern.* Munich: Verlag Peter Erd.

Wiedemann, Inga. 1992. *Cocataschen aus den Anden.* Berlin: Haus der Kulturen der Welt.

Wieshammer, Rainer-Maria. 1995. *Der 5. Sinn: Düfte als unheimliche Verführer.* Rott am Inn: F/O/L/T/Y/S Edition.

Wohlstein, Herman. 1959. Heilige Bäume und Pflanzen. *Ethnos* 1–2: 81–84.

Zimmerer, E. W. 1896. *Kräutersegen.* Donauwörth: Auer.

Zoozmann, Richard. 1927. *Pflanzen-Legenden: Schlichtfromme Erzählungen von Blumen, Büschen und Bäumen.* 2nd ed. Karlsruhe: Badenia A. G.

Zohary, Michael. 1986. *Pflanzen der Bibel.* 2nd ed. Stuttgart: Calwer.

INDEX

Books of Related Interest

Shamanism and Tantra in the Himalayas
by Claudia Müller-Ebeling, Christian Rätsch, and Surendra Bahadur Shahi

Witchcraft Medicine
Healing Arts, Shamanic Practices, and Forbidden Plants
by Claudia Müller-Ebeling, Christian Rätsch, and Wolf-Dieter Storl

The Encyclopedia of Psychoactive Plants
Ethnopharmacology and Its Applications
by Christian Rätsch
Foreword by Albert Hofmann

Plants of the Gods
Their Sacred, Healing, and Hallucinogenic Powers
by Richard Evans Schultes, Albert Hofmann, and Christian Rätsch

Marijuana Medicine
A World Tour of the Healing and Visionary Powers of Cannabis
by Christian Rätsch

Christianity: The Origins of a Pagan Religion
by Philippe Walter

Magic Mushrooms in Religion and Alchemy
by Clark Heinrich

The Mystery of Manna
The Psychedelic Sacrament of the Bible
by Dan Merkur, Ph.D.

Inner Traditions • Bear & Company
P.O. Box 388
Rochester, VT 05767
1-800-246-8648
www.InnerTraditions.com

Or contact your local bookseller